W9-BNQ-456

DISCARDED

JUST JACKIE

HER PRIVATE YEARS

JUST JACKIE

HER PRIVATE YEARS

Edward Klein

BALLANTINE BOOKS • NEW YORK

A Ballantine Book
Published by The Ballantine Publishing Group

Copyright © 1998 by Ed Klein, Inc.

www.randomhouse.com/BB/

Grateful acknowledgment is made to the following for permission
to reprint previously published material:

Criterion Music Corporation: Excerpt from the lyrics of "Tiny Bubbles"
by Leon Pober. Copyright © 1966 Granite Music Corporation.
© Renewed 1994 Granite Music Corporation. Reprinted by permission of
Criterion Music Corporation.

Harcourt Brace & Company and Random House UK Ltd.: Excerpts
from "Ithaca" from *The Complete Poems of Cavafy* translated by
Rae Dalven. Copyright © 1961 and renewed 1989 by Rae Dalven.
Reprinted by permission of Harcourt Brace & Company
and Hogarth Press, Random House UK Ltd.

PolyGram Music Publishing Group: Excerpt from "Little Green Apples"
written by Robert Russell. Copyright © 1968 PolyGram
International Publishing, Inc. Copyright renewed.
Used by permission. All rights reserved.

PolyGram Music Publishing Group and Ms. Carly Simon: Excerpt from
the lyrics of "Touched by the Sun" by Carly Simon. Copyright © 1994
C'est Music. Used by permission. All rights reserved.

LIBRARY OF CONGRESS CATALOGING-IN-PUBLICATION DATA
Klein, Edward, 1936–
    Just Jackie : her private years / Edward Klein.—1st ed.
        p.   cm.
    ISBN 0-345-42102-7 (alk. paper)
    1. Onassis, Jacqueline Kennedy, 1929–1994.   2. Celebrities—
United States—Biography.   3. Presidents' spouses—United States—
Biography.   I. Title.
CT275.O552K57 1998
973.922'095—dc21
[B]   98-26133

Text design by Holly Johnson

Manufactured in the United States of America

First Edition: October 1998

10   9   8   7   6   5   4   3   2   1

To Michael Sacks

ACKNOWLEDGMENTS

I first began writing about Jacqueline Kennedy Onassis almost a decade ago, in a cover story that appeared in *Vanity Fair* in the fall of 1989. Over the years, many people have helped me separate the wheat of truth from the chaff of tabloid invention about Jackie. Such guidance proved to be even more important for this book, which is about the least documented—and most controversial—period of Jackie's life, her private, post–White House years.

Of the several hundred people who agreed to speak on and off the record for this book, I owe a special note of appreciation to Stelio Papadimitriou, Niki Goulandris, John Carl Warnecke, John Loring, Jack Anderson, Les Whitten, Ralph Graves, Peter Beard, Michael Beschloss, and Robert Lindsey.

In addition, contributions were made by Elizabeth Folberth, Linda Puner, Alfred Fariello, Deborah Creighton, Molly Ginty, Justine Fontinell, Anita Goss, and Amy Steiner.

My research assistants and I were steered in the right direction by Eulalie Regan at the *Vineyard Gazette*, Claudia Anderson at the Lyndon Baines Johnson Library, and Jane Payne at the John F. Kennedy Library.

At Ballantine Books, I want to thank Judith Curr, who shared my vision from the outset, as well as Peter Borland, Ellen Archer, and Emily Grayson.

My agent Robert Gottlieb and his associate at the William

Morris Agency, Marcy Posner, provided wise counsel throughout the project.

My editors, Walter Anderson at *Parade* and Graydon Carter at *Vanity Fair*, were unstinting in their encouragement.

Finally, I want to express my gratitude to my wife, Dolores Barrett. Her intelligence, insight, and loving kindness sustained me throughout the long months that it took to research and write this book.

JUST JACKIE

HER PRIVATE YEARS

ONE

THE SUNDOWN
OF CHIVALRY

Friday Evening, November 29, 1963

THE STORYTELLER

A giant thunderbolt split open the night sky, and in the shuddering light a car emerged from a swirl of fog and raced on through the storm. Slumped in the backseat was the journalist Theodore White, a stubby little man in his late forties with thinning hair and an owlish expression. He took a slug from a plastic bottle that contained a decanted pint of Scotch whisky—his self-imposed allotment of alcohol for the long hours that lay ahead.

There was another huge flash of lightning, followed this time by a thumping crash of thunder. White peered out the window at the flooded stretch of highway. It was coming down in solid sheets of water, just the way it had rained a week ago on the night President Kennedy's body was brought back from Dallas in a dark bronze coffin.

White had covered the assassination and the three-day pageant of Kennedy's funeral for *Life* magazine. He was still physically exhausted and emotionally drained from the experience. Now, however, he found himself in a rented limousine, with a strange chauffeur, driving at breakneck speed through an old-fashioned northeaster on his way to another assignment for *Life*.

"There is something I want *Life* magazine to say to the country," the President's widow, Jacqueline Kennedy, had told White during a brief phone conversation from her home on Cape Cod, "and you must do it."

White did not know what Jackie had in mind, but he could guess why she had chosen him above all other journalists to carry her message to the American people. He was the author of *The Making of the President 1960*, a book that had caught the mood and the strains of the election campaign, and that helped give birth to the myth of John Fitzgerald Kennedy. Jackie had selected White because he was a storyteller with a talent for hero worship.

The limousine slowed down as it approached the summer resort town of Hyannis on Nantucket Sound. The board of selectmen of Barnstable Township had decked the façade of the town hall with black crepe in memory of the dead President, but the merchants had strung up colored Christmas lights along Main Street in an effort to dispel the gloom. White tossed down another stiff slug of Scotch and instructed the chauffeur to stop at a gas station. He got out, ducked into a telephone booth, and placed a call to New York City.

"How's my mother doing?" he asked.

The thunder and pelting rain drowned out the reply.

"*What?*" White shouted. "I can't hear you."

"She's doing as well as can be expected," Dr. Harold Rifkin, his family physician, yelled back into the phone.

White's mother was gravely ill. It was she who had answered the telephone at her son's East Side town house in Manhattan when Jackie called from the Cape, and in all the excitement, the old woman began having a heart attack. White was forced to make a hard decision: stay with his mother, or answer Jackie's call.

On the phone, Jackie had not spoken to White in her tiny, whispery voice. She had used her other voice, the one rarely heard by strangers, the deep, expressive vibrato that she employed when she refused to take no for an answer. You must do it, she had told White, and he felt compelled to heed her summons. He chose Jackie over his mother, and drove off into the raging storm.

He was afflicted by pangs of guilt as his car pulled up to a checkpoint in front of the Kennedy compound in Hyannis Port. It was not quite eight-thirty on Friday, November 29, 1963. The presidential flag, illuminated by floodlights and tugged by the wind, was flying in the front yard of John and Jacqueline Kennedy's rented summer house on nearby Squaw Island.

The place was crawling with Secret Service men. No one knew if the assassination had been part of a larger conspiracy, or whether a plot existed to murder Jackie and her young children, too. Two agents, dressed in water-stained trench coats and dripping fedoras, shone flashlights into White's face, then waved him through an opening in the barricade.

The car crunched up the long driveway, past broad lawns that swept down to the gray, restless waters of Nantucket Sound. White took another snort of Scotch, cupped a hand over his mouth to check the smell on his breath, and climbed out of the limousine into the pouring rain. He dashed up the steps to the big veranda that wrapped around the white clapboard house belonging to Joseph P. Kennedy Sr., the family patriarch.

He knocked on the door and a maid ushered him into the first-floor parlor, which was filled with comfortable stuffed furniture. In the room, he spotted a number of familiar faces—Dave Powers, the President's political crony; Chuck Spalding, Jack's classmate at Harvard; Pat Lawford, the President's sister; Franklin D. Roosevelt Jr.; and Clint Hill, the agent in charge of Jackie's Secret Service detail. They greeted him with a chorus of friendly hellos, followed by polite inquiries about his mother.

He placed another call to New York City from the phone in the hallway, and while he waited for the long distance operator to connect him to Dr. Rifkin, he snuck another nip from his plastic bottle. He caught sight of himself in a mirror. His pale and frantic face was glistening with perspiration.

His mind reeled with what seemed like a thousand thoughts. The editors of *Life* were holding the magazine's giant presses for him at a cost of $30,000 an hour. He must notify them as soon as possible about what Jackie had to say. His contract with *Life* called for him to be paid $5,000 for long pieces and $1,500 for so-called white-fang pieces—stories that could be done in one quick bite. He wondered whether his editors would try to pay him the lower rate for tonight's work.

"There's no change in your mother's condition," Dr. Rifkin informed him.

White put down the phone just as Jackie entered the room.

Out of the dozens of hours of funeral coverage that White had watched on television and events he had witnessed in person, he retained a few indelible images of Jackie: her swollen eyes behind the sheer veil, her sad black stockings, her firm, long stride as she marched behind the caparisoned horse and the President's catafalque on the way to St. Matthew's Cathedral. Jackie's flawless performance during the President's funeral had transformed her in the eyes of the public into a kind of paragon of virtue, practically a saint, and White half expected to find her here in Hyannis Port still dressed in mourning.

Instead she was turned out in trim black slacks, tapered at the ankles, and a beige pullover sweater. Even in flat shoes, she looked taller than White remembered. This impression of height was enhanced by her long, graceful neck, broad shoulders, and slim hips. Everything about her, even her hands, seemed slightly out of proportion, yet somehow absolutely right.

She had not bothered to fix her hair. It was tucked casually behind her ears, exposing the broad contours of her face with its high cheekbones and full, voluptuous mouth. Without eyeliner or mascara, her eyes seemed to be set even wider apart than they appeared in photos. But that was not what made them look different, White decided. It was their color. They were darker than before. Tragedy had both darkened and deepened her beauty.

"Oh, Teddy," she said, "you came all the way up here in the storm just for me."

He was suddenly stone-cold sober.

His fatigue, his anxiety over *Life*'s idle presses, his concern over his fee—all these worries left him in an instant. Even the guilt about his mother evaporated without a trace. The storyteller in White took over, and he thought: A talk with Mary Todd Lincoln a week after Lincoln's assassination wouldn't have been nearly as compelling as this.

"PARTS TOO PERSONAL
FOR MENTION"

"What shall I say? What can I do for you?" Jackie asked after the others had left the room.

What could she do for *him*?

White was taken aback by the question. He unsnapped the leather case of his tape recorder and placed the machine on a table between them. Then, as the cold, driving rain rattled the windows in Hyannis Port, he flipped open his reporter's notebook and scribbled his first impressions:

> Composure . . . beautiful . . . eyes wider than pools . . . calm voice . . .

"Why don't we pick up from our telephone call," White suggested. "You said that journalists like Arthur Krock and Merriman Smith and all those people were going to write about Jack as history, and that isn't the way you want him remembered. How do you want him remembered?"

Jackie took a long drag on her cigarette, making the tip turn red. As soon as she began to speak, White realized that he was going to hear more than he had bargained for. Jackie regarded him as a friend who also happened to be a journalist, rather than as a journalist who would record everything she said. He felt an obligation to protect her, and he pushed aside his tape recorder—a signal that it was safe for her to speak her mind.

"She poured out several streams of thought which mingled for two hours," White recalled. "There was the broken narrative, the personal unwinding from the horror, the tale of the killing. Then there was the history part of it. And parts too personal for mention in any book but one of her own."

White took eleven pages of notes, but as he confided years later to the author of this book and to one or two other close friends, he did not transcribe many of the most personal things that Jackie told him that night. . . .

. . . How in Fort Worth, on the eve of the President's assassination, Jackie and Jack had separate bedrooms in a suite on the eighth floor of the Hotel Texas. Her room was a hideous green, and it overlooked a neon-lit parking lot. Before turning in, she went into Jack's bedroom. He was exhausted from the day's politicking. Normally she would have said a quick good-night and returned to her room. But something had changed in the chemistry of their relationship, which in the past had been poisoned by Jack's insatiable need for sex with an endless succession of women.

Jackie attributed the change in the relationship to the death three months earlier of their son Patrick Bouvier Kennedy. The premature baby had put up a stirring fight for life, and Jack had said, "Nothing must happen to Patrick, because I just can't bear to think of the effect it might have on Jackie." Then, when the infant died, Jack broke down in tears. It was the first time that Jackie had seen him cry.

Since then their relationship had deepened and been transformed, Jackie told White, and she felt closer to Jack than at any time in their ten-year marriage. And so Jackie slipped into her husband's bed, and in the sickly green reflection cast by the neon light, she aroused him from the depths of his fatigue, and they made love for the last time. . . .

. . . And the next morning, in a light drizzle, Jack addressed an outdoor rally of union men and they shouted, "Where's Jackie?" And Jack pointed to his wife's eighth-floor hotel window and said, "Mrs. Kennedy is organizing herself. It takes her a little longer, but, of course, she looks better than we do when she does it."

The truth was, Jackie was delayed because she had just begun her menstrual period. It was her first normal monthly flow since Patrick Bouvier had been delivered by cesarean section, and she remembered that it filled her with joy.

She and Jack had talked about having more children, but she feared that she might never get pregnant again. So the day that ended in blood had begun in blood, but the first blood was a sign of life. It meant that Jackie could begin to try to have another baby. . . .

And White did not record the personal things that Jackie told him about her time alone with Jack as he lay dead in Trauma Room No. 1 at Parkland Memorial Hospital in Dallas. Or, rather, what White chose to put down in his notebook was a bowdlerized version of the truth.

> They kept trying to get a priest . . . there was a sheet over Jack, his foot was sticking out, whiter than the sheet. . . . I took his foot and kissed it. Then I pulled back the sheet. His mouth was so *beautiful* . . . his eyes were open. They found his hand under the sheet, and I held his hand all the time the priest was saying extreme unction. . . .

There was blood everywhere. Not only on Jackie's hair and gloves and skirt and stockings. Her panties were soaked with menstrual blood, too. She was covered in blood from head to foot. The heartrending Latin words, so familiar to her from her Catholic childhood—*Si capax ego te absolvo* . . . —staggered her, Jackie recalled, and she almost lost her balance. She felt that if she let go of Jack, she would collapse in their commingled blood.

She was determined to hold on to Jack at all costs. She did not see how she could go on without a man in her life, she told White. Her own father was dead. Jack's father, Joe Kennedy, had been left speechless by a stroke, and could not protect her. Her brother-in-law Bobby was as devastated as she was by Jack's murder.

There was no one to look after her.

And so after the tube was withdrawn from the hole they had cut in

Jack's trachea, and after the nurses removed the corset he had used for his bad back, and after they had gone out of the room, leaving her alone with Jack, she bent over the corpse, and showered the body with kisses. She kissed his foot, his leg, his thigh, his chest, and his lips.

"I could not let go," Jackie said.

For a moment, her voice faltered, and as White waited for her to go on, he was aware of the flicker of lightning in the panes of the living-room window. Then Jackie spoke again, but her voice was almost drowned out by the thunder that came rolling in over Nantucket Sound.

She ran her hand along her husband's body, Jackie told White. And she found his penis and caressed it.

GUINEVERE

J ackie's face was drained of color, and she looked as though she might
faint. White reached out to console her.

"No, no," Jackie said, recoiling, "don't protect me now."

For the past week, no one had been able to comfort her. To Father
John Cavanaugh, another priest, who met privately with her in Washington after the assassination to hear her confession, Jackie had said:
"What am I supposed to confess, Father? That I neglected to watch the
calendar and ate meat some Friday three months ago?"

She demanded that the clergyman explain her husband's murder.

"Why, why? How could God do something like that?"

Jackie was a lax Roman Catholic, but in her heart she embraced the
teachings of her church. She believed, for instance, that the universe
was kept in a kind of moral balance by a just God who rewarded the
good and punished the wicked. Now, however, that faith presented her
with a perplexing problem, for over the past few years the God of her
understanding had seen fit to snatch away her husband and two of
her children—one by a stillbirth in 1956, and another in the first few
hours of his life that past summer.

What sin had she committed to deserve such terrible punishment at
the hands of God? Would God now choose to take Caroline and John as
well? The prospect of that happening was too painful for her to contem-
plate, she told White. She could not even talk about it. In fact, talking

about Jack's murder only served to remind her that she was utterly inconsolable. Surely there must be something in these horrible events to salve her pain.

"One thing kept going through my mind," she said, groping for words. "The line from a musical comedy. I kept saying to Bobby, I've got to talk to somebody, I've got to see somebody. I want to say this one thing."

White intuitively sensed that he was about to hear the story he had come for.

"This line from the musical comedy has been almost an obsession with me," Jackie said. "At night before going to bed . . . we had an old Victrola. He'd play a couple of records. I'd get out of bed to play for him when it was so cold. He loved *Camelot*. It was the song he loved the most at the end . . . on a Victrola ten years old . . . it's the last record, the last side of *Camelot*, sad Camelot . . . 'Don't let it be forgot that for one brief shining moment there was Camelot.'

"Jack's life had more to do with myth, legend, saga, and story than with political theory or political science," she continued. "There'll be great presidents again—and the Johnsons are wonderful, they've been wonderful to me—but there'll never be another Camelot."

Camelot, as Teddy White knew, was adapted for the musical stage by Frederick Loewe and Alan Jay Lerner from *The Once and Future King*, the fantasy masterpiece written by T. H. White, a British author with the same initials and last name as his own. It just so happened that White and the lyricist, Alan Jay Lerner, were good friends. They were often invited to the same parties in New York and Washington, where White had heard Lerner boast on more than one occasion that he had attended Choate and Harvard with Jack Kennedy. Yet White could not recall Lerner ever mentioning that his old schoolmate and friend, the President of the United States, went to sleep at night listening to a recording of *Camelot*.

That was enough to make White suspicious of Jackie's story. And it was not the only thing that bothered him about it. If anyone knew Jack Kennedy's mind-set, it was White. While he was researching *The Making of the President 1960*, White concluded that of all the Kennedys Jack was the toughest, the most intelligent, the most attractive—and down deep, the least romantic. "Life is one continuous choice between second bests," Kennedy was fond of saying. And his favorite songs were "Heart of My Heart," "Bill Bailey (Won't You Please Come Home?)," and "That Old Gang of Mine."

White suspected that the metaphor of Camelot said more about Jackie than it did about Jack. She was a woman with an artistic temperament, one who knew little and cared less about politics. She had not even bothered to vote before she married John Kennedy, and her political influence had seemed so slight to White that he had mentioned her only three times in his exhaustive chronicle of the 1960 campaign.

During her husband's thousand days in office, Jackie had avoided official functions as much as possible. But she had taken charge of the furniture, the paintings, the flowers, and the food. And she had invited a host of great artists and Nobel Prize–winners to state dinners, transforming the President's House into a glittering showcase of American culture.

Before Jackie became First Lady, most Americans looked across the Atlantic for their serious art, literature, music, and dance. They felt culturally inferior to Europeans, especially to the British and French. But after Jackie entered the White House, all that began to change. She made everyone aware that America was not only the world's major military power, it was its cultural superpower as well. More than anyone else at the time, Jackie was responsible for awakening Americans to their rich cultural endowment.

While Jack was engaged in the pragmatic business of the presidency, Jackie was creating a brilliant illusion—a stage set upon which gallant men danced with beautiful women, and great deeds were performed by heroes who changed history. "There'll never be another Camelot," Jackie had said, and White sympathized with her desire to portray the Kennedy years as the sundown of chivalry.

But White had been educated at the prestigious Boston Latin School and at Harvard College, and he was familiar with the classics. Stripped of its knightly ideals and courtly romance, Camelot was the tale of flawed humanity. At the heart of the legend was the story of how King Arthur's wife Guinevere betrayed him with his best friend, Lancelot, and brought disaster and ruin to her husband's magic kingdom.

What, White wondered, was a storyteller to make of that?

"LORDS OF IT ALL"

Around midnight, White disappeared into a maid's room and began the job of sorting out his notes. As he wrote years later in his memoirs, he saw himself at this juncture of his career as a sort of court musician, a modern troubadour, who sang his stories for attention, applause, and a fee. His immediate audience was composed of the millions of middle-class, middlebrow readers of *Life*, but in his heart of hearts he knew that he was singing for the men of politics, diplomacy, and finance who ran America.

Many of these men were White's close friends, and they expected him to lay a respectful wreath on the grave of John F. Kennedy. And so, as he sat down in front of his portable typewriter, White made an important decision. He would not expose Camelot as a misreading of history. Nor would he try to explain Jackie's comparison of herself to Guinevere, a woman who was responsible for betrayal and disaster. He would leave the riddle of Jackie's true identity to her future biographers.

Instead, Jackie's farewell to Camelot would stand as a sad good-bye to a golden age of America, a time never to be recaptured. White had always been attracted by the notion of such a golden age. He liked to quote the lines in Archibald MacLeish's poem *Conquistador*, in which Bernal Díaz, MacLeish's storyteller, is made to say: "but I . . . saw Montezúma: I saw the armies of Mexico marching, the leaning Wind in their garments: the painted faces: the plumes. . . . We were the lords of it all."

Americans had felt like the lords of it all during the brief reign of John F. Kennedy, and the storyteller who had made them feel that way was Theodore H. White. In 1959, after writing two novels that received lukewarm critical receptions, White returned to his first love, public affairs, and embarked on a nonfiction book about the coming 1960 presidential campaign. He cast Richard Nixon as the villain of his story. The hero who emerged from White's yearlong adventure on the campaign trail was John F. Kennedy, who, as White wrote,

> was the first postwar American leader who could see how changed were the circumstances in the country which he had left for war twenty years earlier. Moreover, and just as importantly in terms of a popular story, Kennedy was young, rich, heroic, witty, well read—and handsome.

White, of course, was the physical opposite—a homely little man with short arms and thick glasses. And from the moment he laid eyes on the tall, gleaming figure of John Kennedy descending the steps of the *Caroline*, his campaign airplane, White fell into a journalistic swoon. The future President was all the things that White wished to be, but was not: graceful, immaculate, wry and witty, and irresistibly attractive to women.

What was more, White had grown up as a poor Jewish boy in the ghettos of Boston, and like millions of people who felt that they had been excluded from the American Dream, he admired Kennedy because he had unlatched the door of opportunity. Through that door, as White wrote in a typically hyperventilating passage,

> marched not only Catholics, but blacks, and Jews, and ethnics, women, youth, academics, newspersons and an entirely new breed of young politicians who did not think of themselves as politicians—all demanding their share of the action and the power in what is now called participatory democracy.

White would always remember that he was lunching with an old war-correspondent acquaintance when a waiter came over to their table, and told them, "The radio says Kennedy has been shot." At that moment, White believed, America passed through an invisible membrane of time that divided one era from another. Kennedy's murder marked a great divide in history, separating an era of hope and idealism from an era stained by assassination, Vietnam, racial strife, sexual permissiveness, Watergate, and national disillusionment.

Or so White chose to believe.

But like so many other Americans who adored John Kennedy, the awestruck White had shut his eyes to certain facts. During most of his presidency, Kennedy was a grave disappointment as a leader. He was an inexperienced executive who was woefully unprepared for great office. It was only through a series of missteps and blunders that he began to learn the complicated art of statecraft. And just when it looked as though he was finally getting the hang of it, he was struck down in Dallas.

It was those facts that concerned Jackie. She did not want her husband to be judged as a president who had been cut off at the promise, not after the performance. Camelot was her effort to rescue John Kennedy from the merciless inquest of history. And White became a willing collaborator in her fanciful version of history.

FRIENDS OF
THE KENNEDYS

White took a long snort of whisky, then began pounding out the first draft of his story:

It rained hardest in Hyannis Port on the Cape, in those sheets of rain that Verlaine called in his poetry the "sobbing of the autumn."

His clacking portable woke up Clint Hill, Jackie's Secret Service man, who had gone virtually sleepless for days. Hill burst into the room.

"For Christ's sake," he snarled, "we need some sleep here."

Forty-five minutes later, White was finished. He returned to the living room and handed the manuscript to Jackie.

She wrote across the top of the first page: "A Conversation with Jacqueline Kennedy." Then she crossed out the first two paragraphs, including the pretentious literary reference to the French poet Paul Verlaine. Soon she was slashing out lines, adding words, changing tenses, sharpening phrases. On the last page, she found that White had ended his story with the line:

But she did not want them to forget John F. Kennedy or read of him only in dusty or bitter histories.

This did not satisfy Jackie at all. And so she added a new kicker in her own handwriting:

For one brief shining moment there was Camelot.

From a wall phone in the kitchen, White placed a call to David Maness, *Life*'s articles editor, who was standing by in the Time-Life Building on Fiftieth Street in New York City. Maness immediately patched the call through to the magazine's fastest stenographer-typist, who was stationed on a different floor, and to Ralph Graves, the assistant managing editor, who was in his own office.

As White began to dictate the piece, Jackie leaned against the kitchen wall, smoking a cigarette. When White was finished, he asked his *Life* colleagues:

"As a friend of the Kennedys, is there anything you think is in bad taste, or will give a bad impression?"

He held the phone away from his ear so that Jackie could hear the response from New York.

"Yes," said Graves, "I think the gesture of kissing his foot is too intimate for good taste."

White must have found Graves's objection ludicrous, given the fact that he had left out Jackie's far more shocking gesture with an intimate part of the President's anatomy.

"Just a minute," he said.

He put his hand over the mouthpiece, and discussed the editorial request with Jackie.

"Right," he said when he came back on the line. "Take out the foot kissing."

"Hey," said Maness, "is she listening to this now with you?"

White ignored the question.

"Anything else?" he asked.

"Yes." It was the voice of assistant managing editor Ralph Graves again. "I think Camelot is mentioned too many times in such a short story—at least one time too many. I suggest that you delete the last reference in the last paragraph."

White muffled the phone again, and conferred with Jackie. Did she want to soften the focus on Camelot?

She shook her head violently.

"No," White told his editor, "that last Camelot stays in."

TWO

BEYOND HER WILDEST DREAMS

November 1963

"HE'S DEAD, ISN'T HE?"

Early the next morning, after Teddy White had departed, Jackie
stood at her bedroom window, gazing across the lawns that sloped
gently down to the beach. Huge white clouds scudded across a putty-
colored sky. The *Honey Fitz*, the presidential yacht, and the *Marlin*, the
Kennedy family power launch, rode high on the angry waves that roiled
Nantucket Sound.

Off in the distance, Jackie could see that someone had ventured out
onto the dunes. It was several moments before she realized that the figure was her daughter, who was sitting by herself at the edge of the beach,
staring out to sea. Caroline's arms were locked around her legs, and her
chin rested on her knees. Her blonde hair, cut in a pageboy, was lashed
by the harsh wind. She made a bleak picture, lonely and despairing.

Jackie slipped into wool slacks and a cable-knit turtleneck, and
went downstairs. The smells of freshly brewed coffee and frying bacon
filled the house. Louella Hennessy, the Kennedy family nurse who had
been called back into service after the assassination, could be heard
arguing in the kitchen with George Thomas, the President's valet. Everything was just as it had been in the past, except for one thing. Providen-
cia Paredes, Jackie's Dominican maid, had set the breakfast table for
only three people. The fourth was dead.

Jackie's home on the Cape was called Bambletyde. A shingled house
on Squaw Island, not far from the Kennedy family compound, it was

furnished very simply. There were a few upholstered chairs, and some woven rugs scattered on the bare wood floors. The dominant color was yellow—one of Jackie's favorites—and the walls were covered with landscapes by André Dunoyer de Segonzac and with several seascapes that had been painted by Jackie herself.

She pulled on a pair of knee-high Wellingtons and went outside. As she strode down the long sweep of lawn toward Caroline, her soles sank into the wet grass and made sucking noises. When she reached the dunes, she stood behind Caroline for a moment, hesitating to interrupt the girl's thoughts. Then she sat down beside her daughter, and they remained side by side, not touching, only looking out toward the colorless rim of the horizon.

Caroline had been her daddy's girl. The first words of more than one syllable that she had spoken were "New Hampshire," "Wisconsin," and "West Virginia"—names of the key presidential primary states responsible for her father's long absences. Whenever he returned home from his political travels, Caroline would ask him to tell her a story. He had invented a fictitious character, a white shark that ate people's socks. "Where's the white shark, Daddy?" Caroline would ask, and he would say, "Well, I think he is over there, and he's waiting for some socks to eat."

She had just turned six, and unlike her brother John, who was only three, she was old enough to understand what had happened to her father in Dallas.

"He's dead, isn't he?" she kept on saying. "A man shot him."

After a while, Jackie could feel Caroline begin to shiver. She gave her a gentle nudge, and the little girl struggled to her feet and offered a hand to her mother. They stood silhouetted against the gray sky, and the wind struck against their bodies. Caroline leaned hard against her mother, and Jackie wrapped both her arms around her and pressed her close.

METAMORPHOSIS

When Jackie returned from the dunes with Caroline, she placed a call to Erik Erikson, the famous child psychoanalyst. She told friends she was haunted by the fear that the assassination would inflict permanent psychological damage on her children. They needed help right away.

Erikson spent weekends and holidays in Cotuit, a few miles from Hyannis Port. He taught at Harvard, and was friendly with many of the brainy types who ran the New Frontier. His telephone number had been given to Jackie by Richard Goodwin, one of JFK's closest advisers, who had an amazing network of friends and acquaintances.

"The children have been through a terrible experience, as you know," Jackie told Erikson. "I would like to bring them to see you."

"I teach full-time now, and haven't practiced in years," Erikson explained in his slight German accent. "I'm not taking formal patients."

"It might be well for the children to see a person like you," Jackie persisted.

Erikson did not find it any easier to say no to Jackie than had Teddy White.

"Of course," he said. "You can bring them here if you like."

That afternoon, as Jackie was hustling Caroline and John out the door for their appointment with Erikson, she caught sight of a Marine guard lowering the presidential standard in the front yard. The wind was still blowing hard, and the flag dipped and slapped against the flagpole, resisting the guard's efforts to retire it from service for the last time at Hyannis Port.

The White House message center at the Cape was located in the basement of the Yachtsman Hotel, but there was also a communications trailer just beyond the tall cedar fence that marked the boundary of the presidential property on Squaw Island. As Jackie piled Caroline and John into the back of a two-toned Buick, she saw workmen hauling away that trailer.

Jack had once told Jackie, only half in jest, that when they left the White House, the thing he would miss the most would be the White House telephone operator, who was a wizard at finding and connecting you to anyone in the world within a matter of seconds. Now, just as Jack had predicted, the red telephone with the direct line to the White House switchboard was gone.

Jackie climbed into the front seat of the Buick next to Clint Hill, her tall, curly-haired Secret Service agent. He and the other bodyguards were all that was left. Her husband had been taken away from her; now she was being stripped of her identity.

She had undergone a dramatic metamorphosis in the White House. At first she felt as though she had been stuffed into a tight cocoon, and she tried to extricate herself by staying away from Washington as much as possible. She spent the three months of each summer in Hyannis Port and in Newport, Rhode Island. She left on weekends for her Virginia horse-country retreat. Christmas and Easter were passed in Palm Beach. And she went for long stretches of time abroad—five weeks in India and Pakistan, four in Italy, two in Greece. White House reporters began to sign off their stories on Jackie with the line "Good night, Mrs. Kennedy, wherever you are."

Jackie was terrified of snoopy aides who, as she said, "hit the White House with their Dictaphones running." She feared that she was a political liability to her husband, and told him, "Oh, Jack, I'm sorry for you that I'm such a dud."

"She was such an innocent girl when she first came to the White House in 1961," said Robin Duke, the wife of JFK's chief of protocol, Angier Biddle Duke. "She didn't know how to talk on television. She was so inexperienced that she put on that wispy little baby voice, which none of us had ever heard her use before."

But by 1962 Jackie had gained a voice. People began to notice a striking alteration in her attitude. The crowds that shrieked "Jack-ee, Jack-ee, Jack-ee!" no longer seemed to terrify her. She came to understand that the public loved her as much as they loved Jack. Her poll numbers were sky high, higher even than Jack's; this so impressed his Irish mafia ("the Murphia," she called them) that they started to treat her like a key player in the Administration.

More comfortable in her role, she began to change the face and character of Washington. Nothing symbolized that change as much as the parties she gave at the White House.

"[Jack] loved the gaiety and spirit and ceremony of a collection of friends, especially beautiful women in beautiful dresses," wrote Benjamin Bradlee, then the Washington bureau chief of *Newsweek* magazine. "They liked to mix jet setters with politicians, reporters with the people they reported on, intellectuals with entertainers, friends with acquaintances. Jackie was the producer of these parties. Jack was the consumer."

Behind her back, the women of the press corps started calling her the Cleopatra of the Potomac. And it was true that she assumed an almost regal air. She was looking forward to continuing in power during Jack's second term. She was confident that it would be a triumph. There would be more parties, more beautiful dresses, more trips abroad. And Jack would have the opportunity to answer the great questions he had posed when he first entered the White House: What kind of people are we Americans? What do we want to become?

By 1963, she had achieved a life beyond her wildest dreams. She had the love of the most powerful man in the world; a mansion with a staff of servants who catered to her every whim; a fleet of limousines, airplanes, and helicopters to take her wherever she wanted to go; round-the-clock security; a wardrobe created by her own couturier; and the adoration of millions of people around the world.

Then, in a split second, she lost it all. And she was left to ask: Who am I? And what do I want to become?

As agent Clint Hill headed west on Route 28 toward Cotuit, he kept the speedometer below forty miles per hour and turned on his parking lights. The wind had dispelled the rain and fog, but the temperature was near freezing, making the surface of the roads treacherous. The Secret Service had just lost a president, murdered before the eyes of the world, and Hill did not want to be responsible for another national tragedy.

When Hill reached Cotuit, he followed Main Street out past the town to a spit of land on the water. The Erikson house, which stood at the end of a long, pebble driveway, was a modern brown wooden structure in the shape of a hexagon. The famed psychoanalyst was waiting for them on the steps of a screened-in porch.

Erikson looked like a well-groomed, Nordic version of Albert Einstein. He had a high forehead, and his fluffy white hair blew every which way in the wind. His large, sparkling-blue eyes and permanent little smile gave him an approachable air. He came forward to welcome his guests.

The Kennedy children had been trained by their mother to watch their manners, and even in their time of grief, they did not need to be reminded to shake the doctor's hand.

Erikson patted John's head and said, "I remember the picture of this little boy dressed in his formal coat, and saluting his father's coffin."

He led them into the house, where he introduced Jackie to his attractive wife Joan, who was also a psychotherapist. Mrs. Erikson seemed less than thrilled to meet Jackie Kennedy.

"My mother was taken completely by surprise by Jackie's visit," according to Erikson's daughter, Sue Bloland, who followed in the family tradition and became a psychotherapist herself. "My mother was an elegant woman in her own right, and she was the type who would be envious of anybody with Jackie's image. Knowing her, I suspect that she interpreted the fact that my father hadn't told her ahead of time about Jackie as a sign that he considered Jackie more important than his own wife."

While the two women were trying to decide what they thought of each other, Erikson put the children at ease by offering them soft drinks, as well as some toys to play with.

Erikson's personal experiences made him an especially appropriate therapist for Jackie's children. When Erik was three—exactly John's age—his Danish mother married a German-Jewish pediatrician named Theodor Homburger, and little Erik Homburger was raised believing that he was Jewish, and that his stepfather was his birth father. "This loving deceit," as the psychoanalyst later put it, was a prime reason for his interest in identity problems, and it gave him a deep empathy for children who had lost their fathers.

He had other identity confusions as well. Was he Danish or German? Jewish or Gentile? His anti-Semitic German classmates considered him Jewish, and rejected him. His peers at synagogue called him "the goy" because of his Nordic features, and did not accept him, either. Finally, setting out for Boston in 1933 to escape the Nazis, he created a new identity, and gave himself the name Erikson, becoming Erik the son of Erik—his own creation.

Through his practice and teaching, Erikson had met many famous people, but none as famous as Jackie. She was an interesting study for him—a shy, vulnerable woman with the determination of a drill sergeant. He had written about the particular struggles women had in establishing their identities. He said that married women who hoped to find their identities through their husbands, without first establishing a firm sense of self, often ended up woefully unhappy.

"What seems to be the problem with your children?" he asked Jackie, knowing full well that her answer would reveal a great deal about herself.

"A CHAIR
HANGING IN SPACE"

"More than anything else," Jackie told Erikson, "I want life to go on as normally as possible for my children. They were born in the same week, three years apart this month, and after the assassination I held birthday parties for them in the White House. But since then, things seem to have unraveled."

For Jackie, it had become a major effort to get through each day. She was taking large doses of the tranquilizer Amytal, which left her speech slurred and her mind disoriented. Erikson could see, without being told, that Jackie was existing in a shell of grief. She evidently felt guilty that she was neglecting her children at the very moment they needed her the most.

Jackie told Erikson that the assassination had transformed Caroline from a bright and lively little girl into a dour and lethargic child. Jackie was concerned about Caroline because of her daughter's deep attachment to her dead father. Even under normal circumstances, Caroline was not nearly as outgoing as John, but now she walked around with her hands clenched in angry little fists. She refused to play with other children, and at dinnertime she toyed with the food on the plate. She did not say much, or show any emotion, and she seemed to be pulling away from her mother.

Jackie had read many of Erikson's books, including *Childhood and Society*, and was familiar with his theories. He believed that there were eight stages of human development, and that each of them involved an "identity crisis." It was necessary for a child to resolve each crisis successfully in order to go on to the next stage, and become a whole person.

At age six, Caroline was entering stage four, which Erikson characterized as reflecting the conflict between "industry" and "inferiority." The little girl was beginning to figure out the rules of the larger society beyond the walls of her home. But how did a six-year-old integrate personal lessons of right and wrong with the moral outrage she must have felt about her father's assassination? Was this the beginning of a conflict between a public and a private self that would bedevil Caroline for the rest of her life?

Jackie identified with the sudden change in her daughter's personality. The same thing had happened to her when she was a child. Jackie had grown up in a home torn by bitter discord. She often saw her father, John Vernou Bouvier III, sprawled drunk on the living-room sofa. Dressed in nothing but his underwear, socks and garters, and shoes, he ranted against "kikes" and "micks" and "wops." He cursed God for the unfair way the world had treated him, and hurled abuse at Jackie's mother, Janet Lee Bouvier.

Janet generally gave as good as she got, hurling the family china at her husband. She denounced him in front of Jackie and her younger sister Lee as "a no-good drunk," and constantly threatened to leave him. Sometimes the fights went beyond words, and there were blows, blood, and black eyes.

As the older, more responsible daughter, Jackie was expected to help her mother carry her drunken father into the bedroom and undress him. Before they put him to bed, they had to clean up the mess left by his night of debauchery—his semen, vomit, and urine. The next morning, Jackie would watch in shame and pity as her father poured out his tearful apologies and begged his wife for one more chance.

When he was sober, her father was a totally different man. He was especially warm and compassionate toward Jackie, whom he favored over Lee. Jackie responded to his affection by secretly siding with him in the explosive marital battles. She came to see her father as a victim. If she had been his wife, she would not have driven him to drink. She would have known how to make him happy.

In later years, Jack Kennedy joked that Jackie had "a father thing." Her friends agreed; they said that the men Jackie found attractive bore a striking resemblance to her roué of a father, whose dark good looks accounted for his nickname, Black Jack. She was drawn to older men, piratical types with rampant sexual appetites.

However, that was only part of the story. Black Jack Bouvier was Jackie's first and greatest mentor in the art of life. He had an eye for color, shape, and form, and he delivered lectures to his daughter on everything from architecture and art to antiques, interior decoration, and fashion.

For Black Jack the most interesting art of all was the mating game between men and women. Pay attention to everything a man says, he told Jackie. Fasten your eyes on him like you are staring into the sun. Women gain power by affiliating themselves with powerful men.

He called her "Jacks"—a sexually ambiguous term that stuck as her family nickname. And in many ways they were more like sexual confidants than father and daughter. He engaged her in sexually stimulating conversations and bragged about his conquests. Jackie was flattered, because her father made her feel as though she was his most important girl.

When Jackie was a teenager, her father visited her at her boarding school, Miss Porter's School in Farmington, Connecticut. They played a lewd game in which Jackie would point to the mothers of her classmates.

"That one, Daddy?" she would ask.

And if Jack Bouvier had not slept with the woman in question, he would reply to his daughter, "Not yet."

And Jackie would point to another mother and ask, "That one, Daddy?"

"Oh, yes," he would say, "I've already had her."

"And that one, Daddy?"

"Yes."

"And that one, Daddy?"

"Yes."

As the child of an alcoholic—and a verbally incestuous alcoholic at that—Jackie sought ways to deny the existence of the painful and ugly. She did not hear things she did not want to hear; she did not see things she did not want to see.

"If something unpleasant happens to me, I block it out," she once said. "I have this mechanism."

Jackie's father provided her with the mechanism: style.

"Style is not a function of how *rich* you are, or even *who* you are," Black Jack told Jackie in what was his most important lesson. "Style is a habit of mind that puts quality before quantity, noble struggle before mere achievement, honor before opulence. It's *what* you are. It's your essential self. It's what makes you a Bouvier."

It was the Bouvier in Jackie that had prompted her to enter *Vogue* magazine's famous Prix de Paris writing contest when she was in college. The first-prize winner was offered a trial period as a junior editor on French *Vogue*, and a permanent position on the staff of New York *Vogue* if she made good.

Asked by the organizers of the contest to write an essay on "People I Wish I Had Known," Jackie chose three unusual artists: the French poet Charles Baudelaire, the Irish author Oscar Wilde, and the Russian ballet impresario Sergei Diaghilev. Her choices reflected her father's influence.

"If I could be a sort of Overall Art Director of the Twentieth Century, watching everything from a chair hanging in space," Jackie wrote in her essay, which won first prize, "it is [the theories of Baudelaire, Wilde, and Diaghilev] that I would apply to my period, their poems that I would have music and painting and ballets composed to."

Here, in her own words, was the best definition the world would ever get of Jackie. She saw herself as a detached observer safely suspended in space, a sort of celestial figure who employed the power of male gods to make things turn out her way.

"It was a sensibility best described as 'artistic' in that it was her own 'version' of things," wrote her stepsister Nina Auchincloss Straight. "Sometimes it was caught in her caricatures—simple, yet detailed, intimately funny pen, ink, and watercolor sketches of family and friends. But her singular view of life could best be seen in a photograph. Pictures were about being beautiful, brave; they were about family relations and friends. Her photograph of choice would have been the kind selected for a postcard: what to *look* like in life. Jackie knew what kind of a 'postcard' she wanted to send, as well as what message she wanted to deliver on the flip side."

Jackie's genius for staging artistic effects was apparent from the moment she entered the White House, her "chair hanging in space," where she reigned as a supreme, if detached, first lady. She became an inspiration to a generation of postwar Americans, who yearned to be shown what to do with their newfound affluence. She taught these ambitious but socially insecure Americans how to dress, decorate their homes, raise their children, and become confident consumers of culture.

In years to come, it became popular to dismiss Jackie as a woman of great personal style but little real accomplishment. She was no Eleanor Roosevelt, it was said. Some people sneered at her interest in interior design, flower arrangement, and fancy sit-down dinners.

But that was not only unfair, it was untrue. Jackie wielded great power. But she wielded it indirectly, like an art director, and through men. If the primary role of a president's spouse is to generate popular support for the man who occupies the Oval Office, then Jackie had to be ranked as one of the most effective first ladies in American history.

With her art director's skills, she became John Kennedy's most potent political ally. She transformed a White House that brimmed with rampant sexual infidelities and secret assassination plots against foreign leaders into a storybook place called Camelot. She established for all time the ideal of a golden age in American politics, making people yearn for the kind of heroic leaders who were probably no longer possible. And, in the words of the poet Archibald MacLeish, she "made the darkest days the American people had known in a hundred years the deepest revelation of their inward strength."

All this was done on such a grand scale that it was easy to overlook Jackie's other great achievement, which came *after* she left the White House. In her private years, Jackie suffered an ordeal by the media such as no other woman in this century, with the possible exception of Britain's Princess Diana, has had to undergo. But even as the public's image of Jackie was dulled by gossipy sludge, the private flesh-and-blood Jackie developed into an ever more appealing, self-confident person.

Over the next thirty years, Jackie struggled to recapture her old life, with all the power and the glory, only to discover that the key to her happiness lay where she least expected to find it: in the simple pleasures of family, friendship, work, and nature.

"It's queer how her public persona and her real self are so unlike," one of her oldest friends, Charles Whitehouse, told the author toward the end of Jackie's life. "I've given a lot of thought to this, and I think it is because she didn't become connected in the public mind with any virtuous cause. She is not perceived like Lady Bird Johnson, planting and making things beautiful, or like Barbara Bush with reading. And, you know, being involved with a national problem might have eased Jackie's situation.

"So why didn't she do it?" Whitehouse continued. "It may have been connected in some way with her being fiercely independent, and not willing to be involved superficially in something just for the sake of the press. Jackie is clearly not gripped by children with rickets. What she is, is a fascinating, somewhat perplexing human being—lively, sporty, affectionate, youthful. Not at all like the acquisitive monster that was portrayed in the press."

Erik Erikson was fascinated to listen to Jackie talk about herself and her children. Rarely had he encountered a woman who seemed so soaked in guilt.

"There are children who mourn invisibly," Erikson told her, speaking about her feelings as much as those of her children. "These children may show little emotion, but they are often concerned with the idea that some aggressive or sexual act or wish of their own might have been the cause of the death."

Jackie had no doubt harbored such aggressive wishes herself, especially when Jack Kennedy wounded her with his public displays of philandering and his callous disregard for her feelings. Her best friend, Bunny Mellon, called Jackie "a witch with supernatural powers," and there were times when Jackie must have wished she was a sorceress so she could punish her rogue of a husband for all the pain he had inflicted upon her.

"Jack would walk into a room and spot a young, attractive girl, and make a beeline for her," Jackie confided to a friend.

But then, in the last few months of their marriage, she and Jack had reached a new understanding, which was why she had agreed to go with him to Texas. And there in the blinding sunlight of Dallas, the third bullet from Lee Harvey Oswald's rifle had torn away the back of Jack's head, leaving Jackie with chunks of his brain quivering in her hands.

She would surely have given anything to obliterate the memory of her shameful wishes. But of course she was powerless to change the past. All she could do was deal with the present, and especially with the assassination's impact on her children.

Jackie was even more concerned about John than she was about Caroline. She worried that John might somehow be damaged in his masculine development by the absence of a father figure. Her son had always been a handful, but he was growing more difficult to control. He was wild and impulsive, and unwilling to listen to anybody. Managing him was becoming a chore.

At age three, John was in the midst of Erikson's stage three—the conflict between "initiative" and "guilt." John was trying to figure out which of his independent moves were socially acceptable, and which were not. It was the duty of his mother to help him internalize socially correct behavior through loving discipline. At the same time, according to Erikson's theory, she was to encourage free expression, and not raise a little automaton.

Erikson talked about the shooting in Dallas. A child's early concept of his body was often related to mechanical objects, and a great deal of childhood was devoted to working out the desires to retain and eliminate. So it might be important to learn how little John viewed the gun, the bullet, and the hole in his father's body.

Erikson then excused himself, and led John into his private study and closed the door. The room had an analyst's couch with a throw, and was filled with books and paintings by friends, including a couple of seascapes by a Cape Cod artist named Gyorgy Kepecs. Erikson had also brought back art from his trips to India. He had won a Pulitzer Prize for his biography *Gandhi's Truth*, and he believed in the concept of nonviolence—another reason he was deeply affected by John Kennedy's assassination.

There was a pile of toys on the floor—blocks, bears, marbles, cars, a broken bowl, a pinwheel, clay, paint, and small dolls made to look like male and female adults and children. Erikson got down on the floor and asked John to build a house. For several minutes, the white-haired therapist remained silent, allowing John to concentrate on his play undisturbed.

For all Erikson knew, John's participation in the events following his father's assassination had not been as traumatic for the little boy as most adults might have imagined. In a certain sense, the funeral, with its drums and flags and Scottish pipers, could have been exciting and fun for him. The whole experience might have given John the chance to perform on a large public stage. And besides, with his father's disappearance, John no longer had to compete with another male for his mother's attention.

"What kind of house is that?" Erikson asked John. "And why is that doll outside the house?"

"Because the doll went away," John replied.

"And why did he go away?" Erikson asked.

"Because," said John, "he doesn't belong in the house anymore."

THREE

NO PLACE
TO GO

December 1963

HER OWN PRIVATE
GREY GARDENS

A bitter wind was blowing off the Potomac when Jackie's Air Force C-131 transport touched down at Washington National Airport the next evening. Caroline came down the ramp first, dressed in the same blue overcoat she had worn at her father's funeral. She hopped into the waiting limousine, and Jackie followed with John; Maude Shaw, the children's nanny; and one of the family dogs, a blue roan cocker spaniel named Shannon.

The drive to the White House took them within a half mile of Arlington National Cemetery. The children could see the Eternal Flame fluttering on their father's hillside grave. Maude Shaw said that their father was in heaven looking after Patrick, and the flame seemed to confirm her words as it winked at them in the clear, cold air.

John was sleepy and out of sorts, and Jackie was anxious to see him tucked safely into bed for the night. She herself would sleep hardly at all. Her wounds were too painful. The world might marvel at her strength and indomitable spirit, how she had orchestrated Jack's funeral and held the nation together for three days of mourning. But as she confided to her sister Lee and to Bobby Kennedy, she felt that her usefulness to herself and others was coming to an end.

She had nothing more to give. Some days, she could not even get out of bed. She cried all day and all night until she was so exhausted that she could not function. She drowned her sorrows in vodka, and was slipping into depression. She feared that she might be turning into an alcoholic. Or was she losing her mind?

Madness ran in the family. Jackie's aunt Edith Bouvier Beale lived in a ramshackle mansion called Grey Gardens in East Hampton, on the south shore of Long Island, where she wandered like a crazed woman through rooms filled with rotting rubbish and piles of cat and raccoon excrement. Would that be Jackie's fate? She felt it was possible.

After all, Jackie remarked ruefully, she was already living in her own private Grey Gardens.

"THE MOMENT I
WAS ALWAYS SCARED OF"

After the children were asleep, Jackie came down from the Family Quarters, and peeked into the Oval Office. Jack had always wanted a red rug, and while they were in Texas, she had instructed the White House decorators to lay a new scarlet carpet.

The refurbished office now belonged to Lyndon Baines Johnson, who had been urged by Secretary of State Dean Rusk and Secretary of Defense Robert McNamara to move in as quickly as possible to minimize the shock of transition. But things had not gone as smoothly as expected. On the day after the assassination, as Johnson approached the Oval Office for the first time as President, he had been surprised to find John Kennedy's personal secretary Evelyn Lincoln still sitting at her desk in the anteroom.

"Can't you clear out of here so my girls can come in?" Johnson said.

Mrs. Lincoln reported the rude remark to Robert F. Kennedy, the Attorney General. Bobby Kennedy was so outraged that he virtually ordered Johnson to stay out of the Oval Office until after his brother's funeral. Not wanting to look like a usurper, Johnson acquiesced, and waited three days before moving in.

During that time, word spread that the new President had been barred from the Oval Office by the Kennedys. It was said that Johnson was being forced to conduct the nation's business from across the street in the vice president's office in the old Executive Office Building. Even after he took possession of the Oval Office, Johnson had to return each night to the vice president's residence to sleep, because Jackie and her children were still occupying the Family Quarters.

"I can't even live in my own house," Johnson complained to a companion one day while he was doing laps in the White House swimming pool.

Pressure mounted on Johnson to get Jackie and the rest of the Kennedys out of the White House.

"You're the President," Harry Truman scolded Johnson. "Clear this bunch out, and move your people in."

Jackie had promised Lady Bird Johnson that she would move within a week after her return from Hyannis Port. Her shock and sorrow were etched in every word of the memo she sent to the new First Lady.

> Maybe I will be remembered as the person who start[ed] restoring the White House—but you will be remembered as the one who *PRESERVED* it—and made sure for all time it would be cared for. That was the moment I was always scared of—Would the next President's wife scrap the whole thing as she was sick to death of hearing about Jacqueline Kennedy.

The women of the White House press corps, whom Jackie had dubbed "the harpies," had never warmed to the aristocratic Mrs. Kennedy, and they were eager to see her go. In the dispatches they sent back to their local newspapers, they noted that Eleanor Roosevelt had vacated the President's House the day after Franklin's death. When, they asked Liz Carpenter, Lady Bird's press secretary, would Jackie make way for the Johnsons?

"So I went to Mrs. Johnson and I said, 'They just keep asking when are we moving in,' " recalled Liz Carpenter. "It's the first time I've ever seen Mrs. Johnson really angry. She turned and said with rather intense indignation at the question, 'I would to God I could serve Mrs. Kennedy's comfort. I can at least serve her convenience.' "

"Everything was in a jumbled state as we were packing for the move," recalled Mary Barelli Gallagher, Jackie's private secretary. "The third floor was the busiest those days, fairly buzzing with activity. All the storage rooms had been opened and the things brought out to be packed. That moved smoothly enough. But the complication was Jackie's clothes: special tall cartons had to be made to hold the closets full of gowns."

"Now that I look back on it," Jackie admitted later, "I think I should have gotten out the next day. But at first I didn't have any place to go."

HALF-FORGOTTEN
DREAMS

Jackie received a call from Mrs. Averell Harriman, the wife of JFK's patrician undersecretary of state, offering the use of her house on N Street in Georgetown until Jackie could make more definite plans about a place to live.

Marie Harriman had attended Miss Spence's School with Jackie's mother, and she was a popular figure in Washington social circles. She had an appreciation for expensive Impressionist and Postimpressionist artists—van Gogh, Gaugin, Picasso—and for rich, handsome men. She was the kind of woman who could amuse a man for an entire evening by telling off-color jokes in a husky voice out of the side of her mouth. Jack Kennedy had been very fond of her.

"You need a place to live while you get your act together," Marie told Jackie.

It was a generous offer, and Jackie immediately accepted it. But she knew that the Harriman house, like all the houses she had lived in since her marriage, would be just one more way station in her life. She clearly yearned for something more permanent.

During the Depression, when her father lost most of his money, the family had been forced to move a number of times. They lived a rootless existence until Janet Bouvier's father, James T. Lee, a real-estate investor whom everyone called Old Mister Lee, let them borrow an apartment he owned in Manhattan, a grand Art Deco duplex at 740 Park

Avenue, which had been designed by the famous architect Rosario Candela.

"Remember, you're living rent-free in my house," Old Mister Lee barked at Black Jack, humiliating him in front of Jackie.

After Jackie's parents divorced, Janet had married Hugh Dudley Auchincloss Jr., an heir to the Standard Oil fortune and a prominent member of the hereditary WASP ruling class that had set the standard of behavior in America for nearly three centuries. But Janet and Black Jack had continued to carry on their bitter feuding. Mostly, they argued about money. As one of Jackie's biographers wrote:

> Perhaps it was the growing-up years in the Depression, her mother's complaints about the size of her alimony payments, her parents' constant bickering over dentists' bills, the graveside quarreling among the Bouviers over wills, estates, and trusts— whatever it was, [Jackie] had learned to draw an equation between money and peace of mind.

Jackie's teenage years were spent at Merrywood, the Auchinclosses' storybook estate in Virginia just across the Potomac River from Washington, D.C. But even there, she was aware of the disparity between her luxurious surroundings and her own fragile financial state. Five of the seven children at Merrywood were the direct descendants of her stepfather Hughdie Auchincloss; they bore his family name, and they received trust funds from the matriarch of the family, Grandmother Auchincloss, the former Emma Brewster Jennings. By contrast, Jackie and her sister Lee were impecunious Bouviers.

Jackie considered herself an outsider. Born into an aristocratic Catholic family, she never felt at home in the narrow-minded world of the WASPs. But as much as she wished to be emancipated from that world, she loved Merrywood—and everything it stood for. To her, Merrywood was a golden place of idealized beauty, splashed with sunlight and provided with every comfort and convenience.

What she remembered most about this lost Camelot of her youth was her bedroom. It was located on the third floor of the imposing Georgian mansion. The ceiling of the room slanted sharply beneath a gambrel roof, which gave the space a cozy feeling. The furnishings were simple: a few pieces of painted furniture, twin beds, and fleur-de-lis wallpaper that also ran across the low ceiling. An easel stood near a window. On the dresser, there were scrapbooks bulging with newspaper clippings, society columns, and hundreds of photos of Jackie.

After John Kennedy's assassination, the place that made Jackie feel the safest was the bedroom in her home in Hyannis Port. It was an almost exact replica of her bedroom at Merrywood: gambrel roof, patterned wallpaper on the ceiling, bulging scrapbooks. There was even an easel, which Jackie used when she and Caroline painted in the afternoons.

With only three days to go before she would move into the borrowed Harriman house, Jackie asked her maid Provi Paredes to bring the President's clothes to the third floor. After Provi put them on racks and laid them out on couches, Jackie looked them over, deciding what to keep and what to give away. It made her even more depressed to see Jack's things go.

"I suppose I was in a state of shock, packing up [in the White House]," Jackie said. "But President Johnson made you feel that you and the children [could stay], a great courtesy to a woman in distress. . . . It's funny what you do in a state of shock. I remember going over to the Oval Office to ask [President Johnson] to name the space center in Florida Cape Kennedy. Now that I think back on it, that was wrong, and if I'd known [Cape Canaveral] was the name from the time of Columbus, it would be the last thing that Jack would have wanted.

"The reason I asked was, I can remember this first speech Jack made in Texas . . . that there would be a rocket one day that would go to the moon. I kept thinking, That's going to be forgotten, and his dreams are going to be forgotten. I had this terrible fear then that he'd be forgotten."

Ever since Jack's murder, Jackie had been searching for ways to secure his place in history. She had asked her old friend Teddy White to write the authorized account of the death of the President. But White had respectfully declined, as had another Kennedy family favorite, Walter Lord, the author of A Night to Remember, the story of the sinking of the Titanic, and Day of Infamy, an account of the Japanese attack on Pearl Harbor. Jackie finally settled on William Manchester, who had won her trust with a fawning book on JFK, Portrait of a President. Unlike

White and Lord, Manchester was willing to sign an agreement ceding to Jackie and Bobby Kennedy the right to approve his manuscript before it was published. He gave every sign of being a malleable author.

But Jackie's desire to art-direct her husband's death had begun even earlier. It was on the flight back from Dallas that a picture had formed in her mind—a beautiful, brave picture of what Jack's funeral should look like. She recalled seeing an old woodcut in a bound copy of *Harper's Weekly* in the White House library that showed the East Room during Lincoln's funeral.

She observed parallels between her husband and the assassinated Civil War President. Both were inspiring leaders; both had died victims of hate. She sent instructions to Angier Biddle Duke that she wanted the President "laid out as Lincoln had been," with the same black cambric fabric. Jack's funeral was to be a carbon copy of Lincoln's.

In the course of his research, Duke learned that before Lincoln became president, he had lost a child, just as Jack had lost a child when he was a senator. While in the White House, Lincoln had lost a second child, just as Jack had lost Patrick Bouvier. And when Lincoln died, he was buried next to his children at Oak Ridge Cemetery in Springfield, Illinois.

As Jackie packed away Jack's things, she decided to follow Lincoln's example one more time. She made two telephone calls—one to her mother, in Georgetown, and the other to Richard Cardinal Cushing, in Boston.

Exhume the bodies of my dead children from their graves in New England, she instructed them, and have them reburied beside their father at Arlington National Cemetery.

"WHY, GOD? WHY?"

Janet Auchincloss was met at Washington National Airport the next morning by Ed Zimny, a veteran World War II aviator. Zimny was used to flying charters for wealthy people, but he was unprepared for Janet, a woman with lovely pink-and-white skin and dark eyes, her face framed by a thick head of hair. She was wearing a pair of white kidskin gloves, and looked as though she was on her way to a lady's tea rather than to a grisly exhumation.

Janet was not squeamish. She had spent many nights cleaning up Black Jack's mess. But the idea of digging up the bodies of dead children was too grotesque for words. Janet told Zimny that she had tried to talk her daughter out of her bizarre scheme, but nothing she said could change her mind.

Zimny was flying an Aero Commander 600, a small twin-engine six-seater, and it took him less than two hours to reach Newport, Rhode Island. There Janet was greeted by John F. Hayes Jr., the director of the Hayes-O'Neill Funeral Home. They drove in his hearse to St. Columba's Cemetery, overlooking Narragansett Bay.

At the entrance, a few stubborn leaves still clung to the branches of the maple trees. The cemetery looked gray against the gray sky. The hearse made its way along a winding drive to Section 40, a gentle hillside where Jackie's stillborn girl had been buried on August 25, 1956, by Father Murphy, a priest from St. Augustine's Church, in the presence of Bobby Kennedy and Kenny O'Donnell, Jack's right-hand man.

Two gravediggers were waiting in front of the marker, an upright headstone, about thirty inches high. Jackie had picked out a name, Arabella, for her stillborn daughter, but the gravestone simply read "Baby Girl Kennedy."

At a signal from Hayes, the gravediggers shoved their spades into the ground, and earth began flying over their shoulders. While they dug away, Hayes removed a brand-new infant's casket from the back of his hearse and placed it near the hole that was appearing in the ground.

It was a shallow grave, and the workmen quickly reached the lid of the coffin. They dug around its sides, creating a trench, then tried to lift it out of the ground. The moldy wood crumbled in their hands. Inside, maggots and beetles crawled over what remained of Arabella—a few muddy shards of bone, and tiny bits of soft tissue. The decomposed body was so thoroughly leached by water and bacteria that it was hard to identify any part of the skeleton.

Piece by piece, the gravediggers dragged out whatever they could. Everything went into the new casket. The small mass of putrefying matter gave off a horrifying stench. John Hayes, the undertaker, attempted to engage Janet in conversation to distract her during the gruesome proceeding. But she refused to speak. Nor did she utter a word as Hayes sealed the new coffin and slid it back into his hearse.

Janet spent the night at Hammersmith Farm, the Auchincloss country seat in Newport. Once Janet had acquired the Auchincloss name and money, she had become quite grand. She had always been a mercurial woman with a cyclonic temper, but during Jackie's teenage years, Janet's violent outbursts seemed to know no bounds. She thought nothing of strafing Jackie across both cheeks with her open hand.

After witnessing examples of Janet's cruel behavior, many of Jackie's school friends assumed that she hated her mother. But that was not true. Jackie admired her mother's spirit and courage (Janet's nose had been broken three times in horseback riding accidents), her passion for art, her personal discipline in diet and grooming, and her talent for household organization. Jackie may have loved her father more, but she spent her life trying to please her mother.

Her parents' messy divorce left a lasting mark on Jackie. She was ashamed that her schoolmates could read newspaper accounts of the divorce, in which her father was described as an adulterer. Her shameful feelings of exposure would color Jackie's attitude toward the press for the rest of her life.

Once a carefree and happy-go-lucky child, Jackie became stiff and introverted. She began a lifelong habit of biting her nails. She retreated into a life of fantasy and seemed to relate better to books than to people. She identified with legendary heroines who were sought after by powerful men, and whose beauty brought betrayal, war, and disaster: Helen of Troy; Persephone, the mythological queen of the underworld; and, most of all, Queen Guinevere.

It was difficult for Jackie to show her feelings. She found it even harder to form attachments. She became a loner; she had no real friends. People said it was almost impossible to get to know her. One young woman remembered being introduced by Jackie as "my best friend," when in fact they had not seen or spoken to each other in years.

Jackie's shyness never left her, and her childhood wounds started to heal only after Caroline was born. She began to develop the capacity to get outside herself, to understand pain and joy, kindness and pity, and to interpret them more movingly than she ever could before. Through Caroline, she came to realize that someone other than herself was real.

The night of the exhumation of Baby Girl Kennedy, Janet called Jackie and in some detail described her ordeal at the cemetery. It must have sounded hellish to Jackie, who had tried so hard to be a good wife and mother, but whose own life was spoiled and corrupted, just like the tiny bodies that were being disinterred from their graves.

Jackie had been pregnant five times in the ten years of her marriage. She lost one child in a miscarriage. The second, Arabella, was stillborn. The third, Patrick, died shortly after delivery. Two more—Caroline and John—survived, John only barely. Over and over, Jackie asked: Why, God? Why?

Whether she wanted to admit it or not, Jackie must have known the answer to that question. After Jack's assassination, Jackie had not wanted the doctors who performed the autopsy on his body to mention any diseases that might have been present. She feared that a thorough

examination would uncover evidence of the President's chronic venereal disease.

From the earliest days of her marriage, Jackie was aware that Jack
took enormous amounts of antibiotics to eradicate the bacteria that
caused his sexually transmitted disease—nongonococcal urethritis, or
chlamydia. She lived in deadly fear that he would infect her.

"Where you have a man who carries nongonococcal urethritis," according to Dr. Atilla Toth,* a specialist in the relationship between infections and infertility, ". . . after the first intercourse, the woman always
becomes infected, and the bacteria usually stays behind and multiplies,
and her subsequent pregnancies can be affected. Her second baby might
come to term immature, and subsequent pregnancies can be miscarried."

More than likely, this explained Jackie's difficult birth pattern. But
what of Jackie herself? Was her health affected by the venereal infection, too?

"These bacteria," explained Dr. Toth, "do not stay inside the
woman's uterine canal solely; they go through her tubes, her pelvic
cavity, her ovaries, and they interfere with ovarian function. Those slug-
gish ovaries do not produce the normal complement of hormones.
These are the women who, after deliveries, after miscarriages, develop
hormonally related emotional problems, and go through hormonal
withdrawal and severe depression that can last for months."

This explained why Jackie suffered from severe bouts of postpartum
depression after her pregnancies. And why she had felt so despondent
after giving birth to John.

*Dr. Toth never treated either Jack or Jackie Kennedy. His comments to the author were
based on his knowledge of many apparently similiar case histories.

AT A LOSS
FOR WORDS

It was dark and beginning to sleet when Richard Cardinal Cushing left his Boston Archdiocese residence and drove to Holyhood Cemetery in nearby Brookline, where Patrick Bouvier Kennedy was buried. Patrick was born five and a half weeks prematurely by caesarean section, and weighed four pounds, ten ounces at birth. He was the first to be placed in the large family plot, a wedge of land with a gray granite gravestone that had been purchased by Joseph Kennedy.

The Cardinal was a tall man, with a square jaw and a seamed face. He possessed a big personality and a big Boston Irish voice—"the harshest in Christendom," said McGeorge Bundy, JFK's national security adviser. Cardinal Cushing had delivered the invocation at John Kennedy's Inauguration.

"I thought it was a pretty good prayer," he said, "but less than three years later Jack was killed. So it didn't seem to do any good."

The prelate was dressed in black vestments. He watched as Patrick's intact casket was exhumed from its shallow grave. Then he sprinkled it with holy water and said a short prayer:

"Blessed be the name of the Lord, now and forever."

The Cardinal had officiated at Patrick's funeral, and witnessed the spectacle of the President of the United States slumped over his son's coffin, his body wracked by tears. He watched as Jack encircled the tiny coffin with his arms. Now, in an impulsive reenactment of the moment,

Cushing reached down, picked up Patrick's little casket, carried it over to his car, and placed it in the backseat.

It was midnight when he left Holyhood Cemetery and set off on the eighty-mile journey to Newport. There, the Cardinal met Janet Auchincloss at the Naval Air Station and turned the coffin over to her.

It was an especially poignant moment for Janet. As a consequence of her divorce from Black Jack, she had been excommunicated from the Catholic Church, and though in her heart she still felt like a Catholic, she knew that in the eyes of that church, she had irrevocably lapsed. Like Jackie, she had a Catholic sense of her own sinfulness, and whenever she was in the presence of high Catholic officials, like Cushing, she was uncharacteristically at a loss for words.

And so Janet did not say more than a terse thank-you to the Cardinal before she boarded the *Caroline* for the flight back to Washington. Inside the narrow cabin, Patrick's coffin rested beside the coffin of Baby Girl Kennedy.

IF ONLY . . .

At eight-thirty the following night, Jackie stood shivering in Arlington National Cemetery and watched as a crane lowered the coffin of Baby Girl Kennedy on the right side of the President's grave. There was something so final about seeing your own flesh being put into the ground.

Jackie's father was buried in East Hampton, Long Island, and she and her sister Lee had plots in the same cemetery. But now that Jackie's husband and two of her children were laid to rest in Arlington, it seemed more than likely that this would be the site of her last resting place, too.

The reinterment ceremony had been kept secret from the press. The only other people present were Jackie's mother; the surviving Kennedy brothers, Robert and Edward; and the Most Reverend Philip Hannan, the auxiliary bishop of Washington, who said the Lord's Prayer:

". . . and lead us not into temptation, but deliver us from evil . . ."

Jackie had told friends that Jack's death and the deaths of her children were all interlaced in her mind. Why did Jack have to die so young? she asked. Even when you're sixty, you like to know your husband is there.

She might have known that it was expecting too much to grow old with Jack and see their children grow up. That dream was now being buried along with the bodies of little Patrick and Baby Girl Kennedy.

Could she have saved the children? Could she have saved Jack?

She played the events in Dallas over and over in her mind. She told friends that she hoped the assassination had been part of a conspiracy, and that Oswald had not acted alone. That way, Jack's death would have an air of inevitability about it. For even if Oswald had missed, the conspirators would have gotten Jack anyway.

She did not want to accept Jack's death as a freak accident, for that meant that his life could have been spared—if only the driver in the front seat of the presidential limousine had reacted more quickly and stepped on the gas . . . if only the Secret Service had stationed agents on the rear bumper . . . if only *she* had insisted on a bubbletop . . . if only *she* had turned to her right sooner . . . if only *she* had done something to save him.

And so, as Jackie later remembered it, she went over and over the last three minutes in the car in Dallas, and there in the flickering shadows of the Eternal Flame, she wondered whether she was the cause of all the ruin and destruction: *What could I have done? How could I have changed it?*

FOUR

THE FREAK OF
N STREET

January 1964

"MORE THAN I CAN STAND"

Toward the end of January, Jackie moved out of the Harriman house and into a home of her own, a handsome, three-story Georgian structure at 3017 N Street in Georgetown. At her behest, Billy Baldwin, the famous interior designer, flew down from New York to help her with the decorating.

"Look, I have some beautiful things to show you," Jackie told Baldwin, producing a few small fragments of Greek and Roman sculpture. "These are the beginnings of a collection Jack started. . . . It's so sad to be doing this. Like a young married couple fixing up their first house together. I could never make the White House personal. . . . Oh, Mr. Baldwin, I'm afraid I'm going to embarrass you. I just can't hold it any longer."

She collapsed into a chair, and buried her face in her hands while she wept.

"I know from my very brief acquaintance with you that you are a sympathetic man," she said after she had recovered her composure. "Do you mind if I tell you something? I know my husband was devoted to me. I know he was proud of me. It took a very long time for us to work everything out, but we did, and we were about to have a real life together. I was going to campaign with him. I know I held a very special place for him—a unique place. . . . Can anyone understand how it is to have lived in the White House and then, suddenly, to be living alone as the President's widow?"

Decorating the house helped Jackie begin the long journey back to life. So did the excitement of going out and buying new clothes. She was no longer using Oleg Cassini, the temperamental couturier who had dressed her as First Lady. Once again, she turned for fashion guidance to *Vogue's* flamboyant editor Diana Vreeland, who had put her together with Cassini in the first place. But as always, Jackie was involved in every detail of her own attire, down to the size of her hats.

"The smaller the better," she told Vreeland, "as I really do have an enormous head, and anything too extreme always looks ridiculous on me."

After two months of bleak seclusion, she was ready for company. She invited Benjamin Bradlee and his wife Tony to spend a weekend with her at Wexford, her 166-acre property on Rattlesnake Mountain in Atoka, Virginia, adjoining the Oak Spring estate of Paul and Bunny Mellon.

A secret passageway had been built for the President in Atoka, leading from the master bedroom to a bomb shelter beneath the stables. But Jack and Jackie had stayed at Wexford only two weekends before his death.

Bradlee recalled that he, his wife, and Jackie all tried—with no success—to talk about something other than Jack Kennedy.

"Too soon and too emotional for healing, we proved only that the three of us had very little in common without the essential fourth," Bradlee wrote in his memoirs. "Only four weeks after the assassination, after the last of these weekends, we received this sad note from the President's widow."

Dear Tony and Ben:

Something that you said in the country stunned me so— that you hoped I would marry again.

You were so close to us so many times. There is one thing that you must know. I consider that my life is over and that I will spend the rest of it waiting for it really to be over.

With my love,
Jackie

There were other friends in Jackie's life. During the Kennedy Administration, an informal group consisting of the President, his cabinet officers, and some close advisers had met once a month for lively policy debates at Hickory Hill, Bobby Kennedy's estate in McLean, Virginia. Now, members of the so-called Hickory Hill Seminar—Arthur Schlesinger Jr., Franklin D. Roosevelt Jr., Charles Bartlett, McGeorge Bundy—made it a point to stop by for late afternoon tea at Jackie's new house to buoy up her spirits.

One day, Robert McNamara came calling. As he stepped from his chauffeured car, the bespectacled Secretary of Defense was greeted by an astonishing sight: a vast throng of shivering people had gathered in the snow in front of Jackie's house. They filled both sidewalks and spilled onto the street for as far as the eye could see. Some of them carried binoculars. Others had brought boxes and ladders to stand on. They were silent and sad-faced, watching reverently. A couple of photographers, perched on tree limbs, snapped McNamara's picture as he crossed the street carrying a large package in brown-paper wrapping.

He was almost run down by one of the smoke-belching diesel buses that plied N Street day and night with tourists eager for a glimpse of the former First Lady and her children. The front door was raised high off the street by several flights of stairs, and McNamara had to push his way past a group of tourists who were taking each other's pictures on Jackie's front stoop. He rang the doorbell, and was ushered inside by Secret Service agent Clint Hill.

"I'm a freak now," Jackie told McNamara as she escorted him into the living room. "I'll always be a freak. I can't take it anymore. They're like locusts, they're everywhere. Women are always breaking through the police lines trying to grab and hug and kiss the children as they go in and out. I can't even change my clothes in private because they can look into my bedroom window."

Jackie had not counted on becoming a national institution as a result of her televised performance after Dallas. She walked over to the living-room windows and drew the curtains, then turned back to McNamara. Her eyes were rimmed in red. Her uncombed hair looked dry and brittle.

McNamara felt pity for her. She had been elevated to the position of a mythical folk heroine, and yet she was a virtual prisoner in her own home. In the first few weeks after the assassination, she was inundated by several hundred thousand letters of condolence. Congress voted to give her office space for one year, and secretarial expenses of $50,000 to handle the bales of letters that arrived daily. She was assigned ten Secret Service agents—the first time the widow of a president had been given round-the-clock protection.

Jackie was the widow of the wealthiest man ever to occupy the White House, and people assumed that she was rich. But in fact she had been left with relatively little money. In his will, President Kennedy had given her a lump-sum payment of $70,000 in cash, plus all of his personal effects—furniture, silverware, dishes, china, glassware, and linens. In addition, there was the interest income from two trusts, valued at $10 million, which he had established for his wife and children. Jackie's annual income came to less than $200,000—a handsome sum by most people's standards, but an inadequate amount for a woman who was now expected to play the role of Her American Majesty.

Like most of the men who came to visit Jackie, McNamara was a little bit in love with her. Eager to please, he wasted no time in unwrapping his present. As the brown paper fell to the floor, an unfinished oil portrait of John Kennedy was revealed. The painter had completed the President's face and shoulders, but had left a large part of the canvas blank.

"This artist came to me, and said that he had been working on this portrait from life," McNamara told her. "He had a few more sittings to go when the President died. He said he didn't intend to complete it, and that he knew of my love for the President, and thought I'd find the painting appealing, and that I could buy it. So I did. If you want it, Jackie, it's yours."

Jackie was extremely fond of McNamara. He had played a key role in picking out the site of Jack Kennedy's grave in Arlington National Cemetery, a spot just below the Curtis-Lee Mansion that was in a direct line of sight between the Lincoln Memorial and the Washington Monument. It was the perfect place. But as Jackie examined the gift that McNamara had brought her today, she realized he had been the victim of a hoax. Jack had never sat for an oil portrait. The painting was copied from a photograph. And it was not a very good copy at that.

"Oh, Bob," she said, smiling through her tears, "it's lovely. Thank you so much."

After McNamara arrived home, however, there was a phone message waiting for him from Jackie.

"Bob," she said when he returned her call, "I can't keep the portrait. You must take it back."

"For heaven's sake, why?" he asked.

"Because I had it on the floor in the dining room, leaning against the wall where I was going to hang it," she said. "And Caroline and John came in and saw it. They kissed it. It's more than I can stand."

"DANKE SCHOEN"

As hard as she tried, Jackie could not escape the morbid pull of the past. The crowds in front of her home on N Street thickened by the day. The Speaker of the House of Representatives, John McCormack, insisted on presenting her with no fewer than six flags that had flown over the capitol during the weekend of her husband's funeral. Lyndon Johnson considered appointing her ambassador to France or Mexico, which, if she had accepted, would have made the new President wildly popular with the legions of Jackie admirers. It would also have had the added benefit of getting Jackie out of Johnson's way.

Johnson feared a kind of Kennedy government-in-exile, with Bobby as the heir presumptive and Jackie as the dowager queen. But Jackie did not want a public life. She wanted a private life, and the companionship of men on whom she could lean for support. The trouble was, if she ventured outside her house with a man who was considered a possible suitor, people began to talk.

That was what happened one night when her sister Lee Radziwill suggested that she and Jackie have dinner with Marlon Brando and his best friend, George Englund, with whom Lee was involved. The four of them went to the Jockey Club, Washington's most exclusive restaurant, where they drank martinis and got uproariously drunk.

Jackie and Lee sat together on the banquette, whispering conspiratorially into each other's ear. The sisters had almost identical voices—

rough, whispery vibratos—and the same gestures. They were having a splendid time until someone tipped off the press, and a group of photographers suddenly appeared in the restaurant.

Jackie, Lee, Marlon, and George fled through the kitchen exit and went back to Jackie's house. There they mixed a fresh batch of martinis, and Jackie turned down the lights and put a song on the record player so they could dance. She chose Wayne Newton's rendition of "Danke Schoen." Lee and Englund started dancing and necking. Jackie and Brando got up to dance, too.

No one in America was as famous as Jackie, but Brando came pretty close. He still had the perfectly chiseled forehead and jaw line from his *Streetcar Named Desire* days, but at age forty, he was beginning to lose his hair and put on some weight. His latest movie, *The Ugly American,* which Englund had directed, had been a big disappointment at the box office. Still, when he chose to, Marlon Brando could be a sexual tidal wave, on or off the screen.

Many of Jackie's acquaintances thought that she was a prude, the kind of repressed Catholic girl who ran the faucet when she went to the bathroom, but as Brando later told a friend, this was not the way she behaved with him. As they danced, she pressed her thighs against his and did everything she could to arouse him. When the music stopped, she went over to the record player and dragged the needle back to the beginning of the record. The room was filled again with the sound of Wayne Newton singing "Danke Schoen."

> Danke schoen, darling, danke schoen,
> Thank you for all the joy and pain. . . .

Jackie slipped back into Brando's arms. They talked about going away on a skiing vacation together, just the two of them. Brando could feel Jackie's breath on his ear. He felt that Jackie expected him to make a move, try to take her to bed.

However, Brando was not a big drinker, and liquor had more of an impact on him than it did on most people. A friend of Brando's speculated that the actor was concerned that if he got Jackie into bed, he might not be able to perform sexually. The fear of impotence might not have inhibited another man, but it was enough to stop Brando, who worried about his reputation as a great lover.

At the next break in the music, Brando abruptly excused himself and bid the sisters good night. With Englund at his side, Brando staggered drunkenly out of Jackie's house, slipped, and almost fell. The Secret Service men stationed in front of the house rushed forward to catch him, but Brando caught himself at the last moment and managed to walk stiffly down the stairs to the street, then climb into a waiting car.

At the open door, a totally bewildered Jackie watched Brando disappear into the night.

BIZARRE
BEHAVIOR

More and more, Jackie was thrown back on the company of the one man in Washington who did not seem to excite any prurient gossip, her Secret Service man, Clint Hill. Tall, handsome, and as laconic as a movie cowboy, Hill had all the attributes of an American hero. He had been a football star at Concordia College in his native North Dakota, and married his high school sweetheart, Gwen Brown, who still sang in her church choir.

Among his Secret Service colleagues, Hill was considered to be an agent's agent. One time, Jackie asked him if he would like to bring his children, who were about the same ages as Caroline and John, to the White House to play. Hill gently explained to her why he thought that would not be the professional thing to do.

In Dallas, Hill had hurled himself onto the trunk of the presidential limousine as Jackie was reaching for a piece of her husband's skull that had been blown away by Lee Harvey Oswald's bullet. Hill grabbed her and pushed her into the backseat, then crawled on top of her and lay there protecting her.

Since then, Jackie's feelings toward Hill had passed beyond the realm of gratitude to a kind of deep and dependent affection. She had asked President Johnson to give Hill the Treasury Department's highest award for the exceptional bravery he displayed in Dallas.

Hill did not believe that he deserved the medal. On the night before the assassination, he and eight other Secret Service agents had stayed up into the small hours of the morning drinking at the Fort Worth Press Club. They claimed later, rather implausibly, that they had not drunk a lot. In any case, Hill got only four hours' sleep, and was not at the top of his form the next day in Dallas. He was convinced that if he had reacted only five tenths of a second or perhaps a second faster, he would have taken the third shot, the one that killed the President. It was Hill's job to take that bullet, and he had failed.

His closeness to Jackie only intensified his feelings of guilt. Over the past couple of years, he had traveled with Jackie to India, chauffeured her from appointment to appointment in Washington, and become involved in the daily routine of her life. After their withering experience in Dallas, they had developed an even closer bond, the kind that exists between people who escape together from a brush with death. They were like two soldiers returning from the front. No one else could understand what they had been through.

Like Jackie, Hill wandered around in a shell-shocked state, often unaware that people were talking to him. He was teetering on the brink of a nervous breakdown, and should have asked for a medical leave. But he was too loyal to Jackie to abandon her to their dark memories.

One evening, about two months after the assassination, Jackie and Hill drove to the Embassy Row section of Washington and parked in a dark and deserted lot. They slipped through a back entrance of the Fairfax Hotel, an unpretentious, family-style establishment that housed such permanent tenants as Senator and Mrs. Prescott Bush, Admiral Chester Nimitz, and the family of a future politician by the name of Al Gore.

Jackie and Hill were greeted by Jack Scarella, the maître d' of the hotel's famous restaurant, the Jockey Club, where she had dined recently with Marlon Brando. Scarella escorted them through the bustling kitchen to the dimly lit dining room. It had beamed ceilings, dark paneling, and equestrian paintings. The restaurant was crowded with customers. Five captains in tuxedos and ten waiters in black pants and red bolero jackets hovered over the tables, serving the Jockey Club's renowned crab cakes, and its pièce de résistance, a half-vanilla, half-chocolate soufflé.

With Scarella leading the way, Jackie and Hill walked through the front section, known as the Royale, where celebrities normally liked to sit so they could see and be seen. Jackie had telephoned Scarella in advance and asked him to reserve an area in the back room, which customers called "Siberia."

After they were seated, Jackie ordered a vodka martini. As the evening wore on, she drank two or three more. At one point during dinner, she got up from the table and staggered to the powder room. She did not look any steadier when she came back.

"Then something really crazy happened," said a diner who was sitting with a friend in the Royale section, and had a clear view of Jackie and Hill from his table. "Jackie and Clint began engaging in what appeared to be a lot of heavy necking and petting. At first, I couldn't believe my eyes. Maybe Jackie was just crying on Clint's shoulder. Maybe he was just comforting her.

"After a bit, they slumped down in their red-leather banquette and disappeared from sight," the diner continued. "Every once in a while, they would appear, then disappear again. This went on from eight-thirty to ten-thirty. Jackie's hair was all messed up, and she looked like a mental wreck. But she didn't seem to care who saw her.

"In those days, people treated Jackie like a national institution, and newspapers bent over backward never to take a picture of her doing anything undignified, not even smoking a cigarette. So, for her to indulge in this kind of display at the Jockey Club in front of the crème de la crème of Washington society was totally bizarre behavior."

FIVE

"A GATHERING OF THE WRECKAGE"

March 1964

BUNNY

"I remember kneeling at the foot of the President's coffin in the East Room of the White House, and feeling utterly drained," Bunny Mellon was saying. "The tears would not stop. It was like the fall of all the hopes of youth. As though youth had tried and been thwarted. It seemed to me that the country had symbolically killed something."

"It had," said Jackie.

It was early one evening during Easter week, four months after the assassination, and a group of friends were having cocktails on Bunny Mellon's terrace on the grounds of the exclusive Mill Reef Club in Antigua.

Jackie's sister Lee was there with her husband Prince Stanislas Radziwill. Stas (whose name was pronounced "Stash") was the son of a Polish nobleman, and he was a favorite of Jackie's and the other ladies' because of his impeccable old-world manners.

Then there was Jack's old college chum, Chuck Spalding, a well-born advertising executive. He was at the bar, fixing another daiquiri for Lee.

Bobby Kennedy was slumped in his chair. He appeared to be listening to the conversation. But nowadays, Bobby was often lost in his own world, deep in grief over the loss of his brother.

And finally, there was a tall figure standing in the shadows. This was Clint Hill, who was keeping an eye on "Mrs. Smith," the code name the Secret Service had given Jackie during her stay in Antigua.

The Mellon house was made of native white limestone, and was surrounded by a mortared wall, six feet tall and three feet thick, that dripped with bougainvillea and hibiscus. Bunny had transformed the grounds into a lush tropical paradise. To irrigate her extraordinary gardens, her husband, the millionaire horse breeder and art patron Paul Mellon, had built a private water supply system that was larger than all of the public reservoirs that serviced the arid island.

A bright Caribbean moon was reflected in the water of Half Moon Bay one hundred feet below the terrace. A recording of "The Days of Wine and Roses" was playing somewhere inside the house.

"We were a gathering of the wreckage," recalled Chuck Spalding. "Jack's assassination was still very much on everybody's mind. Everybody was trying as hard as they could to shake the blues."

After Dallas, Jackie had turned for comfort to her closest friend, Rachel Lambert Mellon. "Bunny," as she was known to everyone except her servants, had helped Jackie design the grand visual spectacle of John Kennedy's state funeral, and she personally took charge of the flowers at the President's grave site.

Jackie's other female mainstay was Lee, who had hardly left her side since the assassination. Though the Bouvier sisters were known for their competitive relationship, their dealings had actually become much more complex in recent years, as sibling rivalry mixed with mutual admiration, emulation, and camaraderie.

Jackie's tragedy happened to coincide with a crisis in Lee's own private life. Lee was involved with Aristotle Onassis, the Greek shipping tycoon, and had petitioned the Vatican to annul her marriage to Stas.

"Lee and Ari had plans to marry, while Stas Radziwill was supposed to get hitched to Charlotte Ford," recalled the gossip columnist Taki. "It was all very cozy, and things would have gone as planned except that JFK asked Lee not to divorce Stas until after the 1964 election. Dallas and November 22, 1963, changed all that."

Like her mother Janet Auchincloss, Lee was interested in high society and money—and not necessarily in that order. She had conducted a number of famous love affairs with rich and powerful men, and in recent years had begun to compete with the aging opera singer Maria Callas for Aristotle Onassis's attention.

Lee and Ari were seen dining alone at Onassis's table at Maxim's in Paris. She was a frequent guest on his yacht, the *Christina*. And when in Greece, she stayed at his sister Artemis's spacious seaside villa in Gly-fada, near the airport in Athens. Lee and Ari became the object of international gossip. Shortly before the assassination, their names had been linked in a widely syndicated *Washington Post* column written by Drew Pearson.

"Does the ambitious Greek tycoon hope to become the brother-in-law of the American President?" Pearson asked.

Now in Antigua, Bunny's guests whiled away the cocktail hour by peppering Lee with questions about Onassis. A third daiquiri had loosened Lee's tongue, and she was going on about the superabundance of wealth and luxury that she hoped awaited her as the future wife of the Golden Greek.

"People talk about Ari's airline, his ships, and his private island," said Lee, "but what they don't know is that he controls Monte Carlo through his interest in the Société des Bains de Mer et Cercle et Étrangers. He controls his own kingdom."

"Perhaps one should start calling him Prince Onassis," said Stas, who insisted on using his own royal rank, even though Communist Poland had long since abolished its hereditary nobility.

Lee ignored her husband's sarcasm.

"Ari has homes in so many countries that he maintains duplicate wardrobes all over the world," she went on. "He never has to bother with luggage when he travels."

"They say the barstools on his yacht are covered with the scrotums of whales," Chuck Spalding said.

"The skin of the scrotums of *mature* whales," said Lee, as if the age of the whales somehow made a difference. "The sunken bath in his master stateroom is an exact replica of the one in a palace in ancient Crete. The temperature of the seawater in his swimming pool is regulated so that it's maintained a few degrees below air tempera-ture. Ari's business is no longer a means for him to make money; it's a vehicle for his personal pleasure. He's rich beyond the dreams of avarice. Nothing I've ever experienced compares to the luxe of his life."

"Nothing," Jackie corrected her, "with the exception of Bunny's life here on Antigua."

Everyone laughed—including Bobby—because what Jackie said was true.

"Oh, Bunny," Jackie said, "tell us how you picked out the color in your living room. It's such a good story."

"Well," said Bunny, happy to oblige, "I was trying to describe to my interior decorator the salmon-pink color that I had in mind. And I simply told him, 'You know how it is when you get up at five o'clock in the morning, and go into your garden, and the sun is just coming up? Well, it's not the color of the light on the first petal of the rose. And it's not the color when you pull off the second petal. It's the color on the *third* petal. *That's* what I'm trying to achieve!' "

Bunny was eccentric, even a bit nutty, but to Jackie she was the beau ideal of all that was romantic, exquisite, and fine. Jackie held her friend in such high esteem that she had even called Jack by her nickname, Bunny.

Jackie admired her friend's taste in French fashion (Bunny spent tens of thousands of dollars each season buying Hubert de Givenchy's entire couture line). Jackie respected Bunny's opinion on how things should look in a home ("nothing should be noticed," she said). Jackie subscribed to her friend's definition of what was boring and vulgar and a nuisance, and to her determination to keep the world at bay. And Jackie appreciated how Bunny dealt with the fact that her husband had had the same mistress for as long as anyone could remember (Bunny lived her own life, apart from Paul Mellon, and even kept her financial assets separate from his).

Most of all, Jackie admired the fact that Bunny was unbelievably rich. Bunny showered Jackie with presents, everything from the finest handmade stationery to a $5,000 Schlumberger bracelet from Tiffany's. This generosity may have been Bunny's special way of overcoming her feelings of timidity. As a young girl, she could not bear for anyone to look at her. She had such low self-esteem that her parents took her to a psychotherapist, who gave her a special exercise to overcome her problem. Bunny was told to stand in front of a mirror and repeat over and over that she was the most glamorous child, the most wonderful child, the prettiest child on earth.

Bunny never talked about the things that she collected. For instance, Jackie never heard Bunny say, "Oh, isn't that silver tureen beautiful," or "Isn't that a great painting," or "Aren't those chairs wonderful." Bunny did not focus on things as such. She was interested in what people *did* with those things.

She took being rich for granted, as her due. Her father, Gerard Barnes Lambert, had built the family fortune on Listerine mouthwash and Gillette Blue Blades, and he instilled in his daughter a view of money that Jackie found captivating.

"[W]ith the acquisition of almost unlimited funds, all the joy of getting new things disappears. . . . ," Gerard Lambert wrote in his memoirs, *All Out of Step*. "You are completely bored with the things for which those less comfortably off would give their souls. In desperation you seek new thrills through material purchases, but find them disappointing when you get them. It is like a Pyrrhic victory, better not achieved. . . . Wealth has a sort of Siamese twin, satiety, of which it cannot rid itself."

To stimulate the jaded appetites of her guests in Antigua, Bunny flew in her chefs and butlers from the mainland to help her local staff with the cooking and serving. Her servants' uniforms were designed by Hubert de Givenchy, and were of different colors and patterns for each day of the week. When she noticed that the potato chips in the pantry weren't perfectly round, she dispatched her private Gulfstream jet to fetch ones that were.

No one could match Bunny's talent for creating an atmosphere of rarified luxury without a hint of vulgarity. Adjoining her dining room in Antigua was a little slat house, where she grew orchids and seedlings and kept three tree toads that serenaded Jackie and the other guests all evening long.

Much of what Jackie had accomplished as first lady was done with Bunny's artistic guidance and financial support. Bunny had donated $485,000 (several million dollars in today's money) to the United States Park Service to restore Lafayette Square. It was Bunny's loose, mixed Flemish-style flower arrangements that Jackie had used in the White

House. For the state dinner that Jack and Jackie gave for Pakistan's President Ayub Khan at Mount Vernon, Bunny provided the gold vermeil cachepots on the tables, and the chairs, which she had re-covered in fabric that cost $24 a yard. The White House Rose Garden was designed and executed entirely by Bunny.

In the months after Dallas, when Jackie was at her most vulnerable, Bunny gained a great deal of control over her. Jackie tried to please Bunny, as she had once tried to please her mother, and she frequently asked Bunny for advice. One question that weighed heavily on Jackie's mind was whether she would ever be able to shake off her melancholy, and feel pleasure again.

She talked this over with Bunny, and they agreed that she would eventually recover. But a life of refined pleasure, such as Bunny's, required a great deal of money. And, of course, a very rich husband.

"I wrote Ben and Tony Bradlee that I would never marry again," Jackie said to Bunny. "Do you think what I said was right? That I will never want to marry again?"

Before Bunny had a chance to answer, Lee broke in.

"Jacks," she said, "I see no reason why you would ever want to marry again. You have already had a great love affair with a wonderful man. You have children. You have already had everything—love, romance, and all that marriage can offer. Why would you ever want to marry again?"

"AS CLOSE AS
YOU CAN GET"

"While we were in Antigua over Easter, Jackie and Bobby were as close as you can get," said Chuck Spalding. "What do I mean by that? Just anything you want to make of it."

One person who did not know what to make of it was Clint Hill. The Secret Service agent's nerves were shot, but he insisted on accompanying Jackie to Antigua anyway. He never let her out of his sight, and what he saw, day after day, was the spectacle of Jackie clinging to Bobby like a moonstruck lover.

One time, after they had waterskied on Nonesuch Bay, Jackie threw her arms around Bobby's neck and hugged and kissed him. Another time, on Mill Reef Beach, they strolled arm in arm, heads together, reading aloud to each other from a copy of one of Jackie's favorite books, Edith Hamilton's classic study of ancient Greece, *The Greek Way*.

"I'd read it quite a lot before, and I brought it with me," Jackie said. "So I gave it to him and I remember he'd disappear. He'd be in his room an awful lot of the time . . . reading that and underlining things."

Bobby was seeking solace in ancient Greek literature, and he compared his underlined passages with Jackie's. His favorite, which reflected the anguish he was suffering over the loss of his brother, came from Aeschylus's *Agamemnon*:

He who learns must suffer. And even in our sleep, pain that cannot forget falls drop by drop upon the heart, and in our own despair, against our will, comes wisdom to us by the awful grace of God.

Bobby exhibited all the classic symptoms of a severe depression. He had trouble sleeping at night, and was preoccupied with thoughts of death. He appeared physically diminished by his brother's assassination, as though he had actually shrunk. He was forever wearing Jack's old garments, as if he was trying to grow into his brother's clothes.

Deep creases were etched across his forehead and down the sides of his mouth. His thick mop of hair was suddenly splashed with gray. His blue eyes, which had once seemed so bright and steely, were now dimmed by sadness. There was a tentative quality to the way he talked. He groped for words, unable to express the things he felt.

"[A] large part of Robert Kennedy's agony stemmed from his fear that one of his campaigns—whether organized crime, union racketeers, Castro, or white supremacists, or right-wing forces within the government itself—had invited retaliation upon his brother," writes James W. Hilty, a Bobby biographer.

"I thought they would get one of us," Bobby confessed to a friend on the afternoon of the assassination. "But Jack, after all he'd been through, never worried about it. . . . I thought it would be me."

Guilt weighed heavily on Bobby, and he lost his old vigor and zest for life. He had trouble keeping up with Jackie on the beach, because he had recently injured a leg in a touch football game at the Florida home of Treasury Secretary C. Douglas Dillon.

"It was the roughest, wildest game I have ever seen," Pierre Salinger, JFK's press secretary, recalled. "Everybody was trying to get the hate and the anger out of their system. There had never been anything like it at Hyannis Port, Hickory Hill, or anywhere else. Bobby was absolutely relentless. He attacked the man with the ball like a tiger, slamming, bruising, and crushing, and so did everyone else. One guy broke a leg, and you couldn't count the bloody noses and contusions. It was murder. I was never so battered in a game before. For a week I could hardly walk. Every bone in my body hurt."

Bobby's adjustment to life after Jack was eased by the attention he showered on Jackie and her children. It helped him get out of himself. He talked to Caroline and John about the greatness of their father. He took Jackie with him wherever he went. In February, she had accompanied him to the Waldorf Towers in New York City for a visit with ex-President Herbert Hoover.

"Bobby bossed his sister-in-law around, and said, 'Jackie, sit there,' 'Jackie, do this,' 'Jackie, do that,' " Hoover's nurse said.

Bobby had always been a commanding presence in Jackie's life. He was the best man at her wedding in 1953. He was at her side three years later when Jackie had a stillbirth, and Jack could not be found on the yacht he had chartered in the Mediterranean. Bobby was at Andrews Air Force Base in Washington in November when Jackie brought Jack's body back from Dallas. He put an arm around her and said quietly, "I'm here, Jackie."

"Bobby's the one I'd most gladly put my hand in the fire for," Jackie said. "I wish Bobby were an amoeba, so he could divide in two. . . . He's always there—helpful, willing . . . a blessing."

All the sympathy, guilt, and hope that people felt for the dead President were now focused on Bobby. He was the repository of the Kennedy mystique, what Jackie called Camelot. High public office was available to him, though not the one he wanted the most, the vice presidency. Lyndon Johnson made sure of that. In order to avoid having Bobby on his ticket in 1964, the new President announced his intention to bypass all the members of his cabinet for the position.

Richard Goodwin, who was now writing speeches for LBJ, told Bobby, "If Johnson had to choose between you and Ho Chi Minh as a running mate, he'd go with Ho Chi Minh."

Aloof, shy, and a poor public speaker, Bobby was not a natural politician. He was once described as "the least poised, the least articulate, and the least extroverted of the Kennedy brothers." His high-strung personality, with its flashes of ruthlessness, seemed better suited to dark, smoke-filled rooms than to the bright lights of television. In Antigua, he talked with Jackie about retiring from the public arena.

She begged him not to quit, arguing that the country needed him now more than ever. As they talked, Bobby slowly came around to Jackie's way of thinking. He told her that there was an opening for a Senate seat from New York. But he would have to establish his legal residence in the state. Jackie could not imagine living away from Bobby, and he urged her to follow him to New York if he made the move.

There were many who thought that Jackie secretly wished to replace Jack with Bobby. And it was true that if Bobby could have been divided in two, Jackie might have considered marrying the half that was allotted to her. But Bobby was not divisible; he was singularly devoted to his wife Ethel, who had just received the news that she was pregnant with number nine—tying Rose Kennedy's record for childbearing.

Until the assassination, it was Ethel, not Jackie, who was the center of Bobby's emotional life. But Ethel had stayed behind in Stowe, Vermont, skiing with her children, while Bobby flew down to Antigua to be with Jackie.

"Well, what are you going to do about it?" Bobby's sister Eunice asked Ethel. "He's spending an awful lot of time with the widder."

A small court of friends gathered around Ethel to lend support. It was composed of such Washington social stalwarts as Martha Bartlett and Joan Braden, who resented Jackie's husband-stealing ways. The Bobby-Jackie-Ethel triangle became the talk of the nation's capital.

"I was aware of the appearances," said the columnist Charles Bartlett, a great friend of the Kennedy family, who had introduced Jackie to Jack. "I don't understand why Bobby wasn't more concerned about appearances. This wasn't the Bobby that I knew. I knew a Bobby who was pure, while everyone else was playing around."

"I don't know if [Bobby] became infatuated or not," said Paul "Red" Fay, Jack Kennedy's old PT-boat buddy from World War Two. "[Jackie's] a fascinating woman. If she'd throw her charm at you, why, you'd be emotionally swayed."

Was it possible that in their grief and crushing sorrow Jackie and Bobby had fallen in love? Were they sleeping with each other? Was Bobby the Lancelot in Jackie's Camelot?

Many people believed that when it came to understanding the Kennedys, you had to forget all the ordinary rules of behavior. In this view, the Kennedys did exactly as they pleased, and their family motto should have been: If you want to—why not?

This attitude did not sit well with J. Edgar Hoover, the director of the FBI, who knew that any dirt he could dig up on Robert Kennedy would be welcomed by the new man in the White House, Lyndon Johnson. Hoover had FBI memoranda in his private files linking Bobby to Marilyn Monroe. Unfortunately for Hoover, the source of those rumors proved to be totally unreliable.

Nonetheless, Hoover sicced his agents on Jackie and Bobby. After weeks of surveillance, the agents came up empty-handed. There was not a single incriminating note or memo about Bobby's relationship with Jackie in Hoover's bulging files.

"I was talking to Bobby one day about Jackie," said his friend, the journalist Murray Kempton. "I was saying something—it wasn't a probing question—and Bobby said in that sad voice of his, 'Oh, she'll never be happy.' You can say that about someone with whom you've slept. But that's one thing I could not imagine Bobby doing—knowing how he felt about his brother—that he would sleep with his widow. To the extent that he was a very Catholic person, I think he would regard it as a cardinal sin."

One person who had a chance to study the subject at close hand was the author William Manchester, who was writing the authorized account of the assassination.

"When I flew to Washington . . . for preliminary discussions with Bobby at the Justice Department, I was shocked by his appearance," recalled Manchester. "I have never seen a man with less resilience. Much of the time he seemed to be in a trance, staring off into space, his face a study in grief.

"Bob said of the book that the family was anxious to avoid flamboyance and commercialism," Manchester continued. "I replied that he should let me know what was acceptable to him. I did suggest that since the project had apparently originated with Mrs. Kennedy, it might be wise for me to discuss it directly with her. That would be unnecessary, he answered; he represented her."

To Manchester, it seemed clear that Bobby and Jackie were enveloped in some kind of love relationship. Each recognized in the other his or her soul's counterpart. They were both recovering from a terrible trauma, slowly coming back to life, and if love was the exquisite pain one felt for being truly alive, then Jackie and Bobby felt that emotion.

But that was a long way from sexual consummation. Manchester was a student of the Middle Ages, and the behavior of Jackie and Bobby reminded him of medieval courtly love—passionate but chaste.

What was more, Bobby was not the type to carry on an extramarital affair. He had once planned to enter the priesthood, and he had a Catholic sense of right and wrong. His fierce self-righteousness had led him to become a prosecutor. Any overt sexual act with his dead brother's wife would have been antithetical to his nature.

"The difference between the brothers was that Jack had a voracious sexual appetite, while Bobby was the exact opposite," said Manchester. "He channeled all of his sexual energies into his marriage with Ethel. An affair with Jackie would have been a violation of every moral fiber in Bobby's character. It would have been a desecration of his brother's memory."

PUBLICITY
MACHINE

B y now, the moon had disappeared behind the clouds, casting Half
Moon Bay into complete darkness. Bobby got up from his chair on
Bunny Mellon's terrace and disappeared without a word. Soon the
strains of "The Days of Wine and Roses" could be heard once again
coming from inside the house.

Chuck Spalding handed Lee her fourth daiquiri. When she drank a
lot, there was no telling what Lee might say.

"I've just bought a co-op at 969 Fifth Avenue," she said after a long
sip. "And I've been trying to convince Jackie that she should leave
Washington and buy an apartment in New York, too. That way, we can
live close to each other"—she paused, took another long, slow sip, then
added—"after I marry Ari."

There was silence.

Then Stas, who was the intended target of his wife's remark, chimed
in. "But, my dear, what makes you so certain that Ari wants to marry
you?"

"I'm certain that Ari will be more than happy to help us in any way
that he can," Lee said.

Jackie suspected that Lee was living in a dreamworld when it came
to Aristotle Onassis. Most of the published accounts of Lee's romance
with the Greek shipowner had been generated by Ari's own London-
based public-relations consultant, a young New Zealander by the name

of Nigel Neilson. Neilson placed articles on Onassis in the better news-papers in England and America, and he kept his employer's name linked to personalities like Winston Churchill, Douglas Fairbanks Jr., Cary Grant, and King Farouk of Egypt.

Onassis's affairs with some of the world's most desirable women were all part of this publicity machine. Like Donald Trump in years to come, Onassis had a natural talent for feeding the public's fantasies about his life as a libertine. Onassis believed that the public liked a man who lived on a large scale, with large appetites and large loves. He projected an image of potency: powerful in bed, and in the larger world. It was his way of impressing his bankers and customers, and making himself a brand name.

But Onassis was a narcissist, and his interest in women was essen-tially a reflection of his interest in himself. As he told friends, he loved women—plural—but found it hard to love any one of them in particu-lar. And that included Lee. He had never broached the subject of mar-riage to Lee.

"There is an affinity between us," he said of his relationship with Lee. "No more than a friendship."

SIX

AN UNERRING SENSE OF STARDOM

April 1964–October 1965

MISTER
MANCHESTER

A t a few minutes before noon on April 7, 1964, the day after Jackie returned from Antigua, she slid open the mahogany doors in the living room of her Georgetown house, and made a grand, sweeping entrance.

"Mr. Manchester!" she exclaimed.

William Manchester, the tall, pipe-smoking Wesleyan University history professor, whom she had chosen to write the authorized version of Jack's assassination, bolted from his seat. He stared at Jackie as though he could not believe his eyes. She was dressed in a black jersey top and yellow stretch pants.

"She was beaming at me," Manchester recalled years later, "and I thought how, at thirty-four, with her camellia beauty, she might have been taken for a woman in her mid-twenties. My first impression—and it never changed—was that I was in the presence of a very great tragic actress.

"I mean that in the finest sense of the word," he continued. "There was a weekend in American history when we needed to be united in our sadness by the superb example of a bereaved First Lady, and Jacqueline Kennedy—unlike Eleanor Roosevelt, a more extraordinary woman in other ways—provided us with an unforgettable performance as the nation's heroine.

"One reason for this triumph was that her instincts were completely feminine. If she met your plane at the Hyannis airport, she automatically handed you the keys to her convertible. Men drive, women are driven: that was the logic of things to her, and it is impossible to think of her burning a bra or denouncing romantic love as counterrevolutionary."

Jackie motioned for Manchester to sit down, then asked, "Are you just going to put down all the facts, who ate what for breakfast and all that, or are you going to put yourself in the book, too?"

"I can't very well keep myself out of the book," Manchester replied.

"Good," said Jackie.

She offered to pour him a daiquiri from an icy pitcher, then took a nearby chair.

"Future historians may be puzzled by odd clunking noises on the tapes," Manchester noted. "They were ice cubes. The only way we could get through those long evenings was with the aid of great containers of daiquiris."

Over the next several hours, Jackie got quite drunk, and proceeded to pour out her heart.

She described how in Fort Worth, on the eve of the assassination, she had slipped into her husband's bed, and aroused him from his fatigue, and made love to him for the last time. . . .

She described sitting at a dressing table, looking for lines in her face, and musing about the tall Dallas blondes who had caught her husband's eye. . . .

She told Manchester all the "gruesome stuff"—about Jack's brains, and the way he looked on the table in Parkland Memorial Hospital in Dallas. . . .

She told him how she had spent the night of her husband's death alone in bed at the White House, writhing and tossing while under sedation from large doses of the tranquilizer Amytal. . . .

She described for him the sounds of Caroline crying when she heard the news of her father's death. . . .

She reconstructed a scene in the limousine on the way to Arlington National Cemetery, when Bobby looked down at young John and said, "You've got those sissy white gloves on—take them off," but Jackie made her son keep them on. . . .

"I had carefully put the Wollensak recorder where I would see it and she wouldn't," Manchester wrote. "I didn't want her to worry about the machine. Also, I had to be sure that the little light on it was winking, that the reels were turning, and all this wasn't being lost.

"It was a good plan," he went on. "Its defect was revealed to me when she took the wrong chair. Then the only way I could check the light was by hunching up. It was an odd movement; I needed an excuse for it. A cigarette box on a low table provided one. Before that evening, I hadn't smoked for two years. At the end of it I was puffing away, and eight more years would pass before I would quit again."

Manchester was deeply moved by Jackie's candor. Like Teddy White five months earlier, he realized that he was hearing more than he had bargained for. And he, too, felt an obligation to protect her. He worked out a hand signal that she could use when she wanted him to turn off his Wollensak recorder. But she seldom resorted to using the signal.

"It is true that she . . . withheld nothing during our interviews," he wrote. "It is also true that none of that sensitive material found its way into any draft of the book."

Manchester protected Jackie out of a tender regard for her feelings, as well as out of his deep respect for her dead husband.

"I couldn't disdain Kennedy," he said. "He was brighter than I was, braver, better-read, handsomer, wittier, and more incisive. The only thing I could do better was write. I never dreamed that one day I would write his obituary—the longest presidential obituary in history, and, in the end, the most controversial."

DISGUISES
AND SMILES

One fine fall day in September, Bobby entered the lobby of 1040 Fifth Avenue, Jackie's new home in New York City. Her building was one of those massive limestone palaces that had been designed by Rosario Candela, the leading apartment architect of the 1920s, who had also done 740 Park Avenue, where Jackie had lived as a child.

Bobby stopped to speak with Clint Hill, who had stationed himself inconspicuously in the back of the lobby. Hill seemed confused and distracted. Unnerved by the agent's appearance, Bobby got into the elevator and ascended to Jackie's apartment.

He stepped off on the fourteenth floor, directly into Jackie's foyer. A black-and-white marble floor led him into a large rectangular gallery, which served as the hub of the fifteen-room apartment. He went into the living room, a square room with a Palladian sense of light and serenity, and stood at one of the tall French windows and looked out over a spectacular view of Central Park and the reservoir.

Jackie had found the co-op by scouring the real-estate market with Nancy Tuckerman, her old roommate from Miss Porter's School, who had served briefly as her social secretary in the White House after Letitia Baldrige had left. Whenever they inspected the available New York co-ops together, Nancy dressed up, pretending that she was a rich matron, while Jackie disguised herself as a British nanny.

Upon finding the apartment at 1040 Fifth Avenue, Jackie had called

André Meyer, the senior partner of the investment banking firm Lazard Frères and a brilliant spinner of fortunes. Jackie had come to depend on the gnome-like French banker, who enjoyed playing the role of father confessor to beautiful women who were not too sure of themselves.

"It's perfect," she told Meyer, "and if you think it's a good investment, I'll buy it."

Meyer looked over the apartment, which was conveniently located near the best private schools, and only a few blocks away from the apartments of Bobby and Lee, and pronounced the $200,000 asking price a fair one.

After Jackie bought the apartment, she turned to her friend Bunny Mellon for advice on decorating it. Bunny favored light, airy French furniture, sophisticated subtlety, and comfort. Nothing must be gold, nothing dark, nothing frilly. Everything had to be "undercooked."

To achieve that look, Jackie once again hired the designer Billy Baldwin, who had not had time to finish her N Street house before she left Washington. In Jackie's New York living room, Baldwin used the Louis XVI bureau on which President Kennedy had signed the Limited Nuclear Test Ban Treaty in 1963, and her father's ormolu-mounted Empire fall-front desk. He hung John Fowler curtains over the tall windows and placed Jackie's collection of animal drawings and Indian miniature paintings on the walls. On a commode, he displayed Jackie's most treasured possession, an ancient Hellenistic alabaster head of a woman. The result was pure Bunny: rarified luxury without a hint of vulgarity.

"The day Jackie moved into the apartment," Nancy Tuckerman recalled, "we spent the day unpacking, emptying cartons, putting books in bookcases. Around eight o'clock in the evening, the doorbell rang, and Jackie, in her blue jeans and looking quite disheveled, opened the door. There stood two distinguished-looking couples in full evening attire. When they recognized Jackie, they were taken aback. They said they were expected for dinner at Mrs. Whitehouse's. It turned out that the elevator man, unnerved by the mere thought of Jackie's presence in the building, was unable to associate the name Whitehouse with anyone or anything but her."

Bobby wandered through the sprawling apartment, looking for Jackie. He passed Caroline's bedroom, and caught a glimpse of the little girl through the half-open door. She was cutting pictures of her father out of a magazine and sticking them on the wall.

The first anniversary of Jack's assassination was a couple of months away. In the past ten months, 7,740,000 people had visited the slain President's burial place—more than all the tourists who visited the Lincoln Memorial and the Washington Monument combined. Sixty books about JFK had already been published, and more were on the way. Two dozen phonograph records had been issued, most of them containing the text of his speeches. The mania for all things Kennedy continued unabated.

So did the family's penchant for tragedy. In June, Bobby's younger brother Ted was in a plane crash in Massachusetts. Two of those on board lost their lives—Ted's legislative assistant, and the pilot, Ed Zimny, who had flown Janet Auchincloss to Rhode Island on the day Baby Girl Kennedy's body was exhumed. Ted fractured his back, and was still recuperating.

Bobby found Jackie and Nancy in the master bedroom, putting away books. The walls were covered in ivory silk, as were those in the adjoining master bathroom. Bookcases held Jackie's collection of Persian miniatures. The iron four-poster was a gift from Bunny, who had ordered it from her own ironsmith on her estate in Middleburg, Virginia. It was covered by a rare guanaco fur spread that had been given to Jackie by Jack. A photograph of Jack rested on the bedside table next to a small vase with fresh flowers. Apart from Caroline's clippings, it was the only picture of the dead President in the entire apartment.

Nancy went over to shake Bobby's hand, and he winced in pain. His hand was swollen and tender from campaigning.

Bobby's campaign for the Senate was his first attempt at winning elective office. He was running on an idealized version of his brother's legacy. Whereas Jack had been a give-and-take politician comfortable with compromise, Bobby preached the liberal ideals of youth and public service.

"President Kennedy," Bobby told the New York crowds, "was more than just president of a country. He was the leader of young people everywhere. What he was trying to do was fight against hunger, disease, and poverty around the world. You and I as young people have a special responsibility to carry on the fight."

Jackie was delighted with Bobby's noble message. She had attended the Democratic Party's national convention that past summer in Atlantic City, and was thrilled when the crowd gave Bobby a twenty-three-minute standing ovation. His emotional reception was interpreted as a humiliation of President Johnson. Everyone in the convention hall was aware that war had broken out between Bobby and Johnson. Bobby was eager to score a landslide victory in the 1964 New York Senate race so that he could challenge Johnson for the presidential nomination in 1968.

As the art director of Camelot, Jackie played an important role in Bobby's political plans. She had recently learned that, despite her efforts to stop him, Jim Bishop intended to publish a book called *The Day Kennedy Was Shot*. She wrote Bishop, appealing to him to abandon the project.

> As you know—it was my fear as long ago as December—that all sorts of different and never ending, conflicting, and sometimes sensational things would be written about President Kennedy's death.
>
> So I hired William Manchester—to protect President Kennedy and the truth. He was to interrogate everyone who had any connection with those days—and if I decide the book should never be published—then Mr. Manchester will be reimbursed for his time.

Bobby objected to Jackie's use of the words "hired" and "reimbursed," and so she sent a second letter to Bishop.

> I chose Mr. Manchester because I respect his ability and because I believe him capable of detachment and historical accuracy. . . . I exercise no surveillance over what he is doing, and I do not plan to. He will present his finished manuscript and it will be published with no censorship from myself or from anyone else. . . . I have no wish to decide who writes history.

That, of course, was untrue. Jackie had called in Manchester for the express purpose of stopping Jim Bishop. As always, she was trying to be the puppeteer who controlled the strings of history. She envisioned Manchester's book not only as a beautiful and brave account that re-flected her version of her husband's murder, but as one that would also serve as a manifesto for Bobby's long march to the White House.

"You must win," Jackie told Bobby of the Senate campaign. "You *will* win."

One way of assuring an impressive victory was for Jackie to cam-paign by his side.

"You could do it with dignity," Bobby told her. "An appearance here, a few TV spots there."

But Jackie, who occasionally showed up for private fund-raisers for Bobby, had other ideas.

"What if I attend some of your rallies in disguise?" she asked. "You know, wearing a wig or a turban or something? I could lend moral support."

"That's not exactly what I had in mind," Bobby said. "What about the children? Can I use Caroline and John?"

"I don't think so," she said.

"This campaigning is a lot tougher than I expected," Bobby said. "All that smiling . . ."

"You could turn on a very low-level smile," Jackie said. "It's the really broad smiles that wear you out. A gentle little smile would wear better."

LESSONS IN
SELF-IMPROVEMENT

A smiling Oliver Smith was waiting for Jackie when she arrived by limousine at his yellow town house on Willow Street in Brooklyn Heights. It was the dead of winter in 1965, and Jackie was wearing a tailored wool coat that looked like it came from Halston. She stepped past the ornately carved black door that Oliver Smith held open for her, and entered his house.

"Welcome to the house that Sam Goldwyn built," Oliver Smith said, helping her off with the coat. "I bought this place with the earnings from my first Hollywood film, *Band Wagon*."

Oliver Smith was a theatrical designer, and everything about him was theatrical in an understated sort of way. A tall, lanky figure with closely cropped hair, he was dressed in a custom-made double-breasted blue suit from Dunhill. A cigarette dangled from a long, delicate hand that emerged from a cuff fastened with a small gold cuff link. He looked like a Noël Coward creation, a man who knew how to live in grand style.

He led Jackie into the living room, and began mixing martinis. He had spent the past ten years restoring the four-story, Federal-style house, and the place was a marvel of visual imagination. The high-ceilinged room featured a spectacular spiral staircase, a silver chandelier, and an ornate Chippendale mirror over a black Belgian marble fireplace. Two cats snoozed in front of a blazing, stagy fire.

Oliver Smith handed Jackie her drink, then sat down facing her. Once he had a martini in hand, he needed a cigarette, and he lit another Marlboro. When he crossed one long leg over the other, it touched the floor.

Jackie came to Oliver Smith's house once a week to take drawing lessons. She had always possessed a talent for drawing amusing figures in the children's-book style of Ludwig Bemelmans, the creator of the *Madeline* series. In fact, Jackie and Bemelmans had once corresponded about collaborating on a children's book, possibly with Madeline visiting the White House. Bemelmans had also urged Jackie to keep a daily journal with her personal thoughts and illustrative sketches.

Bemelmans died before he and Jackie had a chance to carry out their project. After she moved to New York, she embarked on a self-improvement kick with another visual artist, Oliver Smith.

"What's new with Truman?" Jackie asked.

"Pardon me?" Smith said. He was hard of hearing.

"*Truman,*" Jackie repeated, louder.

She was referring to the writer Truman Capote, not the ex-President. Jackie and Smith had been introduced by Truman Capote, though introductions were hardly necessary for two such well-known people. Oliver Smith was a legend in the theater. He had scored his first major success back in 1942, designing the scenery for Agnes de Mille's *Rodeo*. He then went on to do the sets for *On the Town*, *My Fair Lady*, *West Side Story*, and *The Sound of Music*, as well as for a number of productions of the American Ballet Theatre, where he was now codirector.

A little over a year before, Smith had brought the American Ballet Theatre to Washington, where Jackie and the President saw the company perform in a decrepit movie theater near the White House. Jackie was dismayed by the contrast between the evening's brilliant performance and its down-at-heels surroundings, and it got her to thinking about a center for the performing arts in Washington that would be modeled after Lincoln Center in New York City.

"The arts had been treated as a stepchild in the U.S.," she later recalled. "When the government had supported the arts, as in many WPA projects, artists were given a hand and some wonderful things emerged. I had seen in Europe how proud those countries were of their arts and artists. Of course, they had a longer tradition of patronage, going back to kings, popes, and princes, but modern governments continued this support. Our great museums and great performing companies should be supported, but the experimental and the unknown should also be thrown a line."

After her famous 1961 trip to Paris, when she had met President Charles De Gaulle and his culture minister, André Malraux, Jackie was determined to create an American department of the arts. As a first step in that direction, she persuaded her husband to appoint August Heckscher as a "special consultant to the President on the arts." And Kennedy had been scheduled to sign an executive order realizing one of Jackie's greatest goals: the appointment of Richard Goodwin as the first special assistant to the President for cultural affairs. Her dream was ultimately realized when President Johnson created the National Endowment for the Arts and the National Endowment for the Humanities. The notion that government should take a leading role in promoting the arts became a permanent part of the American cultural landscape.

Oliver Smith's most celebrated accomplishment was his over-the-top design for the Lerner-Loewe musical *Camelot.* When Jackie told Teddy White "there'll never be another Camelot," she was thinking of Smith's pastel jousting fields and golden castles. She shared Smith's talent for turning reality into a stage set.

Oliver Smith's ability to create the perfect mise-en-scène was on permanent display in the garden in the back of his house. The garden was a masterpiece of landscaping, with its splashing fountain, heavy slate patio, and arbor laden with thick, twiny wisteria. In the spring and summer, the feeling was very Southern, like a miniature Tara, and indeed the house appealed to many Southern writers, such as Truman Capote, who for a time lived in the basement apartment on Willow Street with his lover Jack Dunphy. Billy Baldwin helped Capote decorate it with dark green wallpaper, and a pair of gold mirrors in the shape of butterflies.

"He was just an alley cat that wandered around the neighborhood eating whenever he could," Oliver Smith said of Truman Capote. "He was thin—very thin—and he would stand on the porch looking wistfully into the kitchen. He was determined to get into the house, but I didn't want him. I had four other cats, which was a big enough feline population."

"Do you remember?" Jackie said. "At lunch in your dining room, Truman told me, or at least strongly implied, that the whole house was his."

"I remember," Smith answered.

"And then in the middle of lunch I got the idea that it wasn't his," she said. "That it was yours."

Oliver Smith's house figured prominently in the social life of New York's influential community of homosexual artists, writers, and musicians. Smith gave famous parties, and he was known as a brilliant raconteur, a man brimming with the latest bawdy gossip. He had a dry wit, and talked in a slow, thoughtful way about art, style, and having a good time.

Many of the friends Jackie made after she moved to New York were gay. There were, of course, heterosexual men in her cultural circle, too, men like Mike Nichols, Jason Epstein, and Norman Podhoretz. But with gay men, there was no layer of sex, which meant that there was one less thing for Jackie to worry about. Once, for example, when Truman Capote visited Jackie in her Fifth Avenue apartment, she invited him into her bedroom while she dressed to go out for the evening.

Jackie's friendship with gay men like Oliver Smith, Truman Capote, Tennessee Williams, and Leonard Bernstein had a profound effect on her outlook. When she was a young girl, she had heard her father heap contempt on "faggots." The nuns and priests taught her that homosexuality was a sin. Later, the Kennedys scorned any behavior that lacked manly strength and purpose.

As part of her New York education, however, Jackie saw all the harm that was done by this effort to stigmatize homosexuality. She came to believe that no good would ever come from trying to sanitize or standardize behavior.

She was growing more broad-minded and tolerant, even about herself. She started to accept the fact that, like homosexuals, she herself was not what most people considered "normal." In a way, she was "almost normal," just like her gay friends.

After Oliver Smith and Jackie finished their drinks, they went upstairs. On the second floor there was another guest apartment, which was frequently used by Tyrone Guthrie, the artistic director of the Shakespeare Festival in Stratford, Ontario.

"Tyrone must be six foot six, and his wife is a big woman, too," said Smith. "It is always a puzzle to me how two such huge, flamboyant figures can fit into such a small room."

Smith's studio was on the third floor, and it was here that he and Jackie worked side by side at his drafting tables. Smith had studied architecture, and was an accomplished illustrator. But his real skill was as a teacher.

"What do you think of this?" Jackie asked, pointing to the landscape she was working on. "It's terrible, isn't it?"

"Not at all," he said. "Just a trifle primitive. It looks like a fried egg."

"A fried egg!" Jackie said, horrified. She looked at her work again, and started laughing. "Well, I suppose it does," she said.

While they drew, Smith spoke of art and literature. Art was his whole life, and his words flowed in a languid, unforced stream of consciousness. He was a great traveler, too, and extremely well read in most of the world's literature, and his conversation jumped without a hitch across centuries and disciplines and cultures.

Before Jackie knew it, their time was up. She put away her things and stole a glimpse at Smith's drawing.

"Why, that's wonderful, Oliver," she said.

"This?" he said with a vehemence that Jackie rarely heard in his voice. "This doesn't mean a thing. It won't last. What I do is fleeting, and I'll be forgotten tomorrow. A great painter or writer—now *their* work will last forever."

YOU CAN'T KNOW ONE
WITHOUT THE OTHER

In April of 1965, Lee gave Jackie a New York coming-out party. She cleared away the furniture in her dining room and placed a five-piece Lester Lanin ensemble at one end of the room beside the windows. She brought in huge bouquets of multicolored spring flowers, and lots of champagne. And she invited all the beautiful people to toast "Her Elegance," as *Women's Wear Daily* had recently christened Jackie.

By ten-thirty, however, all but one of the guests had departed.

"The party was a flop," Lee moaned.

She was standing in the kitchen of her Fifth Avenue duplex, dressed in a lime-green silk crêpe Yves Saint Laurent ball gown. She and Stas lived in what many people considered to be the most spectacular apartment in all of New York. Friends were stupefied when they entered the drawing room, which was like a stage set worthy of an Italian opera. Created by the interior designer Renzo Mongiardino, the room had elaborate carved wood paneling and walls upholstered in raspberry-colored velvet, with a painted band of scrollwork up and down the corners and around the top and bottom of the room.

"Oh, God, the party was such a *flop!*" Lee repeated.

"Well, darling, it was just one of those evenings," said the actress Kitty Carlisle Hart, who was a regular panelist on the television program *To Tell the Truth* and knew when to be candid with friends. "Something just didn't click."

"It was a *big* flop, all right," Stas agreed. "Jackie's presence put a crimp on things."

Lee did not want to admit it, but Stas was right. Jackie *had* put a crimp on things. For the few hours that she had deigned to stay at the party, Jackie had acted like a queen, making everyone feel self-conscious and uncomfortable. It was almost as if Jackie had *wanted* Lee's party to fail. Jackie could never stand to share the spotlight with Lee.

"Lee was utterly impatient with the public sentiment that had turned her sister into a monument," wrote Diana DuBois, Lee's biographer. "As Jackie's sibling, she knew all too well the weak spots in her character, and the chinks in her psyche. If the key to Lee was held by her relationship to her sister, then the reverse was true, and one could never truly know the one without knowing the other. Once, in an unguarded aside, Lee told a friend, 'You should see that woman! She wakes up in the morning, and goes through all the newspapers looking for her name, and if she doesn't find it, she just throws them all away, and when she sees her name, she cuts it out immediately!' "

"How about some champagne?" Stas asked. He popped open a fresh bottle.

"I've got wonderful news," Kitty said, trying to inject a note of gaiety. "I'm going to play *Marriage-Go-Round* in summer stock. Stas, how would you like to be in it with me?"

"Of course," Stas said, going along with the joke. "I would be very good."

"But you'll have to learn your lines, Stas," said Kitty, a veteran trooper, who had appeared with the Marx Brothers in *A Night at the Opera*, and whose recently deceased husband, the famous playwright Moss Hart, had directed the musical *Camelot*.

"Oh, I can't be bothered learning lines," Stas said.

"Then you can't be in my play," Kitty said. "How about you, Lee?"

"Oh, Kitty, I would *love* to be in it," said Lee. "*Desperately*. Why don't you send me the script so I can read it."

Caught off guard, Kitty took another sip of champagne.

"Well, darling," she said, "you *should* be on the stage. I'm sure you'd be marvelous. I'll send the script around tomorrow morning."

Lee did not know what to do with herself these days. Her marriage to Stas was on its last legs. And she was falling farther and farther behind in her competition with Jackie.

When they were growing up, Lee had been the beautiful one, and the one with a firmer grasp of fashion and style. As a young woman, she worked as a special assistant to Diana Vreeland, the legendary editor of *Harper's Bazaar* who later moved on to run *Vogue*. Then Lee lived in England, traveled with the jet set, and had the richest and most glittering friends. Even when Jackie was First Lady, and went around trying to look like Audrey Hepburn in Givenchy interpretations made by Oleg Cassini, Lee consoled herself with the thought that it was she, not her older sister, who lived the life of a true sophisticate.

Now, however, everything was topsy-turvy. Lee was about to become an impoverished divorcée, and Jackie was being celebrated as the most beautiful and stylish woman in the world. A poll of American newspaper publishers disclosed that the story that would get the widest readership among their female readers would be entitled, "Jacqueline Kennedy Remarries."

Magazines were not waiting for that day. *Photoplay*, the magazine of Hollywood celebrities, put Jackie on its cover with the headline TOO SOON FOR LOVE? *Movie TV Secrets* featured her in a piece called "Jackie's New Neighbors Tell All . . . WHERE SHE GOES, WHO SHE SEES, WHAT SHE DOES!" *Modern Screen's* March issue offered "Jackie Kennedy Changes— Her New Life, Her New Look, Her New Love. . . ."

Jackie was stealing all of Lee's old friends: Vivi Stokes, Truman Capote, Diana Vreeland, Rudolf Nureyev, Baron and Baroness Fabrizio Serena. The gossip columns kept track of Jackie's escorts: economist John Kenneth Galbraith, set designer Oliver Smith, Defense Secretary Robert McNamara, British diplomat Sir William Ormsby-Gore, man-about-town Roswell Gilpatric, and director Mike Nichols, who had brought her to tonight's party at Lee's apartment.

People said that Jackie was more famous than any movie star, perhaps the most famous woman of the twentieth century. She was asked to lunch by United Nations Secretary General U Thant. She was invited to England by Queen Elizabeth II, who planned to dedicate a square mile of Runnymede, where the Magna Carta was signed, as a memorial to President Kennedy. Jackie had become such an important figure that even her private decision not to vote in the 1964 presidential election became a major political issue.

"People in my own family told me I should vote," Jackie explained. "I said, 'I'm not going to vote.' This is very emotional, but maybe you can understand it. You see, I'd never voted until I was married to Jack. I guess my first vote was probably for him for senator, wasn't it? Then this vote would have been—he would have been alive for that vote. And I thought, 'I'm not going to vote for any [other person], because this vote would have been his.' . . . Bobby said I should vote, and I said, 'I don't care what you say, I'm not going to vote.' It was just completely emotional."

Lyndon Johnson, who viewed Jackie as the dowager queen in the Kennedy government-in-exile, did not see it that way. And his fears seemed justified when Jackie turned down his invitation to attend the dedication of the White House Rose Garden in her honor.

"I'd rather go to Dallas than ever return to Washington while Lyndon Johnson is in the White House," she told friends in confidence.

"She is a queen in exile on Fifth Avenue, who waits for the restoration of the dynasty," noted a British journalist.

"Suddenly there [is] a new, beautiful, internationally famous polestar to whirl about, a new peer-person to play status hide-and-seek with, a new 'In' personality to invite and hope to be invited by," Liz Smith wrote about Jackie. "More than anyone else in New York, Jacqueline [typifies] the new society of the metropolitan Eastern Seaboard."

Lee was driven crazy by the thought that she would have to spend the rest of her life in Jackie's shadow. She was desperate to steal back some of the spotlight. A career in the theater sounded like just the ticket. After all, hadn't Kitty Carlisle Hart said that she would be marvelous on the stage?

AUDITION

E arly the next morning, Lee called Kitty.

"Where's the script?" she asked. "I'm going to try out for a part."

"It'll be right over," Kitty said.

Kitty then called Lee Guber, the producer of *Marriage-Go-Round*, who owned a string of summer playhouses.

"Lee Radziwill intends to come for a tryout," she warned him.

To her surprise, Guber sounded interested. "I'm producing a play in Chicago," he said, "and there's a cameo role she might be able to do."

A few days later, Lee Radziwill showed up at the Morosco Theater in a driving rain, clutching a damp copy of the script that Kitty had sent her. She got up on the stage and did a reading for Guber, who was sitting in the empty auditorium.

"I could sell out instantly if I announced your name," Guber told her when she was through. "But I think it's important that you don't go out and fall on your face. Do some studying first, and acquire technique."

Lee promised to start taking acting lessons. Truman Capote had told her that he could get Milton Goldman, who represented Laurence Olivier and John Gielgud, to be her agent. There was nothing like starting at the top.

That same day, Kitty received a call from Jackie.

"Lee told me that you arranged for her to get a part in a play," Jackie said.

"Yes," Kitty said brightly, anticipating a thank-you.

But Jackie was not amused. She thought Kitty was *her* friend, not Lee's. Why was Kitty going out of her way to help Lee? Why would *anyone* help Lee become a professional actress? Lee did not have the slightest chance of making a go of it on the stage. She had no talent. She was trying to steal the spotlight, literally and figuratively, from Jackie. It was just one more example of that old stupid sibling rivalry rearing its ugly head.

"Kitty," Jackie said, "what the hell are you doing!"

It was hard to tell which sister was the more jealous of the other.

CAROLINE'S
MOUSE

Jackie had enrolled Caroline as a student at the Convent of the Sacred Heart on Ninety-first Street and Fifth Avenue. The school was housed in a large Italian Renaissance–style mansion that once served as the home of millionaire Otto Kahn. One day in the fall of 1965, Jackie came by, along with the other mothers, to pick up her daughter.

"This is Teresa Gorman from Great Britain," the mother superior told Jackie, who was dressed in a cream-colored Chanel suit. "She's a gift from God. We were all praying for a science teacher, and here she is."

As a biology teacher, Teresa made good use of Central Park.

"Almost every day I took a group of pupils there," she recalled. "When Caroline came, her two Secret Service agents came, too. . . . Jackie joined in as we turned over stones to find wood lice and earwigs. As our little group of schoolgirls laughed and skipped their way along, she would talk about her childhood in the country. She loved horses."

The frogs, lizards, and white mice in biology class fascinated the children, and they begged to be allowed to take them home for the holidays. Shortly before Christmas vacation, Caroline turned up with a note from Jackie written on a piece of yellow-lined paper that had been torn from a notebook.

"Dear Mrs. Gorman," it said, "Caroline has my permission to bring home a mouse."

Teresa phoned Jackie and asked, "Are you sure you really want this mouse? It could escape."

"Caroline's in love with the idea," Jackie said. "She absolutely insists."

A few days later, Caroline, Teresa, Bobby Kennedy, and two Secret Service agents all went shopping for a mouse cage at Bloomingdale's. Bobby, who had just been elected senator in a landslide, moved down the crowded aisle with both arms extended, allowing people to stretch out and shake his hands. It was a scene of utter pandemonium.

"I don't mind for myself," Jackie told Teresa, "but I'm nerve-wracked about the safety of the children. There are so many nutcases out there."

Caroline chose a cage that looked like a Chinese lantern.

"You'll need some wood chippings, and something for the mouse to nibble," Teresa said.

"I'm beginning to think it would have been simpler to send the children away to camp for the holiday," said Jackie.

A couple of days after the school closed for Christmas, Teresa received a phone call from the mother superior.

"Mrs. Kennedy would like a word with you," she said.

Teresa called Jackie.

"You must come and take this mouse away," she said. "It's stinking up the apartment."

"But won't Caroline be heartbroken?" Teresa asked.

"Yes, she will," said Jackie, "but the mouse is killing my social life."

Teresa smelled the problem as soon as she stepped off the elevator into Jackie's apartment. The mouse had turned out to be a male, and the combination of wet wood chippings and central heating was producing an overpowering effect.

"Ah, the dominance of the male," said a man's voice, which came from the depths of a sofa in the living room.

"This is Andy Warhol," said Jackie, introducing a pale-faced man with large round spectacles and a platinum wig.

At first blush, the pop artist seemed like a strange choice as a friend for Jackie. Andy had won worldwide acclaim by painting portraits of Coke bottles and Campbell soup cans, as well as of celebrities, and he was as starstruck as Jackie was publicity shy.

However, people often misunderstood Jackie's relationship with her public. Her true goal never was to avoid publicity as much as it was to control it. One of her greatest strengths was her own unerring sense of stardom. In this she resembled other strong personalities—Greta Garbo, Charles de Gaulle, Cary Grant—who had the connoisseur's appreciation of their own persona.

Moreover, it was not true that Jackie hated being photographed. In fact, she loved to be photographed—if it was done under her control. She had her own camera, and she was forever asking Jimmy Mason, who was in charge of her horses at her weekend house in Peapack, New Jersey, to take pictures of her mounted on Frank, her jumper. She collected these photographs in bulging scrapbooks, along with the clippings about herself from newspapers and magazines.

On the other hand, she was ambivalent about photography because of the paparazzi who stalked her.

"I remember going out with her," said Karl Katz, a curator at the Metropolitan Museum of Art, "and at the end of the evening, there was always this mess, this barrage of people. We went to the opening of a film once, on Broadway, and got separated. Photographers just got in the center, and I was pushed away. It was violent, and truly frightening for her."

"I understand you're introducing Caroline to the facts of life," Andy Warhol said to Teresa Gorman, "including some we don't talk about in polite society."

Teresa could not think of what to say. She collected the mouse, and Jackie and Andy walked her to the foyer, where she rang for the elevator.

"We're going skiing next week," Jackie said. "With a bit of luck, Caroline'll have forgotten about the mouse by the time we come home. I'll tell her you've taken it to the vet."

Teresa got into the elevator, and as the door began to slide shut, she caught a glimpse of Andy Warhol and Jackie—the artist and his icon—waving good-bye to the mouse in the Chinese cage.

SEVEN

THE OTHER JACK

October 1965–July 1966

ROSEBOWL

"Right after Dallas, Jackie called and asked if I would help her design a permanent memorial grave for the President," said John Carl Warnecke, an architect who had gained considerable fame a few years before the assassination for his design of the American Embassy in Thailand. "The burial site had been put together in haste by Bill Walton, the painter, who was chairman of the Fine Arts Commission and the Kennedys' expert on all things aesthetic. Walton told Jackie that in his view the final design for a monument would be a landscape problem, and so Jackie naturally turned to her friend Bunny Mellon, who was a brilliant landscape gardener.

"Jackie and Bunny agreed that the Eternal Flame should remain the primary symbol at the grave," Warnecke went on, "and that everything else should be kept simple and dignified. They did not want statues or buildings, just some slate tablets engraved with passages from Jack's Inaugural Address. Bunny had in mind the kind of gray slate that was used for tombstones in Colonial New England.

"A couple of days after Jackie called me, she and Bobby picked me up at a barbershop in Georgetown, where I was getting my hair cut, and we drove to Arlington National Cemetery. There must have been at least fifty reporters and photographers waiting for us when we got there. Jackie and Bobby got down on their knees and crossed themselves.

"We walked up the hill to the Lee Mansion. Jackie was quiet. But then all of a sudden she came to life when she saw the view—the axis looking from the Lincoln Memorial to the Washington Monument, and then to the dome of the Capitol. It was a thrilling moment, truly electrifying."

Jackie had chosen Warnecke for this important assignment because, like Teddy White and William Manchester, he was a Kennedy family favorite. Back in 1940, while Jack Kennedy was recuperating from one of his many serious illnesses, he had spent a few months in California auditing writing courses at Stanford University. That same year, the strapping Warnecke—six foot three inches tall and 215 pounds—played left tackle on the famous undefeated and untied Stanford football team that went to the Rose Bowl. The sickly Kennedy worshipped Warnecke from afar as a hero.

The two Jacks did not actually meet face to face until 1956, when Kennedy returned to California to campaign on behalf of Adlai Stevenson, the Democratic presidential candidate. For the occasion, Red Fay, Jack's buddy from his PT-boat days in the Pacific, lined up an attractive young woman for the married junior Senator from Massachusetts. Coincidentally, Red had been Warnecke's fraternity brother at Stanford, and he asked the architect to be the beard for the evening and pretend he was the young woman's date. Kennedy was delighted to meet his old football hero, and before he disappeared with the woman, he dubbed him "Rosebowl" and made him promise that they would stay in touch.

By this time, Warnecke was something of an architectural renegade. As the architecture critic Benjamin Forgey noted in *The Washington Post*, "Warnecke was . . . a Californian who didn't altogether take to the rigid principles of modern architecture advanced by his teachers (the famed Walter Gropius among them) at the Harvard Graduate School of Design. At the University of California campus at Berkeley, and elsewhere in his native state, he had taken great pains to design buildings that fit the historical context, a quality not high on the usual modernist list."

After he became President, Kennedy asked Rosebowl to help Jackie with one of her pet projects—the crusade to save Lafayette Square, the quadrangle of splendid nineteenth-century town houses directly across Pennsylvania Avenue from the White House. The houses had been targeted for demolition by the Eisenhower Administration.

"I applied my theory of contextual design and proposed new buildings that would fit behind and work with the historical structures,"

Warnecke explained years later. "But my design was bitterly opposed by members of the Fine Arts Commission and the architectural community. All of the President's advisers gave up on saving the historic buildings, but Jack gave Jackie permission to make one last-ditch effort. She wrote a letter to the people in charge of the demolition, telling them that she would not permit the wrecker's ball to touch one of those old buildings.

"The night before I was to present my plan for Lafayette Square, I went to a party at the British Embassy, and met Jackie for the first time. I danced with her, and we talked, and of course I fell instantly in love with her. She was full of spirit and play. She was delightful to be with. Inquisitive as hell. She said she wanted to see the design and models I had done.

"So I met her the next morning. She was wearing the same pink suit she would wear in Dallas, or one that looked very much like it. She was thrilled with my plan. She took over the reins of the project for the President, and attended the follow-up meetings. From then on, we got to see a hell of a lot of each other."

Warnecke was a bachelor; he and his wealthy socialite wife Grace Cushing had been divorced in 1960. It was said that he was worth several million dollars. He kept homes in a number of places—on Russian Hill overlooking San Francisco Bay, in the exclusive Georgetown section of Washington, and in Hawaii. He had his own three-hundred-acre ranch on the Russian River, forty miles north of San Francisco, where he went trail riding on his horses.

"Jack Warnecke was very self-assured," said Robin Duke, the wife of JFK's chief of protocol. "Like most great big men, he looked down on people physically, which sometimes gave the impression that he was pompous. But he was not pompous. He understood what the French call *placement*, and knew where he wanted to be. I thought him attractive, and I'm sure that Jackie thought him attractive, too."

Working together on Lafayette Square, Jack Warnecke and Jackie discovered they had a lot in common. She admired his knowledge of design, especially that of the Beaux Arts school, which emphasized historic forms and details. He admired her pluck and determination.

"No one in Washington gave a damn what happened to Lafayette Square," he said. "Jackie was the only one."

In her 1961 book *The Death and Life of Great American Cities*, Jane Jacobs had criticized the destructive American habit of razing large areas of cities and replacing them with sterile, modern buildings. Jacobs was not a preservationist herself, but she did sound a clarion call about the large-scale development that was ruining America's cities.

Before Jackie entered the White House with Jack, public officials thought nothing of destroying beautiful buildings of historic value in the name of progress. By taking a stand on Lafayette Square, Jackie forced people to think in a new way. She was the first person at a high level to give support to the preservation movement that flowered in the early sixties. She legitimized a movement that changed the face of urban America, and she continued to champion it for the rest of her life.

As a result of his work on Lafayette Square, Warnecke became the unofficial Kennedy family architect. He designed Teddy Kennedy's house in Hyannis Port, and Bobby's pool house. He worked on Hickory Hill, Bobby's home in Virginia, and he was designing a new windmill to replace one that had burned down at the Auchinclosses' Hammersmith Farm.

"I got all involved with Jack and the Kennedy Administration," Warnecke said. "I was invited to Jackie's private parties upstairs in the White House. I was a bachelor in the middle of the Kennedy White House, and I took part in some of Jack's womanizing, too. A month before the assassination, I helped Jack pick out a site at Harvard University for the library and museum that would someday house his personal and official papers."

The friendship between Jackie and Warnecke went completely unnoticed for a long time. At first they were so deeply engrossed in the design of the grave site that they themselves were unaware of what was happening to them. The only person who seemed to notice that they were developing feelings for each other was Bobby Kennedy.

"Jackie and I talked a lot about Bobby," Warnecke said. "She'd show me family pictures and say, 'Look, that's Bobby. When he was growing up, they called him the little runt.' She started telling me all kinds of strange things about Bobby. At the same time, she was telling Bobby about me. Bobby and I became close because of Jackie."

As time went on, however, Jackie and Warnecke realized that their relationship was maturing into something more profound. This both surprised and alarmed them. They began to take precautions so as not to arouse Bobby's suspicions. They used private code words, and arranged to meet alone when no one else was around. The need for discretion added a new dimension to their budding romance—the delicious aura of secrecy.

DUMPING THE
SECRET SERVICE

The leaves were a brilliant red and gold along Ocean Drive, the boulevard of Gilded Age dreams in Newport, Rhode Island. John Warnecke turned his car up a long gravel driveway, past a herd of prize Black Angus cattle grazing on a vast lawn, and to the porte cochere of Hammersmith Farm, the Auchinclosses' shingle-style Victorian manor.

A maid greeted him at the door and escorted him into the foyer, where she left him to examine a wall hanging with the Auchincloss coat of arms, which included the motto *Spectemur Agenda* (Judge Us by Our Action). It struck Warnecke as ironic that Jack Kennedy, the President who had unlatched the door of opportunity for so many millions of Americans, had married the stepdaughter of Hughdie Auchincloss, a man who epitomized the tradition of WASP exclusion.

In a few minutes, Janet Auchincloss came down the broad, red-carpeted stairway. She gave Warnecke a long, friendly hug.

"Dear Jack," she said, holding him at arm's length by his broad shoulders and looking him square in the eyes, "it is *sooo* good to see you."

"I could never understand those people who put down Janet," Warnecke said. "They described her treating Jackie like a person whipping a horse. I never saw any of that. Janet had real sparkle, and great spirit. She liked me, and I adored her, and thought she was attractive. Quite frankly, I always felt that she favored the relationship between me and Jackie."

Janet had been thinking a lot about Jackie's future. Her daughter's year of mourning was almost up, and it was time for her to get on with her life. Jackie needed a husband. And as far as Janet could see, Jack Warnecke was made to order.

He was forty-five years old and at the zenith of his personal and professional powers. He was tall and handsome, though not too handsome, the way Jack Kennedy had been. Warnecke was not as rich as the Kennedys, either, but he could afford to keep homes on two coasts. He led the life of a rich man, and he appeared to be in a financial position to care for Jackie and her children.

What was more, he was well-spoken, had good manners, and made the right impression in society. He was not mixed up in politics, which Janet always considered a dirty business. He was a creative person, and he shared Jackie's passion for design, architecture, painting, and nature. They both had an eye for color, shape, and form. They had that most important ingredient for a good marriage—common interests.

If Warnecke harbored any doubts about Janet's feelings toward him, they were dispelled on this visit to Hammersmith Farm. Motioning with the curved index finger of her right hand, Janet led him up the grand staircase to a large bedroom with a view of Narragansett Bay.

"This is where the President used to stay when he came to visit us," she told him. "I want you to sleep here tonight in his bed."

The symbolic meaning of Janet's gesture was not lost on Warnecke. Over the past several months, he had made a great effort to replace Jack Kennedy as the man in Jackie's life. This goal was not as far-fetched as it might have seemed. Warnecke was often described in magazine profiles as a contextual architect, which meant that he designed buildings that fit into their environment, but he could just as accurately have been called a contextual *person*. He had the capacity to put himself into the place of others, to feel their emotions. His talent for empathy was just what Jackie needed at this time.

"In order to work full-time on the grave site memorial, I had moved my office from San Francisco to Washington, and set up my operation in Georgetown, within a block of Jackie's house on N Street," he said. "I moved three of my four kids east for the summer. We were all together that summer of nineteen sixty-four—my family and Jackie's family. We went to Williamsburg together, and visited Civil War battlefield sites.

"Meanwhile, all kinds of people—Jack's friends, and family, and political associates—were visiting my office to look at the design of the grave. Jackie came frequently. Her sense of grieving was always there. The passion we were beginning to feel for each other was all mixed up with the sorrow. We were going through a terrible experience together. I remember, Bobby would come to my office, and just stand there with his mouth open, not able to talk.

"By the end of the summer, I was ready to choose the stone that I would use for the engraved words of Jack's Inaugural Address. I needed a great stone carver, because I did not want any joints in the stone. I found one living in Newport, and hired him. That's why I had come back to Newport just a few weeks before the assassination anniversary, to get final approval of the stone from Jackie."

The next day, Jackie drove down to Newport from Hyannis Port with two Secret Service agents. After lunch, Warnecke took her to inspect the stonecutter's work. She loved it. The approval of the stone meant a great deal to both of them.

"It was really the turning point in our relationship," Warnecke told the author of this book. "Now I could schedule a press conference, and formally announce that the design had been approved before the first anniversary of the assassination. It put a closure to Jackie's year of mourning."

When they got back to Hammersmith Farm, Jackie announced that she planned to return to Hyannis Port the next day.

"Why don't you dump the Secret Service and let me drive you back?" Warnecke said.

"That would be great, Jack," Jackie said.

"I had learned early on how to handle the Secret Service," Warnecke said. "Those guys liked and trusted me, because I was a football player, a jock, and one of them."

The next day, Jackie and Warnecke got into her black Mercury convertible, put down the top, and headed off for the Cape. The Secret Service followed at a discreet distance.

It was a fine autumn day, as crisp as a Granny Smith apple, and Jackie and Warnecke felt exhilarated as they sailed along with the wind in their hair. When they arrived at Jackie's house in Hyannis Port an hour and a half later, they found that Jackie's Italian housekeeper Marta Sgubin had arranged for Caroline and John to spend the night at another house in the Kennedy compound.

"We were all alone," Warnecke said.

Jackie showed Warnecke her collection of landscape paintings by André Dunoyer de Segonzac. Warnecke admired the seascapes that she had done herself. They had dinner, then Jackie gave him a tour of the rooms upstairs.

Warnecke's head almost hit the sharply slanted ceiling in Jackie's bedroom. He stood with Jackie for a few moments at the window, looking out at the choppy waters of Nantucket Sound. Then, wordlessly, he led her over to the bed that she had once shared with Jack Kennedy, and they began to make love.

"After a year of pent-up feelings," said Warnecke, "it was like an explosion. I remember saying to myself, *What am I doing here? What's happening?*

"A lot has been written about Jackie's being cold," he went on. "That image is all wrong. There was nothing inhibited or cold about her. All those aspects that made Jackie so delightful—her sense of fun and joy—were also part of her lovemaking."

Afterward, Warnecke told Jackie that he loved her.

"I fell in love with you the first moment I saw you at the British Embassy," he said.

"I love you, too, Jack," she said.

"She was so excited by what had happened between us that she wanted to tell Bobby at once," Warnecke said. "But I told her that I thought she should wait. I was sure Bobby would think that such a commitment was premature."

A COTTAGE
IN THE WOODS

A few weeks later, Jackie suggested to Warnecke that they spend a night in a cottage on Bunny Mellon's property on the Cape, about twenty minutes away from Hyannis Port. Warnecke hesitated to accept Bunny's invitation.

"I was getting a bit fed up with Bunny," he said. "She had become a problem on the design of the memorial. Jackie had found it too painful to deal with the grave design herself, and she had delegated a lot of authority to Bunny.

"Bunny thought she was in charge," he continued. "Once I entered the picture, and became romantically involved with Jackie, Bunny felt that Jackie had been taken away from her. She had lost her control over Jackie. Bunny was very possessive.

"In any case, Jackie talked me into going to Bunny's place. And when we got to this little cottage deep in the woods, we found that Bunny had decorated it for Halloween with pumpkins and candles and flowers. It was fixed up as only Bunny Mellon could do it. It was perfect, completely romantic. And it was a total surprise to both of us."

HAWAIIAN
WAR CHANT

When school let out in the summer of 1966, Jackie and her children boarded a plane at the newly renamed John F. Kennedy International Airport and flew off to the West Coast with a nanny and two Secret Service agents in tow. In San Francisco, they were joined by Jackie's brother-in-law, the actor Peter Lawford, his children Christopher and Sydney, and his longtime friend John Spierling. Then the entire party got on the United Airlines mainliner *Hilo* and headed across the Pacific for Hawaii.

In the first-class compartment, John played in his stocking feet, while the older children watched an in-flight movie, *Harper*, starring Paul Newman. Jackie relaxed with a drink and chatted with Buck Buchwach, the managing editor of *The Honolulu Advertiser*.

"I hope to get a real rest in Hawaii, almost out of the twentieth century for a little while," she told Buchwach.

But it was not the twentieth century that Jackie was escaping from. It was the black-tie dinners with doddering elder statesmen and their dreary little wives. It was the boring charity events. It was the dreadful committees that supported all those noble causes.

Jackie would have none of it. She liked dressing up in miniskirts. Shopping. Eating out at restaurants. She liked going to nightclubs. Dancing. Smoking. Drinking. Gossiping. Staying up late. She liked having fun. The only trouble was, whenever she had fun, she seemed to inflame the passions of the media.

"It was the year she discovered that, like the huge idol in Nebuchadnezzar's dream, she had feet of clay," wrote Liz Smith. "Or rather, she discovered that a large segment of her ordinarily adoring public now seemed to feel this way. . . . She began to behave like a private person again, like a human being with feelings, passions, desires, opinions, and a penchant for action, rather than a semi-deity to be worshipped from afar."

The first inkling the public had that Jackie had grown weary of playing the saint came when she and attorney William vanden Heuvel gave a midnight dinner-dance in honor of their friend, former ambassador John Kenneth Galbraith, at the Sign of the Dove restaurant, which had just opened in New York. Jackie's guests were a curious mixture—the crème de la crème of old New York–Newport–Palm Beach society, a mélange of jet-setters like Gianni Agnelli and Count and Countess Rudi Crespi, and such denizens of the demimonde as Andy Warhol and underground movie queen Edie Sedgwick. Vogue called them "the Beautiful People," and said that Jackie had invented a new kind of society.

"Somehow, word got out that Jackie was having the party," said vanden Heuvel, "and it seemed like there were fifteen thousand people in the street, trying to get a peek at her."

Jackie had hired Killer Joe Piro and his rock 'n' roll band, and she danced the frug and the jerk until one-thirty in the morning. On her way out of the restaurant, someone stopped her at the door, and she introduced her escort for the evening.

"This is my very, *very* special friend," she said, glancing up at John Carl Warnecke.

A few months later, Jackie took off for Spain to attend the annual fair in Seville, a six-day post-Lenten fiesta of glamorous parties and superb bullfighting that had been made famous by Ernest Hemingway in *The Sun Also Rises*. The Duke and Duchess of Alba installed her in their

Palacio de las Dueñas in a bedroom once used by France's Empress Eugénie, the great-grandaunt of the present duchess.

Newspapers back in America ran headlines like JACKIE AND THE JET SET IN SPAIN. She was shown in photos astride a white horse, wearing a dashing Andalusian *traje corto* riding habit—black-trimmed red jacket, flowing chaps, and flat broad-brimmed hat.

"I don't know what I'm doing," Jackie said as she made a leisurely *paseo* of the fair, "but it's all very exciting."

Some people thought it was a little too exciting for the widow of the slain President. When she attended a bullfight featuring Manuel Benitez, who was known to his devoted fans as "El Cordobés," she was criticized for encouraging the barbarism of bullfighting. When Jackie stayed until three in the morning at a charity ball, Princess Grace of Monaco was said to be piqued at finding herself upstaged. And when Jackie was seen being escorted around town by Spain's ambassador to the Vatican, Antonio Garrigues, a sixty-two-year-old widower with eight children, Spanish newspapers ran stories that she was about to get married.

Angier Biddle Duke, America's ambassador to Spain, issued an official statement quashing the absurd rumors.

"I really felt that you were a knight in armor and I don't know how to thank you," Jackie wrote Angie Duke when she returned home.

Spain had not provided Jackie with the escape she wanted. So now she was on her way to an even more distant destination—Hawaii. The trip took many hours in the four-engine prop plane, and it gave Jackie the opportunity to think about her future.

Jack Kennedy had been dead for almost three years, and Jackie's mother was urging her to make a decision about marriage. However, Bobby had other ideas. He was against marriage for Jackie altogether. If she got married now, Bobby said, she would undermine his chances for winning the White House. Why not wait for the right man to come along?

Jackie herself was torn. John Warnecke reminded her of her father, or at least one side of her father, his aesthetic side. With Warnecke as a husband, Jackie could pursue refined artistic sensations and celebrate the pleasurable effects of art. Warnecke had impeccable taste. He offered a life of private pleasures, as well as a respite from the world's spotlight.

"Jack was highly romantic and very sexy in those days," recalls a woman who knew him well. "He was very creative. He had this artistic vision and saw things in an artistic way. There was also an element of danger about him. He was the kind of person, when he walked into a room, everyone knew he was there. And he was always a notorious womanizer. These were all things that would appeal to Jackie."

Just before the plane landed at Honolulu Airport, Jackie changed into an ivory-colored faille coat and an A-line skirt. She stepped down the ramp into the bright sunshine, bareheaded and wearing a pair of wraparound sunglasses. A crowd of five thousand people was on hand to greet her, and she smiled broadly, holding her hair, which blew in the brisk trade winds.

Mrs. Pat Lam of the Hawaii State Department of Transportation hung two leis around Jackie's neck. A band struck up "Hawaiian War Chant," and a hula troupe began swinging and swaying to the music. Embarrassed by the corny ceremony, Jackie stood stiffly on the tarmac, flashing her patented smile. Then she thanked everybody and ducked into a waiting Lincoln Continental.

She was whisked off to her $3,000-a-month rented house on fashionable Kahala Beach, about a mile from Diamond Head. The four-bedroom redwood-frame house was set back only about forty feet from busy Kahala Avenue, but it had a tall hedge and tropical trees that shielded it from view. Six burly members of the Metro Squad were standing guard as Jackie got out of the car and went inside.

There, waiting for her in the living room, was John Warnecke.

TINY BUBBLES
IN THE WINE

"We had spent a year and a half together before she came out to Hawaii," said Warnecke. "I was with her every weekend. We were together in her apartment in New York, at her place in New Jersey, at Hammersmith Farm, at Hyannis Port. We went to the movies, and to football games. We did everything together. Then I invited her to spend the summer with me in Hawaii."

Warnecke had won a huge commission to design the capitol of the newly admitted state of Hawaii. He knew the governor, the mayor, and the editors of the Honolulu newspapers. He promised Jackie that if she came to visit him, the *Honolulu Advertiser* and the *Star-Bulletin* would leave her alone, and that she would be treated like a private citizen. This was quite a promise to make to a woman who had received more publicity in the years following her husband's death than she did in the years when she shared the spotlight with the President.

"I had to prepare the groundwork for Jackie's Hawaiian trip very carefully so as not to arouse suspicion," Warnecke said. "I asked a local Hawaiian socialite by the name of Cecily Johnston to come to New York beforehand in order to meet Jackie. After they had been seen around town together, and had become quote best friends unquote, Cecily invited Jackie to Hawaii, and arranged for the rental of the house. Just as I had been the beard for Jack Kennedy back in the fifties, Cecily was now the beard for me."

Even so, Jackie felt squeamish about accepting Cecily Johnston's invitation. She asked Peter Lawford to accompany her as a kind of chaperon. Lawford agreed to provide her with additional cover, and be on hand at the nearby Kahala Hilton Hotel if she needed him.

Shortly after they arrived, Cecily Johnston gave a pool party at her home for the Kennedy and Lawford children. The singer Don Ho, who was known as the Sinatra of the Islands, was on hand to warble his favorite song.

> Tiny bubbles in the wine
> Make me happy, make me feel fine.

Christopher Lawford pushed his sister into the pool, and John followed suit by pushing Caroline in. Don Ho got caught up in the spirit of things. He came up behind Jackie and pushed her in, clothes and all. A Secret Service agent leaned over with a helping hand, and Jackie jerked him in.

Just as Warnecke had promised, everyone was having a good time. However, Jackie had failed to inform Peter Lawford's estranged wife, Pat Kennedy Lawford, about the arrangements. And when Pat saw photos of Jackie and Peter getting off the plane together in Honolulu, she called Peter's manager, Milt Ebbins.

"How dare he do that?" Pat screamed.

"Peter was planning to go there anyway," Ebbins said, "and so was Jackie. They decided to go together. So what?"

Next, Pat called Peter directly.

"I won't put up with this," she said. "How dare you go away with this woman!"

"Pat," Peter said, "we've got the children with us."

"How could you go to Hawaii with her?" said Pat. "That's where we went on our honeymoon."

Pat was not the only one who was upset by the arrangements. Caroline and John were confused by their mother's relationship with Warnecke. Three days after their arrival, Caroline cut her left foot on a jagged piece of coral reef while swimming in front of their Kahala guest home. She had to have five stitches. She was on crutches when the family attended the Kamehameha Day Parade in honor of the monarch who united the islands of Hawaii.

Several weeks later, while on a camping trip at Kapuna Beach on the island of Hawaii, John stumbled and fell backward into a pit of hot coals left over from a campfire. He let out a cry, then instinctively stuck his right arm down to push himself up. The hand and part of his forearm suffered first- and second-degree burns. He was flown to Honolulu, where Dr. Eldon Dykes, a plastic surgeon, treated several blisters on his arm and buttocks.

Though Jackie was concerned by these mishaps, she failed to make the connection between her children's accident-prone behavior and her barely disguised love affair with Warnecke. When her month-long lease on the Kahala house expired in late June, she decided to extend her stay in Hawaii for another month.

She and the children moved into a luxurious guest accommodation on the eight-acre Koko Head estate of Henry J. Kaiser, the fabulously rich industrialist, who had made his first fortune building Liberty ships during World War Two, and then a second fortune manufacturing steel, aluminum, and automobiles after the war.

"The part of the estate where Jackie stayed was called the Boathouse," recalled Michael Kaiser, Henry's adopted son, who was home from college at the time. "It stood on a cliff and had a view of the back side of Diamond Head across the bay."

The Boathouse was built in the shape of a horseshoe. The first level was where the Kaisers kept their fifty-six-foot motor launch, which had its own indoor berth. The next level was for storage. And the third had a living room and bedrooms that wrapped around a large oval swimming pool.

"My mother had sent her decorator, George White, all over Asia for a long period of time," said Michael Kaiser, "and he came back with fabrics from India and Indonesia. The cushions and pillows in the Boathouse were covered in this colorful fabric, and they made a wonderful contrast with the modern furniture."

Jackie had brought her own cook, who made breakfast and lunch.

During the day, she took lessons in Chinese painting. At night, she went to the main house for dinner, and to watch screenings of the latest movies.

Mrs. Kaiser took little John to a Pacific Coast League baseball game, and introduced the five-year-old boy to Hank Allen, the batting star in the team's 10–2 victory over Denver.

"This is John-John," Mrs. Kaiser said.

"My name is not John-John," he corrected her. "It's John."

Caroline developed a crush on Charles Kaiser, the younger son in the family, who was in his early twenties.

But for the first time since the assassination, Jackie was too preoccupied with her own life to pay much attention to her children.

"Do I have your permission to have Jack Warnecke land a helicopter on the grounds to take me out from time to time?" Jackie asked Mrs. Kaiser one night.

"Of course," said Mrs. Kaiser.

However, when Mrs. Kaiser informed her husband about this new arrangement, she expressed concern that Warnecke, who had the reputation of being a ladies' man, was not the most appropriate escort for the President's widow. Perhaps, Mrs. Kaiser suggested to her husband, someone should tell Bobby Kennedy.

Henry Kaiser and the Kennedys got on well. A progressive businessman who treated his workers fairly, Kaiser had pleased the Kennedys by keeping the Kaiser Steel Corporation operating during the steel industry crisis in 1962.

Henry Kaiser called Bobby and told him what was going on between Jackie and Warnecke. As soon as Bobby hung up, he called Jackie.

"Bobby was trying to kill off a possible marriage to Warnecke," according to Richard Goodwin. "He knew that's what Jackie was contemplating, and he did not approve of it. I don't know why he felt that way, but obviously he thought Warnecke wasn't the right guy."

Warnecke's chartered helicopter touched down on the front lawn of the Kaisers' main house. He reached out a hand and pulled Jackie on board.

Moments later, they lifted off and disappeared into a perfect blue sky. Jackie's infuriated Secret Service men were left behind.

That day they visited Maui, where they lunched at Lahaina's Pioneer Inn. Another time, they hopped over to the island of Hawaii, which was sometimes called the Big Island, where they enjoyed the privacy of Laurance Rockefeller's guest cottage on the Parker Ranch. Once, they went trekking in the mountains of Kauai, where they hunted goats and wild boar.

"Sometimes we would just go off alone to a remote beach and swim," Warnecke said. "We had endless conversations about JFK. His memory was the thing that had bound us together in the first place. The John F. Kennedy Memorial Grave was nearing completion. I knew that despite the monument, his reputation wasn't inviolable. Stories about his womanizing would be coming out sooner or later.

"I told Jackie about some of those stories involving Jack and other women. I did it so she wouldn't be shocked when she read about them later. She was prepared for the worst when it came.

"I told her stories about my own personal experiences with women, too," he went on. "One story took place when I was in Thailand, designing the American embassy, and one of my Harvard classmates, a Thai, invited me to dinner at his home in the mountains of northern Thailand. At dinner I was told that I would be given twelve beautiful women for dessert, and that I could choose any of them I desired.

" 'Oh,' Jackie said, 'to think you had your choice!'

"And I said, 'Well, it was all very proper. It was arranged by the family. After all, I had to be polite.'

"She loved that, and broke into gales of laughter.

"She teased me with her own stories, except that she didn't have many sexual experiences to talk about. She told me about her first love, John Marquand Jr., the son of the famous novelist, whom she had met during her junior year abroad in Paris.

" 'Were you seduced by Marquand before you married Jack?' I asked her.

" 'Well, just let's say I came very close,' she said.

"I thought maybe she said 'very close' because she couldn't bring herself to admit to me that she had gone all the way when she was so young.

"And we talked about getting married. I had a beautiful five-bedroom house on Black Point off Diamond Head Road. Jackie decided that a room off the living room, a nice soft den, needed remodeling. She did a watercolor-and-ink sketch, and set to work redecorating the room with fabric. She did the whole thing in no time flat. But we talked about starting out fresh, and buying another house after we got married.

" 'I wonder,' she said, 'if we could live in a house on a hill overlooking the harbor?'

"I was a good Presbyterian with a grandmother who had been a Christian Science practitioner, but Jackie was pleased when she found out that I could not remember having been baptized as a child. She thought I could be baptized as a Catholic. She was exultant over the idea.

" 'I'm going to turn you into a Catholic to make you more suitable as a husband,' she said.

"All this time, the Secret Service guys were looking after the kids, and leaving Jackie and me pretty much alone. Our summer together in Hawaii was a fairy tale."

When it was time for Jackie to return to the mainland, she wrote a farewell thank-you letter to the editors of the *Honolulu Advertiser* and the *Star-Bulletin*.

> I had forgotten, and my children have never known what it was like to discover a new place, unwatched and unnoticed. It was your papers that made this possible for us, by deciding at the beginning not to follow our activities. . . . I truly appreciate the extraordinary gesture you made.

But as she prepared to leave Hawaii, Jackie had to face some hard questions. Did she truly want to be unwatched and unnoticed, and pull a disappearing act like Greta Garbo? And even if she could somehow vanish from public view, would she be satisfied by such a life?

She was less sure of the answers to these questions than she sounded in her letter to the editors. No one, perhaps not even Jackie herself, knew exactly what was in her heart. But before she left Hawaii she had a conversation with Mrs. Kaiser in which she alluded to her future.

"My mother told me later about that conversation," said Michael

Kaiser. "Jackie made it clear to my mother that she had no present in-tention of marrying Jack Warnecke."

Of course, Warnecke did not know that.

"Before she left," Warnecke said, "I told her that my goal was to get her back to a normal life. A private life, not a public one. I wanted to let her be her own person. Away from the press. Away from prying eyes. Away from all that pressure. And I was a little surprised by her response.

" 'One of the biggest forces of all between two human beings is the search for power,' she told me. 'Power is a strong force and motivation in people. I don't want to wield power myself, but I've observed that the ul-timate motive in humankind is power.' "

EIGHT

TARNISHED HALO

July 1966–August 1967

"OUT OF CONTROL"

Soon after Jackie returned from Hawaii, she learned that *Look* magazine had bought the serial rights to William Manchester's book, *The Death of a President*, for the astounding sum of $665,000. It was the biggest deal in magazine history (the equivalent in today's money of more than $5 million). Jackie did not think that Manchester had any right to profit so obscenely from her husband's murder.

It was not only the money that bothered Jackie. She and Bobby had enlisted the editorial help of several old Kennedy friends: Edward Guthman of the Los Angeles *Times*, John Siegenthaler of the Nashville *Tennessean*, the historian Arthur M. Schlesinger, former JFK speechwriter Theodore Sorensen, and Jackie's private secretary, Pamela Turnure. When these proxies came back with scores of suggested revisions to the manuscript, Manchester balked. He refused to make many of the changes. Now, to make matters even worse, he had sold his unacceptable text to a popular weekly magazine.

Who was going to choose the excerpts that ran in *Look*? Jackie asked. And what about the photographs? The art director in Jackie always thought in terms of packages—visuals and text together.

The trouble was, Bobby had already approved both the publication of the book and the *Look* serialization. In a telegram that he had sent to Manchester, Bobby promised:

[T]he Kennedy family will place no obstacle in the way of publication of his work.

Jackie did not care what promises her brother-in-law had made. She wanted *Look* to cancel the serialization. In late August, she summoned Mike Cowles, the chairman of the board of the media company that owned *Look*, to Hyannis Port.

Cowles arrived the next day with his lawyer Jack Harding at his side. To their surprise, Jackie was there to greet them at the small airport. She was wearing a pretty smile and a Pucci dress.

They drove to the Kennedy compound, where she served them iced tea and sandwiches and took them on a tour of her house. Then she, Bobby, and her attorney Simon Rifkind, whose law firm was one of the most prestigious in New York, got down to serious business.

"Bobby doesn't represent me," Jackie explained to Mike Cowles. "He sort of protects me."

Jack Harding, Cowles's attorney, pointed out that *Look* had paid $665,000 for the serial rights.

"If it's money, I'll pay you a million," Jackie said.

No, no, said Harding, it was not just the money. *Look* wanted to excerpt the book because it was an important historical document.

It was a huge mistake for Harding to lecture Jackie Kennedy about history.

"You're sitting in the chair my late husband sat in," she said. "I will demand that publication of both the book and the serialization be stopped."

"No," Bobby interjected, "not the *book*."

Jackie turned to Mike Cowles and demanded to know: "Are you going to serialize?"

"First, let me ask a question," Cowles replied. "I sense an undercurrent of feeling that *Look* didn't act in good faith."

"*Look* acted in good faith," Bobby conceded.

"Well, then, yes, Mrs. Kennedy," Cowles said, "we will publish."

No one had dared to say no to Jackie in a very long time. She exploded in a fit of anger.

"You're a son of a bitch!" she told Cowles. "And a bastard! You can't do this!"

The men sitting around the table stared at her, aghast.

"She became quite hysterical and violent, verbally violent," said William Attwood, *Look*'s editor in chief, "to the point that Mike Cowles came back [to New York] a little amazed that the great lady of the funeral and all that could talk just that way. . . .

"I agreed that [Manchester's] prose was very purple," Attwood continued, "and we all decided that the [series] could easily have been trimmed down. . . . But Manchester is a very baroque writer, and he loves to describe the color of the brains on the lapels, that sort of thing. And so, nevertheless, this is what *he* wanted.

"We were caught between two rather neurotic people—Manchester, who is subject to fits of depression, and exhilaration, and all that . . . and Mrs. Kennedy, who had by this time become really out of control."

"US AGAINST THEM"

Desperate now, Jackie turned for help to Richard Goodwin, JFK's old speechwriter and political jack-of-all-trades. With his craggy face, hirsute appearance, and slightly slurred speech, Goodwin reminded some people of a man with a perpetual hangover. But he was one of those brilliant Renaissance men who seemed to know everything and have friends everywhere—in politics, academia, the arts, publishing, medicine, and business.

Goodwin had come to Jackie's rescue once before, when he had arranged for her to take her traumatized children to the psychoanalyst Erik Erikson after the assassination. Since then, Goodwin had become an important member of Bobby's shadow cabinet, and while he waited for the Kennedy Restoration, he had taken a teaching post at Wesleyan University, where—conveniently enough—William Manchester also taught. In fact, the two men were close neighbors in leafy Middletown, Connecticut.

Jackie hoped that Goodwin could make Manchester see the light. And on Wednesday morning, September 7, she dispatched the *Caroline* to La Guardia Airport to pick them up and fly them to Hyannis Port.

"Jackie was waving to us as we came down the ramp," Manchester wrote. "I remember that she was wearing sunglasses and a green miniskirt;

she looked stunning. In the compound, we drank iced tea on the porch of President Kennedy's house. Then Dick strolled off and Jackie and I changed to bathing suits.

"I sat on the back of a towing boat with young John on my lap while she water-skied behind—Jackie at her most acrobatic, at one point holding the tow rope with one foot and zipping along with the other foot on a single ski. After she had tired of this, I dove in, and the two of us struck out for shore. Wearing flippers, she rapidly left me far behind. Wallowing and out of breath, I momentarily wondered whether I would make it. I remember thinking: What if I drowned? Would that be good for the book or bad for the book?"

Like many men before him, Manchester was overcome by an irresistible impulse to please Jackie.

"She's incredible," he recalled. "She's all woman. You've got to spend a little time with her, to see her in the full spectrum. When she looks at you with those big eyes . . ."

But Manchester was in for a big letdown.

"Back on the porch," he went on, "with the three of us seated at a luncheon table in dry clothes, I slowly realized that nothing good for the book could possibly come out of this meeting. The atmosphere was completely unrealistic . . . Jackie was hostile toward *Look*, bitter about Cowles, and scornful of all books on President Kennedy, including [Arthur] Schlesinger's. Repeatedly, she expressed affection for Goodwin and me, saying, 'It's us against them,' and to me, 'Your whole life proves you to be a man of honor.' She was going to fight, she said savagely, and she was going to win: 'Anybody who is against me will look like a rat unless I run off with Eddie Fisher.' "

It slowly dawned on Manchester that Jackie did not want *any* published account of her husband's death—whether in book form or in a magazine excerpt. Beyond the personal revelations that she found so objectionable, Jackie was concerned about the political passages in Manchester's book.

There were many references to discord between Bobby Kennedy and Lyndon Johnson. Manchester portrayed Johnson as a man who had been eager to seize power, and who had been insensitive to the dead President's family. For instance, Manchester described Kenneth O'Donnell, JFK's White House secretary, pacing up and down the aisle of Air Force One, his hands clapped over his ears so that he would not have to hear the judge administering the presidential oath of office to Johnson.

All this could be used against Bobby if he should run for national office. Jackie did not want to offend the thin-skinned Johnson, who was well aware that the Manchester book had been commissioned by her. When Bobby had talked about retiring from the public arena, it was Jackie who had begged him not to quit, arguing that the country needed him. If the book turned Johnson into an implacable foe, and scuttled Bobby's chances for the White House, it would be all her fault. Once again, she would bring disaster upon someone she loved.

TAKING CARE
OF BUSINESS

In the midst of her troubles over the Manchester book, Jackie received a call from John Warnecke. They had not seen each other for several weeks.

"I've just got back to my office here in San Francisco," he told her, "and I'm afraid I've got some bad news."

"What's wrong?" Jackie asked.

"My bookkeeper tells me that I owe the bank six hundred thousand dollars," he said. "The bank says the loan is more like a million dollars. And it's due Monday."

"How could that happen?" Jackie asked.

She had been led to believe that Warnecke was a wealthy man and was insulated from problems like this.

"That's what I asked my bookkeeper," he said. "She says I haven't been paying enough attention to my business, and the office always relied on me in the past to generate the commissions. The last couple of years I've been preoccupied with the memorial grave. Then you and I spent the last two months together in Hawaii. I guess I just let things go."

It sounded as if he was trying to lay the blame for his money problems on Jackie.

"What are you going to do?" she asked.

"I have to spend a lot more time taking care of business."

"What does that mean?"

147

"It means I don't think I can see you quite so much," he said. "Not as often as before, anyway. At least not until things calm down a bit."

It all sounded bizarre. For the past two years, Warnecke had told Jackie over and over again that he loved her. But now, out of the blue, he seemed to have changed his tune. *He could no longer be to her what he had been before*—a man did not say that to the woman he loved.

Obviously, something had changed. And it was not only Warnecke's financial condition. He seemed to have suddenly realized that those fairy-tale weeks in Hawaii were not real, and that he would never be able to change Jackie into a normal person. He could not provide Jackie with what she really needed: total security from the outside world.

There was a long silence on the phone. It went on for so long that Warnecke thought Jackie might have hung up, or that they had lost their connection.

Then Jackie said, "I understand."

"We'll still see each other," Warnecke said. "This isn't good-bye."

"Of course not," she said.

"I still love you, Jackie," he said.

But this time Jackie did not say that she loved him back.

WALTER SCOTT'S
PERSONALITY PARADE

Parade was the first national magazine to run a full-fledged story on Jackie's secret relationship with Warnecke. The piece appeared in early December 1966, and was titled "Jackie Kennedy, World's Most Eligible Widow—WILL SHE MARRY AGAIN?" It was written by Lloyd Shearer, a well-connected journalist, who also wrote the magazine's famous page-two column "Personality Parade" under the pseudonym Walter Scott.*

"The name one hears most frequently in connection with Mrs. Kennedy and romance," wrote Shearer, "is John Carl Warnecke, 47, the architect in charge of the John F. Kennedy Memorial grave now under construction at Arlington National Cemetery. . . .

"One of Jack Warnecke's friends in Marin County, Calif., says, 'They have a lot in common, love of art, architecture, athletics, culture, but I don't think there's a thing to it. My own opinion, for what it's worth, is that Jackie for the first time is enjoying her own freedom, her own identity, indulging in her own tastes too much to give all that up for any guy.' "

Jackie and Warnecke were still sleeping with each other, but things were not the same. In conversations with friends, Jackie had begun to drop hints that her feelings for Warnecke had cooled. That may have

---

*When Shearer retired in 1991, the author of this book took over as Walter Scott.

been part of the reason he was not awarded the design commission for the John F. Kennedy Library. That coveted job would go instead to I. M. Pei, a little-known Chinese-American architect who was recommended by Bunny Mellon.

ACTING
ON HER OWN

Nine days before Christmas in 1966, an emotionally distraught Jackie filed suit against Harper & Row, *Look*, and William Manchester to prevent publication of *The Death of a President*. No one was more shocked and dismayed by her legal action than Bobby. Jackie had placed him in an untenable position. On the one hand, he could not be seen to be favoring censorship. On the other, he could not abandon his brother's widow.

He had begged her not to take the case to court. The fact that she had gone ahead anyway was interpreted by some people as a sign that Jackie was struggling to break free of Bobby's iron control.

The battle of the book pitted Kennedy-lovers against Kennedy-haters, and old friends against each other. James Reston, the influential Washington bureau chief of *The New York Times*, wrote a column entitled "The Death of Camelot," in which he portrayed Jackie as an imperious woman who had launched an assault against the First Amendment's guarantee of freedom of speech. Reston's dear friend Teddy White fired back in a letter to the editor of the *Times*, chastising the columnist for a "rare lapse from excellence," and praising Jackie for her "great courage and honor."

Jackie's action made front-page news all over the world. As *New York Times* reporter John Corry wrote in his book-length account, *The Manchester Affair*, it was the stuff of high political drama. It touched on two presidencies—John Kennedy's and Lyndon Johnson's—and potentially a third—that of Robert Francis Kennedy.

No one enjoyed the squabble more than Lyndon Johnson. Though he looked robust, LBJ had never entirely recovered from his first heart attack back in the late 1950s, and Lady Bird Johnson feared that the gathering domestic storm over the Vietnam War might prove too much for his health. She was urging him not to run for reelection in 1968.

But Johnson did not want to hand over the White House to his old nemesis, Bobby Kennedy. That was something he dreaded almost as much as a second heart attack. As a result, Johnson, who feared Jackie's power, handled the Manchester affair with extreme caution.

He asked his White House image consultant, Robert Kintner, the former president of ABC and NBC, to get him an early copy of Manchester's galley proofs. The thin-skinned Johnson read the book with mounting rage, but he was careful not to say anything that might offend Jackie. On December 16, 1966, LBJ wrote her a letter that dripped with honey:

> Lady Bird and I have been distressed to read the press accounts of your unhappiness about the Manchester book. Some of these accounts attribute your concern to passages in the book which are critical or defamatory of us.
>
> If this is so, I want you to know while we deeply appreciate your characteristic kindness and sensitivity, we hope you will not subject yourself to any discomfort or distress on our account.

Jackie replied to LBJ that she had no choice but to sue. But, she went on, "winning . . . seems a hollow victory—with everything I objected to printed all over the newspapers anyway."

Before the controversy was over, Manchester would flee to a Swiss sanitarium, where, it was later reported, he suffered a mental breakdown. In January 1967, Jackie reached an out-of-court settlement with her adversaries. She forced Harper & Row, *Look,* and Manchester to make most of the changes that she wanted. But as she had pointed out to LBJ, it was a Pyrrhic victory. Shortly after the settlement was announced, the New York *World Journal Tribune* began running a five-part series of articles by Liz Smith under the astonishing headline JACKIE COMES OFF HER PEDESTAL.

"Regardless of whether she was right or wrong," Liz Smith wrote, "Jackie was not escaping from the highly publicized [Manchester] controversy unscathed. From now on, she would never again appear in the limelight with quite all that queenly dignity intact. Things were being said, innuendos repeated, the very deletions from the book itself being magnified and publicized to the point that it had all badly tarnished the Kennedy halo."

Like Liz Smith, many people were puzzled by Jackie's behavior. Why had she risked her spotless reputation to suppress a book? The answer was quite simple: It had never occurred to her that *The Death of a President* was William Manchester's property. After all, it was she who had thought up the idea for the book, she who had chosen the author, she who had given him the most important interviews, and she who had made other witnesses available to him. She had put it all together.

In her eyes, Manchester was merely a tool for expressing her vision. When the manuscript of the book failed to reflect her version of things, she felt that she had no choice but to destroy it.

In the end, Jackie hurt herself far more than she hurt the book. It was one of the rare instances in her life when she acted alone, not through the instrument of a powerful male figure.

Women gain power by affiliating themselves with powerful men, her father had taught her.

She would never forget that lesson again.

AN UNABASHED
LOVE LETTER

Even as her affair with Warnecke was cooling down, another man with connections to Jackie's past had been doing his best to woo the former First Lady. His name was Aristotle Onassis.

From the instant he learned of John Kennedy's assassination, Onassis had lost interest in Lee Radziwill and become obsessed by thoughts of Jackie. As far as he was concerned, she was not only the most famous woman in the whole world, she was the Mount Olympus of women, beyond the reach of mortal men.

Among Greeks, it was considered altogether natural and proper that powerful men should use marriageable women as a way to keep score, and that they should compete with each other to marry these women. If Onassis could win Jackie, he would be elevated in the eyes of his Greek rivals into the pantheon of modern gods. He would also command the world's spotlight, which was his very favorite place to be.

Onassis had first met Jackie at a dinner party in Georgetown in the 1950s, when Jack Kennedy was a senator. The Greek shipowner and the Senator's shy wife only exchanged a few words. A year later, when Jack and Jackie were visiting Jack's parents in the South of France, Onassis invited them aboard the *Christina*, which was docked in Monte Carlo, to meet Sir Winston Churchill.

"Churchill and Kennedy immediately flung themselves into a politically nostalgic conversation that revolved around some of the stories that JFK's father had told him about his experiences as U.S. Ambassador to the Court of St. James's from 1937 to 1941," wrote Frank Brady, an Onassis biographer. ". . . While the two men talked, Onassis gave Jackie a personal tour of the yacht."

Jackie found the *Christina* vulgar. The dining-room walls were covered with murals of naked girls that had been painted by Vertez, a fashionable muralist of the 1930s. The china was bad and the flowers were overdone. Everywhere, there was tacky French reproduction furniture in the Napoleonic style.

"Mr. Onassis," Jackie fibbed as she and Jack left the *Christina*, "I have fallen in love with your ship."

Several years later, when Jackie was First Lady, she and Lee visited Greece, and Onassis was present at a cocktail party given in their honor. But Onassis spent most of his time talking to Lee—with whom he was by then sexually involved—and showed little romantic interest in Jackie.

The turning point came after the death of the infant Patrick Bouvier Kennedy. Lee informed Ari that her sister was in a deep depression. He suggested that Jackie come to Greece for a recuperative cruise.

"Tell Jack that Stas and I will chaperon you," Lee told Jackie. "It will be perfectly proper and such fun. Oh, Jacks, you can't imagine how terrific Ari's yacht is, and he says we can go anywhere you want. It will do you so much good to get away for a while."

Jackie was enthusiastic about the idea. She loved Greek history and mythology, and she saw the opportunity to visit legendary places that she had only read about. In her usual methodical way, she began making notes for the trip on a yellow legal pad: "October 2 arrive Athens by plane . . . Afternoon October 2 depart Athens for boat. . . ."

But Jack Kennedy was dead set against her going.

"For Christ's sake, Jackie, Onassis is an international pirate," he said.

Kennedy had a vivid imagination, and nobody had to tell him what went on during these cruises. In his womanizing days before the White House, he had chartered yachts, and had sailed the Mediterranean with his "girling" companions. They had turned those boats into floating bordellos, ferrying women back and forth, and passing them around freely.

He doubted that things would be any different on board the *Christina*. After all, hadn't Onassis flaunted his affair with Maria Callas? Nowadays, Kennedy might occasionally frolic in the White House swimming pool with a couple of young female assistants, but that was nothing compared to Onassis's life as a sexual predator. Or, at least, that was how Kennedy imagined Onassis's life to be.

Kennedy's objections went beyond mere jealousy, however. He was worried about a political backlash when it became public knowledge that Jackie was cruising the Mediterranean in the lap of luxury with the notorious Onassis. Such a trip could not come at a worse time. In the summer of 1963, Kennedy was laying plans for his reelection campaign, and what he really feared about his wife's proposed trip on the *Christina* was that *he* would be tarred by the brush of Aristotle Onassis.

He ordered the FBI to check into reports that Onassis was violating the American embargo against Cuba by shipping oil to Castro. And he reminded Jackie that during the Eisenhower Administration, Onassis had been indicted on criminal and civil charges of fraud in connection with United States surplus ships that he had acquired. The criminal charges were dropped, and Onassis settled the civil suit by paying a hefty fine. But the scandal continued to plague him for years, and he never quite lived down his reputation for being an amoral businessman who routinely skirted the law.

Nonetheless, Jackie insisted on going on the trip. And rather than fight her about it, Kennedy relented. But he was so concerned about the potential for negative publicity that he personally took charge of drafting a White House press release. The draft, which did everything possible to disassociate the trip from Onassis himself, said that the *Christina* had been "secured" by Prince Stanislas Radziwill from Onassis, and suggested that Jackie would be Stas's guest, not Onassis's.

"If asked, we should state that Onassis is not expected on the trip, at least not in the beginning," Kennedy wrote.

In order to spare Jackie any embarrassment, Onassis told Lee that he would be more than willing to stay on shore. But when Lee conveyed this offer to her sister, Jackie said that she would not think of it.

"I could not accept his generous hospitality and then not let him come along," Jackie explained to Lee.

For weeks Lee continued to act as a mediator between Ari and the Kennedys. To be helpful, Ari suggested to Lee that the White House issue a press release stating that his yacht had been "arranged" by Prince Radziwill, rather than "secured."

"Mr. Onassis thought that 'arranged' was even vaguer," Lee wrote Kennedy's secretary, Evelyn Lincoln. "Please check with the President."

Finally everything was settled, and Jackie flew to Athens accompanied by Kennedy's choice of chaperons—Undersecretary of Commerce Franklin D. Roosevelt Jr. and his wife Susan. On October 4, 1963, Captain Costa Anastassiadis, the master of the *Christina*, set sail from the port of Piraeus and headed for the island of Lesbos.

The *Christina*, a converted 2,200-ton Canadian frigate, consumed thirty tons of fuel a day, and cost nearly a million dollars a year to run, including its insurance and crew of sixty. As usual when there were guests on board, the vessel was stocked with rare vintage wines, and had a sommelier to serve them. There were two chefs—one for French cuisine, the other for Greek dishes, including Ari's favorite, *papatsakia*, eggplant baked with onions, cheese, celery, tomatoes, and peppers. A Swedish masseur and two hairdressers were on call twenty-four hours a day. There were nine double guest cabins, each decorated in a different style and named after a different Greek island. Jackie was given "Ithaca," which was the most lavish, and had been occupied at various times by Lady Pamela Churchill, Greta Garbo, Maria Callas, and Lee Radziwill. Her bathroom was done in solid pink marble.

Late on her first night out at sea, Jackie retired to her cabin and wrote a long, rambling letter to Jack. She began by describing her visit to the palatial villa of Greek shipowner Markos Nomikos and his wife Aspasia, and ended the letter by trying to tell Jack how much she missed him. When she finished, she read it over, and was dissatisfied. She tore it into small pieces, threw it away, and started all over again.

She wrote for the next couple of hours, filling seven pages. It was an unabashed love letter, the most passionate letter of her life. She poured out her heart, telling Jack how much she missed him, how she knew that he had suffered from the death of Patrick, how their relationship had been deepened and transformed by the baby's death. She said that she felt there was a new, stronger bond between them. She loved him more than ever before. She promised to be a better wife, to campaign with him whenever and wherever he wanted. She wrote:

I miss you very much, which is nice though it is also a bit sad—
but then I think how lucky I am to be able to miss you—I know
that I always exaggerate—but I feel sorry for everyone else who
is married—I realize here so much that I am having something
you can never have—the absence of tension—I wish so much
that I could give you that—so I give you every day while I think
of you everything I have to give.

The next morning, she handed the sealed letter to the *Christina's*
purser and asked him to mail it at their next port of call. The love letter
would be postmarked October 6—six weeks and six days before her husband's assassination.

From Lesbos the *Christina* made its way to Crete. Still, none of the
guests had laid eyes on Onassis. He had decided to remain below decks
in his cabin, discreetly out of sight, as a concession to Jackie's reputation, and to John Kennedy's political ambitions. Finally, after they had
docked at Smyrna, the birthplace of Onassis, Jackie sent Franklin Roosevelt Jr. to implore him to join the others. To everyone's delight, their
host sent back word that he would act as their guide.

And with that, Aristotle Onassis made his entrance.

ARISTO

He was a short man, not even five feet six, with a barrel chest, thick forearms, and the face of a gangster. He gave off the impression that he was both dangerous and disreputable, and this sinister aura was enhanced by the tinted glasses he wore to protect his weak eyes.

Jackie had heard all the rumors about Onassis—how he was a skirt-chaser, a star-fucker, and a loud vulgarian. He might not be the richest man in the world, people said, but he was second to none when it came to fraud, deceit, and double-dealing. It therefore came as a great surprise to Jackie to discover that Onassis was nothing like his reputation.

He turned out to be the most completely sociable person she had ever met, not excepting Jack Kennedy, who was no slouch in that department. Ari struck her as a man with a conflicted personality, as insecure and vulnerable as he was egotistical and grandiose. One moment, he could be brash, exuberant, and effervescent; the next, he was plunged into a mood of deep melancholy. He was like a chameleon, constantly changing to adapt to his surroundings.

"His most characteristic stance is with shoulders slightly hunched, arms spread out, and swaying a little on the balls of his feet like a bantamweight watching which way his opponent is going," wrote Randolph Churchill, Winston's son, in an article for the London *Evening Standard*. Randolph went on to note:

As well as Greek, he speaks fluent Spanish, French, and English. Though his choice of words in English is sometimes slightly off-center, his sense of the balance of a spoken sentence is uncannily acute. He is a born orator with a poetic sense and can build up a list of adjectives in an ascending order of emphasis and weight which are as perfect as a phrase of music.

Just as his listener is caught by the spell, he will suddenly bring the whole edifice tumbling down by a deliberate piece of comic bathos. He will burst into laughter at the very moment when almost any other man would be exploding into passion. Sometimes he changes from a gentle whisper to a deafening bellow between two words.

Jackie fell completely under his spell. She hardly noticed that Ari drank heavily—mostly Dom Pérignon champagne and Courvoisier—and that he sweated so profusely that he had to change his clothes frequently throughout the day. After she got over the initial shock of his appearance, she hardly gave it a second thought.

For Ari, talk was the breath of life. And as the cruise continued, Jackie sat with him on the poop deck under the stars, listening to the tales of his youth, which he made sound like an adventure yarn starring himself as the plucky hero. Jackie was especially attracted to Ari's portrait of himself as the underdog.

He lied to her about his origins, repeating the rags-to-riches legend of his childhood. In fact, his father had been a prosperous tobacco merchant in the Turkish port city of Smyrna. The Greek pale of settlement on the western shores of the Ottoman empire was the cradle of the ancient Ionian civilization.

"Ionia is the birthplace of Homer, and of all true Greeks like me," Ari said.

He was the only son, and his mother, Penelope, whom he remembered all his life as being very beautiful, died as the result of a kidney operation when he was six years old. The early loss of his mother was, most likely, the source of his lifelong melancholy, and of the deep insecurities that he always sought to cover up.

When his father remarried, Aristo did not accept his stepmother, Helen, whom he regarded as a usurper. Nor did he develop much affection for the two stepsisters, Merope and Kalliroi, who joined the family over the next few years. He reserved all his love for his full sister, Artemis, and his grandmother, Gethsemane, a deeply religious woman, who regularly scrubbed the little boy's body and washed his mind of sins.

Among Greeks, modesty is not a highly regarded virtue, and when Aristo's rebellion against his stepmother led to cruel beatings by his father, the young boy was determined to show up the old man. He entered a famous athletic contest run by his uncle Homer at the Pelops Club in Smyrna. But he failed to win the top prize, "Champion of Champions."

"A friend told me, 'Cheer up, Aristo, there's always next year,' " Ari told Jackie. "And I said, 'Idiot! Do you think I am going to hang around this piddling town? For me, the whole world is small. . . . You will marvel one day at what I shall do.' "

That day came sooner than expected, for in 1922, when Aristo was sixteen years old, the Turkish army fell upon Smyrna and slaughtered the Greek population in a bloodthirsty campaign of ethnic cleansing. The Onassis tobacco warehouse went up in flames. Aristo's father was arrested. His grandmother Gethsemane perished in the holocaust. The traumatic experience sealed for all time the bond he had with his full-blooded sister Artemis.

When a Turkish officer showed up at the Onassis home to requisition the residence, Aristo convinced him that he could be of service.

"You usually find that if you make things comfortable for people, they like you," Ari explained.

In the midst of the fighting and turmoil, he escaped on a boat, wearing the disguise of a sailor, and carrying a large portion of the family fortune. But later he could not resist embroidering even this dramatic incident. He told Jackie that he had seen his uncle Homer being hanged by the Turks—which was false—and that he had to swim under a withering fusillade of gunfire to reach the boat that carried him to Athens, and to freedom.

"In those days," he said, "overseas Greeks were not particularly welcomed in Greece, where we were known as *Turkospori*—'Turk's sperm.' "

He used the family money that he had smuggled out of Turkey to secure his father's release from prison. But when the old man arrived in

Athens, he showed little gratitude. He demanded that his son give him an accounting of every penny he had spent.

"People forget quickly," Ari said. "Only a few weeks earlier they may have been on the verge of death. Then comes safety and the grumbles and complaints begin—over all sorts of trivialities."

Ari's closest friend was Constantine ("Costa") Gratsos, a tall, handsome man who invariably sported a pipe in his mouth and a pretty young woman on his arm. The ne'er-do-well son of a rich Greek shipowner, Gratsos was an alcoholic who squandered his patrimony, and ended up working for Onassis as a paid companion.

Gratsos believed that Aristo was motivated to succeed by his difficult relationship with his father. It seemed to Gratsos that Onassis developed a passion for money and power as a way of winning the approval of his father and, later, of the entire world.

No one, not even Aristo, could say what his motives were, but there was no doubt that he felt humiliated by his father's rebuke. He packed a battered suitcase, put together a few hundred dollars, and emigrated to Argentina. He traveled steerage class on the twelve-thousand-ton *Tomaso di Savoya*, but he bribed a boatswain to let him sleep in the aft of the ship in a cage that held the ship's stern lines.

In Buenos Aires, the eighteen-year-old Ari added a couple of years to the birth date entered on the documents he carried in his pocket. No longer would he need parental permission to seek work. He had dark hair, dark eyebrows, and an abundance of optimism and self-confidence, and he was an immediate hit with the girls.

"I liked the girls a lot, as do all boys of that age, and I must admit that I did have the gift of attracting them more than any of the rest of my friends," he said. "I spoke Spanish with ease and I suppose they must have found my conversation full of charm.

"You know," he continued, "the first five thousand dollars is always the hardest to make. But I was soon on my way to making my first fortune by importing oriental tobacco leaf from my father in Greece and selling it to local cigarette manufacturers. But money was never an end in itself. I never confused accumulation with enjoyment. Money gave me a sense of power, and I used it for my own pleasure, even when I was a young man."

Buenos Aires was a bustling port city, handling the country's massive exports of beef and grain, and Ari decided to take the money he had made in the tobacco business—about $600,000—and invest it in shipping. It was the midst of the Great Depression, and dry-cargo freighters could be bought for less than their scrap value. Ari gambled that shipping would recover, and would make him what he had always wanted to become—the champion of champions.

THE SPLENDOR
OF GREECE

Jackie was mesmerized by Ari's life story. The other passengers on board the *Christina* could not help but notice that a certain chemistry was developing between her and the Greek shipowner. Every morning at breakfast, there were feverish conversations among Princess Irene Galitzine; Arkadi Guerney, Jackie's old friend from her student days in Paris; and Franklin D. Roosevelt Jr., who had been sent along by Jack Kennedy to watch over his wife.

"Maria Callas wasn't [on board] for the first time in four years," Roosevelt recalled. "Jackie's sister brought Stas Radziwill along, but Stas left during the trip. We began to look like a boat full of jet-setters, and President Kennedy didn't want that image."

Between times with Ari, Jackie sat in the sun reading Greek history. One of her favorite books was *The Splendor of Greece*, by Robert Payne, who wrote:

> This naked rock is bathed in a naked light—a light unlike any other light on the surface of the earth. It is a light that can be drunk and tasted, full of ripeness; light that filters through flesh and marble; light that is almost palpable. It fumes and glares, and seems to have a life of its own. It is in perpetual movement, flashing off the sea onto the rocks, flashing from one mountain to another and back again, spilling over the valleys.

The ancient Greeks, Jackie read, were the first to develop the arts, and to live a full and free life of personal freedom—just the kind of life that Jackie yearned for. Homer's hero in the *Odyssey* reminded Jackie of Ari; they were both great fighters, wily schemers, ready speakers, and men of stout heart. Little by little, the salt air, the warm Ionian sun, the opulence of life aboard the *Christina*, the myths of the ancient Greeks, the stories of Ari's youth—all this began to work on Jackie. Myth, legend, saga, and story became jumbled in her mind.

"[Jackie and Onassis] got along famously, speaking voraciously in English, Spanish and French," Frank Brady wrote. "[Onassis] all at once offered to be her friend, provider, companion, father confessor and possible lover. . . . She was amused and fascinated at his seemingly unending supply of anecdotes, and she was impressed that even on the cruise he was able to constantly conduct and control business throughout the world. Cables and telephone calls arrived from heads of state and the presidents of the world's largest corporations, and Onassis, sometimes even between dinner courses, dictated replies and returned calls that had multimillion-dollar implications. Whereas Jack Kennedy ruled a country, Onassis seemed to rule the world."

On the last night of the cruise, Ari presented Jackie with a magnificent diamond-and-ruby necklace.

"Ari has showered Jackie with so many presents, I can't stand it," Lee joked in a letter to President Kennedy. "All I've got is three dinky little bracelets that Caroline wouldn't even wear to her own birthday party."

THE PRIZE

Onassis was in Hamburg, Germany, overseeing the construction of a new tanker, the *Olympic Chivalry*, when he heard the news that President Kennedy had been shot. He immediately contacted Lee, who was still under the impression that he was going to ask her to marry him. Lee insisted that Ari accompany her to Washington.

There, he presented himself at the gate of the White House and demanded to be admitted. Angier Biddle Duke, the chief of protocol, who was in charge of all foreign dignitaries, balked at letting Onassis in. Duke checked with the Kennedy family, and to his amazement, he was instructed to admit the Greek shipowner.

"My job was to keep the foreign guests penned up in Blair House, and a Greek getting through my fingers bothered me," Duke recalled. "Later, of course, I came to realize that Jackie was making all the decisions about the funeral, and this Greek wouldn't have gotten near the Family Quarters without her say-so."

A kind of Irish wake was taking place in the White House as Onassis made his entrance. Ted Kennedy was doing imitations. Robert McNamara was wearing one of Ethel Kennedy's wigs. After dinner, Bobby Kennedy came down from the third floor, where Jackie was resting, and started to badger Onassis about his yacht and all his wealth. The puritanical Attorney General did not like the sybaritic Greek.

"I have never made the mistake of thinking it is a sin to make money," Onassis said. "I've dealt with a lot of people, and they haven't always been scouts. It's impossible for an entrepreneur, a man like me, not to tread on somebody's toes. All profit is an injustice to somebody. I've made a lot of enemies . . . but what the hell! No excuses. I'm as rich as I know how to be, and rich I know about."

Bobby drew up a bogus document stipulating that the Greek shipowner would give away half of his wealth to the poor of Latin America. Playing along, Onassis signed the document in Greek.

His good humor and patience were rewarded when the phone rang with a call from Jackie. She asked that Onassis come upstairs for a private chat. He was the only visitor outside of family and a few heads of state to be accorded such a special honor by the widow of the slain President.

When Onassis entered the Yellow Oval Room of the Family Quarters, he found Jackie sitting on a sofa. He took a place beside her, and immediately started speaking. He did not ask her any questions—not how she felt, nor if she was all right, nor if there was anything he could do for her. He knew how to talk to a woman. He loved words, had a huge storehouse of facts at his disposal, and possessed a keen intelligence. He consoled Jackie with his facts, and wooed her with his native charm.

John Fitzgerald Kennedy had been dead for less than two days.

After the assassination, and Jackie's move to New York, huge bunches of red roses began arriving at her apartment every morning with cards in Greek signed "Aristotle Onassis." In the evening, identical bunches of roses were delivered with the same good wishes. Ari behaved like a man who had nothing better to do than pay court to Jackie.

"Ari began courting Jackie with all his resources, wooing her with his vast wealth, his vast power, and his earthy charm," recalled Aileen Mehle, who wrote a society gossip column under the name Suzy. "Vulnerable, despairing, and at a total loss after Jack's death, she was overwhelmed by the attention. Here was someone, she thought, who loved her truly, coming to her rescue. He, amazed at his luck at winning the world's most famous and sought-after woman, could not stop crowing over his prize."

Little by little, he gained Jackie's confidence and assumed a many-sided role—father confessor, financial adviser, and potential lover. He made no secret of his desire to replace Bobby Kennedy as Jackie's chief male protector, but he felt that an invisible barrier stood in his way.

One fall day in 1967, they were sitting in the library of Jackie's apartment, and Ari turned to her and said:

"Jackie, you have no right to isolate yourself like this."

Just then, Marta, Jackie's housekeeper, came in with a tray of tea and madeleines, Jackie's favorite sweet. Ari waited until Marta had left, then continued:

"It is not good for you, and not good for the children. You have done all the mourning that anyone can humanly expect of you. The dead are dead. You are the living."

For a long time, Ari attributed Jackie's standoffish behavior to Bobby Kennedy's influence. Bobby simply did not like him. Ari had heard about Jackie's relationships with other men: Roswell Gilpatric, the former undersecretary of defense; David Ormsby-Gore, who was now Lord Harlech; and John Warnecke. But Ari told himself that these men were just friends, and meant nothing to Jackie.

He was right—at least when it came to Lord Harlech and Ros Gilpatric.

"There was a lot of nasty stuff going around town about Jackie and Ros Gilpatric," one of Jackie's closest friends told the author. "Ros's wife, Pam, was an old friend of mine, as was Jackie, so I knew the truth. That story was absolute rubbish. Jackie never had an affair with Ros, who had lots of affairs with other women, but never one with her."

Ari considered himself Jackie's most serious suitor. And yet, Ari had a sixth sense about things, and he must have noticed the change that came over Jackie at about this time of her life. Although Ari did not know it, Jackie had recently stopped sleeping with Jack Warnecke, and she seemed more receptive to Ari's overtures. In turn, he stepped up his campaign to win her over. Shrewdly, he began paying more attention to Caroline and John.

Ari had two children of his own, Alexander and Christina, but he had never bothered to be a real father to them. As they were growing up, they had no home life. Ari hardly ever saw them, and rarely mentioned them to Jackie. He made her feel as if she and *her* children were the only ones he cared about.

LITTLE DADDY

A s Jackie and Ari drank their tea and ate the madeleines, they talked
about her problems with the press. Reporters and cameramen were
camped outside her Fifth Avenue apartment. Each time Jackie made
an exit under the long green canopy, the slavering media beast was
there waiting to devour her. So were women with their hair in rollers,
tourists with Instamatics, and strollers with their dogs. Her public ordeal
brought back tormenting memories of the day they shot Jack.

In the shadows cast by the library fire, Ari reminded Jackie of her
father in his latter years. If Jack Warnecke had represented one side of
Black Jack Bouvier's character, Ari represented the other. He was a
bad boy who held out the promise of raw adventure. He danced and
romanced like a real-life Zorba the Greek. He knew how to break
through Jackie's introverted personality, and make her feel like a bit of a
she-devil.

Ari and Black Jack were both men of the world, men who enjoyed
the drama of the mating game. Like Black Jack, Ari had an endless supply of anecdotes about his sexual escapades, and Jackie enjoyed listening
to them.

There was, for instance, the story of his brief affair with Eva Perón,
the wife of the president of Argentina. This had taken place a very long
time before, in 1947, to be exact, when Eva was touring Europe, and
staying at a villa on the Italian Riviera. After she and Ari made love,

Eva cooked him an omelette, and he wrote out a check for $10,000 as a donation to one of her favorite charities.

"It was the most expensive omelette I have ever had," he told Jackie.

Then there was Ingeborg Dedichen, the beautiful blonde daughter of one of Norway's leading shipowners. Ari called her by the Italian nickname Mamita, "Little Mother," and she called him Mamico, "Little Daddy."

Ari described for Jackie in the most graphic detail his love life with Mamita—how he licked her between each of her toes, embraced every part of her body, covered her with kisses, then devoted himself again to her feet, which he adored. He had a thing about feet, he admitted, and he found Mamita's feet as soft as a baby's bottom.

Despite such candor, he chose to omit some of the less flattering details of his relationship with Mamita. For one thing, he did not tell Jackie that he enjoyed putting on Mamita's clothes now and then and parading around their apartment dressed like a woman. For another, it was not only her feet that fascinated Ari. He was also into bottoms, the anus, and anal humor.

He once told Mamita that he had piles, and would have to see a doctor the first thing the following morning. He then asked her to examine his anus, and when she did so, he let out a loud fart in her face. He found the joke very amusing.

Mamita was older than Ari, and when they met, she was far more sophisticated than he. They lived together for more than ten years, and she taught the refugee from Smyrna about good manners, and how to order food from a French menu. But her real value lay in her connections to the elite members of the oil-tanker business in Britain, Sweden, and Norway.

"In the mid-1930s, tankers were still a comparatively small business," noted *The Times* of London. "Oil accounted for only 15 percent of the world's total energy requirements: coal was king. . . . Onassis was not the first Greek into tankers. . . . One or two other small operators were active during the Spanish Civil War from 1936 onward, supplying both sides impartially. What Onassis perceived most clearly was that tankers could be much bigger than anyone then considered feasible. He envisaged heroic economies of scale in operating costs. Having done so, he had the courage to push his vision through."

Ari and Mamita spent the war years in New York, which was head-quarters for most of the prominent Greek shipowning families. It was about this time that the lovers reached a tacit understanding: they were free to come and go as they pleased. Ari slept with other women, and Mamita liked hearing about these sexual liaisons. They became, as Mamita put it, "accomplices rather than lovers."

"We sat in L.A. screwing the girls, a very pleasant occupation," Ari's good friend Costa Gratsos recalled of those war years. "There were star-lets, semistars, and stars, an endless supply."

"He was very sweet," said Veronica Lake, one of Ari's girlfriends, who spent some Hollywood nights with him at Romanoff's. "But, oh, God, those black eyes! They look like they are going straight through the back of your head."

Meanwhile, Mamita had become friends with the second wife of Stavros Niarchos, who, like Ari, was a parvenu in the Greek ship-owning community.

"It was after dinner with the Niarchoses that Ari, for the first time in their relationship, beat Ingse," an article in *The Times* of London re-ported years later. "There had been an argument on the Chris-Craft over her insistence on wearing a pair of green and yellow plaid pants that he found unbecoming. He was uncharacteristically silent through-out dinner, and on the way back. When they were home again, his pent-up rage turned to uncontrolled violence, and he kicked and hit Ingse until he was finally exhausted and went to bed."

Later, Mamita provided her own description of Ari's violent temper:

He needed some victim on whom he could release his nervous tension. It would not have suited his complicated character to discuss what was at issue between us, and we never did. He was always trying to put me in the wrong, because he always needed to keep his victims within his power . . . he had to have them "in the palm of his hand."

Ari was drinking heavily now, and the beatings continued, some-times leaving Mamita so badly battered—"like a boxer who has just lost a fight," she said—that she had to be treated by a doctor. But Mamita and Mamico had developed a relationship of mutual dependence, and she could not leave him. When Ari proposed marriage, he promised to buy Mamita her own yacht and a private Greek island. He gave her an antique Egyptian necklace to wear at the wedding. First, however, Mamita required an operation to enable her to have children. When the operation failed, she made a botched attempt at suicide.

After the end of the war, Ari phased Ingeborg Dedichen out of his life like a rusty ship. He married Athina Livanos, the younger daughter of Stavros Livanos, one of the wealthiest of the Greek shipowners. Ari was forty years old, and Tina—a petite, blonde tomboy with a passion for horses—was seventeen. Ari was marrying up.

Almost a year later, Stavros Niarchos, who had also been attracted to Tina, divorced his wife, and married Tina's sister Eugenie. The stage was set for the monumental rivalry that would obsess Niarchos and Onassis for the next thirty years.

Tina was attractive and well educated, but like Ingeborg Dedichen, she soon became the victim of her husband's uncontrollable anger. When he was displeased with Tina, Ari disciplined her with the tip of his hot cigar.

"Every Greek, and there are no exceptions, beats his wife," he said. "It is good for them. It keeps them in line."

Jackie enjoyed listening to Ari's stories of his women. But of all his paramours, it was Maria Callas who interested her the most. Ari had carried on a love affair with Maria for more than a decade, and like everyone else, Jackie was curious to know what he thought about the legendary soprano.

In private, Maria was a shy, insecure, and humorless woman. But she was transformed into a commanding presence whenever she walked out onto an opera stage. She was a big woman, with huge black eyes and lustrous black hair, and she held audiences spellbound with her soaring, unconventional voice. Her fiery interpretations of *Norma*, *I Puritani*, and *Tosca* were talked about for years, until they took on almost mythic proportions. Gradually, Maria began to confuse herself with her press clippings, and she turned into a stereotype of the spoiled diva.

"Callas was difficult to live with," said Stelio Papadimitriou, Ari's private attorney, who came to function as his second-in-command.

"When they visited his office in Monte Carlo, Onassis would order the elevator to stop so that Callas could have quiet. The staff had to climb the four floors on foot. But Callas did not like the sound of their footfalls. So they in the upper floors had to take off their shoes."

Ari and Maria shared a common language—Greek—which they used for screaming and cursing at each other. And they shared a common background—they had both come up the hard way.

"I have always had a great admiration for Madame Callas," Ari said. "More than her artistic talent, even more than her success as a great singer, what always impressed me was the story of her early struggles as a poor girl in her teens when she sailed through unusually rough and merciless waters."

Ari and Maria traveled to Istanbul on the *Christina*, and they paid a call on the patriarch of the Greek Orthodox Church there, who blessed them as "the world's greatest singer and the greatest seaman of the modern world, the new Ulysses." After that, Maria began acting like a different woman. Her singing career, which she had treated until now like a religious calling, suddenly seemed unimportant, and she retired from the stage. She allowed herself to be swept into the vortex of Ari's life—drinking until dawn at Régine's, attending other people's opening nights, shopping for new clothes, going to the races, gambling at Monte Carlo.

"[But] Onassis, a master of the art of pleasing women, was no less a master of the art of crushing them," wrote Maria's biographer, Arianna Stassinopoulos. "And there was something in Maria's way of treating him like a sultan or a god that brought out the despot in him. Underneath the easy sophistication of the café society habitué (and not that far below the surface), Onassis had retained all the primitive male impulses of the old-fashioned Greek. . . .

"[A]ll the suppressed violence in him came out in the way he treated her, especially in front of his children," Stassinopoulos continued. "He would walk ahead with them, leaving her behind, and he belittled her constantly: 'What are you? Nothing. You must have a whistle in your throat that no longer works.' "

One of Maria's friends, Maggie van Zuylen, tried to comfort her.

"Of course he loves you," she said. "That's why he yells and abuses you and puts you down. If he didn't love you he would just ignore you and be totally indifferent to you."

Ari's violence and infidelities were not Maria's only problems. She also had to contend with Ari's formidable sister Artemis.

A fragile-looking woman who did not weigh a hundred pounds, Artemis Garofalidis was a tiny dynamo. She was married to a wealthy doctor of orthopedics who spent more time pursuing his favorite hobby, hunting, than he did attending to patients in his office. His long absences were explained by the fact that he and his wife had suffered the loss of their only child, a daughter named Popin, who died of a rare disease at the age of eighteen. Artemis was left to focus her inexhaustible supply of energy on her brother Aristo. She doted on him and made no secret of her contempt for "that opera singer."

"They are both big bosses," she said of Ari and Maria. "Neither one knows how to give in. I do not want my brother to marry Maria. She is not right for him. Her personality is too strong for him. She is not elegant enough for him."

The Onassis-Callas affair fascinated the European press. Wherever Ari went, reporters wanted to know: Did he love Callas?

"Of course, how could I help but be flattered if a woman with the class of Maria Callas fell in love with someone like me?" he told reporters in Venice. "Who wouldn't?"

All this was too much for Ari's wife Tina, who flew off with their children to New York to seek a divorce.

"She has kidnapped the children and is demanding $20 million ransom," Ari complained.

Ari's Greek sense of honor demanded restitution. While he tried to work out the best possible terms of divorce, Costa Gratsos, his friend since the Argentinean days, took matters into his own hands. Gratsos telephoned reporters on several of New York's tabloid newspapers, and fed them outrageous—and false—accusations against Tina, Ari's soon-to-be ex-wife.

Gratsos told the reporters that Tina Livanos Onassis was a heartless woman and a compulsive materialist who was spending Ari blind. Gratsos would use the same smear tactics against Jackie many years later.

Like most ne'er-do-well sons, Gratsos had an inflated sense of his own importance, and he loved the company of glamorous stars like

Maria Callas. When Ari and Maria visited New York, Gratsos made his apartment available, providing them with the privacy they required. He tried to convince Ari that, while Tina might have been unwilling to put up with his long absences and chronic infidelities, Maria loved him enough to tolerate anything.

But Gratsos miscalculated Maria's tolerance for repeated public humiliations. When Maria heard that Jackie Kennedy had been invited for a recuperative cruise on the *Christina* after Patrick Bouvier's death, she refused to go along.

"The watching game was turning deadly serious, and the pain, killing," wrote Arianna Stassinopoulos. "[Maria] knew that Jackie had been given the Ithaca suite, the suite reserved for special guests, the suite that was Churchill's, the suite she herself had stayed in. She knew, because she had lived it so many times, the routine on the *Christina*, the times for lunch and dinner, the ritual cocktails on the deck at sunset; she knew the maids who would look after Jackie, the waiters who would wait on Jackie, the chef who would cook for Jackie. . . . In her private hell, Maria lived their cruise with them. It was at this time that she began to find it impossible to sleep without pills."

When Ari flew to Washington to be by Jackie's side after John Kennedy's assassination, Maria was apoplectic.

"Aristotle is obsessed by famous women," she said. "He was obsessed with me because I was famous. Jackie is even more famous."

However, neither Maria nor anyone else could have predicted what the end of her affair with Ari would be like. It dragged on for years, and it resembled the last scene of an opera in which the heroine dies a thousand deaths.

"TYPICAL JACKIE"

In the summer of 1967, Jackie accepted an invitation from Ari to visit Skorpios, his private island in the Ionian Sea.

"That was the year I went to Skorpios with Gianni Agnelli [the Fiat automobile heir]," said a man who was a friend of the Onassis family. "It was August. We came suddenly . . . ; we were cruising down to Greece in Gianni's boat, pulled up at the island, dropped anchor, and sent a message that we were there.

"Down came Onassis with his car, and just as he arrived, we saw Jackie waterskiing; she never even stopped to say hello. Later, when she was finished, we all had lunch. In those days, she was extremely friendly, extremely nice to me, and she spoke to Gianni in that whispery voice: 'Oh, Gianni.' Typical Jackie.

"Onassis drove us around in his car; he was just building Skorpios then, and I remember that once he backed up and we nearly went off a cliff. He was sweating, and he wore a lot of cologne. I remember it well: it was August 1967. Jackie, not married, spent the summer on Skorpios, the colonels were in power in Greece, my wife was trying to leave me, and I got back together with her, and we had a good time—it was a magical summer.

"Christina [Onassis] was insignificant in the scheme of things; in the presence of her father, she was often silent. In those days, in a Greek household, a talkative child was not tolerated, and she was—what?—sixteen then.

"I'm ninety-nine percent certain that there was another Kennedy on Skorpios that summer as well, either Bobby or Teddy, although I would assume it was Teddy; Bobby was always pulling Onassis's leg, trying to get money out of him. Onassis didn't like the Kennedys, but he was a businessman; he got along with them fine. He would have gone to bed with the devil if it meant getting close to power."

NINE

FALLEN
IDOL

Spring–Fall 1968

"THE CAT AMONG
THE PIGEONS"

A ristotle Onassis was in Paris in the spring of 1968 when he heard the good news: Robert Kennedy, the man who stood in the way of his marrying Jackie, had taken the plunge back into national politics. Bobby had decided to challenge President Johnson and Eugene McCarthy, the leading anti–Vietnam War candidate, for his party's presidential nomination.

"Now the kid's got other fish to fry," said Ari.

America was convulsed by its greatest crisis since the Civil War. The Viet Cong had just launched their Tet offensive, invading the United States Embassy in Saigon, and the streets and campuses of America were exploding in demonstrations.

Other traumas followed in quick succession: Martin Luther King Jr. was assassinated in Memphis, setting off massive rioting by blacks in more than one hundred cities. Students took over the president's office at Columbia University, leaving their own feces as a calling card on his desk. The Poor People's Campaign, led by the Reverend Ralph Abernathy, set up Resurrection City in Washington, D.C., a fifteen-acre campsite between the Lincoln Memorial and the Washington Monument. And on the nightly news, LBJ announced that he was not a candidate for reelection.

While Bobby huddled with his advisers at Hickory Hill, Ari made his move in Paris. At a cocktail reception in the swank George V Hotel, he launched into a flowery monologue about his lifelong search for the ideal woman. Someone asked him for his opinion of Jacqueline Kennedy.

Ari's face lit up. It was the opportunity he had been waiting for.

"She is a totally misunderstood woman," he said. "Perhaps she even misunderstands herself. She's being held up as a model of propriety, constancy, and so many of those boring American female virtues. She's now utterly devoid of mystery. She needs a small scandal to bring her alive. A peccadillo, an indiscretion. Something should happen to her to win our fresh compassion. The world loves to pity fallen grandeur."

The words struck his listeners as indiscreet. But, as usual, Ari knew what he was doing. He believed that Jackie wanted to marry him as much as he wanted to marry her, but that she was still in bondage to Bobby. Bobby was the sole remaining obstacle to the conclusion of the biggest deal of Ari's life—marrying Jackie.

"He needed to make deals," wrote Peter Evans, another Onassis biographer. "Deals had always been essential to him, in some psychic way he needed them; a deal meant an opponent, an opponent meant confrontation, and confrontation was the source of his strength. He could not live without adversaries, no more than a tree can live without soil."

Bobby was the enemy, but he was an enemy Ari did not understand. Why wasn't Bobby upset when Jackie flew off to the Yucatán Peninsula in Mexico and strolled through the moonlit Mayan ruins with Roswell Gilpatric? Why didn't it faze Bobby when Jackie invited Lord Harlech for an intimate weekend at the Kennedy compound in Hyannis Port?

Ari had not slept with Jackie yet, and being Greek, he could not be sure of her until he did. He was seized by feelings of resentment and jealousy. Were Jackie and Lord Harlech lovers? How about Ros Gilpatric? Was there more to that friendship than met the eye? Who else was Jackie seeing on the sly? What about those rumors of John Warnecke?

"He was fascinated by scandal," said Joan Thring, who was Rudolf Nureyev's personal assistant and was up on all the latest gossip. "I knew that whatever I said was important to him. Winning Jackie meant everything to him. It was the only time I ever sensed vulnerability in the man."

It galled Ari that nobody took him seriously as Jackie's suitor. People could not conceive that the dewy queen of Camelot would want to make love to the toadlike Onassis. Her kisses would never turn *him* into a prince. The same gossip columnists who wrote about Ros Gilpatric and Lord Harlech hardly noticed when Ari slipped into Jackie's Fifth Avenue apartment for a quiet tête-à-tête, or when he dined with her and Rudolf Nureyev and Margo Fonteyn at Mikonos, one of his favorite Greek restaurants in New York.

At one of those dinners, Nureyev leaned over to Jackie, and said in his heavily accented English:

"Every fact in world must have been printed about you now. To be this public is not good for soul."

"Oh, they're still on the fanciful embellishments," Jackie said. "The essence is still untouched."

Ari intended to change all that. He was feeling quite smug as he left the cocktail reception at the George V Hotel and climbed into the backseat of his limousine next to one of his henchmen, Johnny Meyer, the former Howard Hughes associate, who helped Nigel Neilson with publicity.

Ari knew that his comments about Jackie's needing a juicy scandal would be picked up by the wire services, and played back to America, and run in all the newspapers there. As his car headed down the Champs-Elysées toward his home at 88 Avenue Foch, he turned to Johnny Meyer and said:

"That should set the cat among the pigeons at Hickory Hill."

LITTLE
GREEN APPLES

A ri kept many henchmen like Johnny Meyer on his payroll, but at the critical moments of his life, he turned to his sister Artemis. She was the only person he really trusted. Unlike Merope and Kalliroi, Artemis shared the same mother and father with Aristotle. They had the same genes, the same blood. And in the end, it is always blood that counts to a Greek.

In May, he telephoned Artemis from the Caribbean and asked her to come to St. Thomas in the Virgin Islands, where the *Christina* would be docked.

"A VIP is coming aboard," he told her.

"Who can be so important that I have to drop everything and get on an airplane?" Artemis wanted to know.

Ari knew that his sister would do whatever he asked of her, and he refused to tell her the identity of his mystery guest.

"I thought the *Christina* was going to St. Thomas to pick up Callas," Artemis recalled. "I was afraid Aristo was going to listen to Costa Gratsos, and ask Callas to marry him. Gratsos and my brother were forever talking about women, and for some reason, Gratsos had taken a strong dislike to Jackie from the start. Maybe Gratsos was jealous that Aristo liked Jackie more than he liked him. Whatever the reason, Gratsos was pushing Callas over Jackie."

Like most Greeks, Gratsos saw romantic love as a destructive force.

Jacqueline, age twelve (right), and Lee with their mother, Janet Lee Bouvier, attend a summer wedding in East Hampton, Long Island. Jackie may have loved her father more, but she spent her life trying to please her mother. (Morgan Collection/ Archive Photos)

Jackie, age eighteen, with her father, John Vernou Bouvier III. As Jackie's greatest mentor in the arts of life, "Black Jack" taught her that women gain power by affiliating themselves with powerful men. (Morgan Collection/Archive Photos)

Less than a month after the assassination of John Kennedy, Jackie stands in the doorway of the Harriman house, her temporary residence in Georgetown, and bids goodbye to visitors Robert Kennedy and his wife, Ethel. The relationship between Jackie and Bobby was passionate but chaste. (UPI/Corbis/Bettmann)

Lee with Prince Stanislas Radziwill, the husband she planned to divorce so she could marry Aristotle Onassis. Jackie suspected her sister was living in a dreamworld when it came to Onassis, whose well-publicized love affairs were part of his publicity machine. (AP/Wide World Photos)

(Left) Author William Manchester in his Middletown, Connecticut, house with some of the foreign magazines that serialized his controversial book The Death of a President. "My first impression [of Jackie], and it never changed," said Manchester, "was that I was in the presence of a very great tragic actress." (Mondadori/Archive Photos)

(Right) Journalist Theodore H. White in his Manhattan town house. White collaborated with Jackie in creating the Camelot myth, but he left the riddle of her true identity to future biographers. (Courtesy of David White)

Jackie whispers to John Carl Warnecke at the seventh annual Robert Kennedy Pro-Celebrity Tennis Tournament in 1978, more than a decade after their love affair ended. The need for discretion added a further dimension to their romance—the delicious aura of secrecy. (Ron Galella/Ron Galella Ltd.)

Despite a tabloid's prediction, wedding bells were not in the cards for Jackie and Jack Warnecke. He came to realize that he would never be able to provide Jackie with what she really needed: total security from the outside world. (Courtesy of John Carl Warnecke)

Jackie tours the ruins of Ankgor Watt with Lord Harlech, former British Ambassador to the United States. Onassis wondered whether there was more to Jackie's friendships with other men than met the eye. (Archive Photos)

New Frontiersman Roswell Gilpatric accompanies Jackie on a trip to Los Angeles, where Bobby Kennedy was fatally wounded by an assassin in June 1968. Jackie's purloined "Dear Ros" letter was used by her enemies to poison her relationship with Onassis. (UPI/Corbis/Bettmann)

Onassis, with his bride by his side, waves to newsmen from his yacht, the Christina, shortly after their wedding on Skorpios. Onassis fulfilled Jackie's deep need for a man who could rescue her from feelings of helplessness. If that was a definition of love, then she loved Onassis. (UPI/Corbis/Bettmann)

Sailing aboard the Christina. For Jackie, Greece acquired some of the mythic attributes of Camelot, and in her mind Onassis became mixed up with her mythological view of John Kennedy, a man who paid with his life for defying fate. (Courtesy of Niki Goulandris)

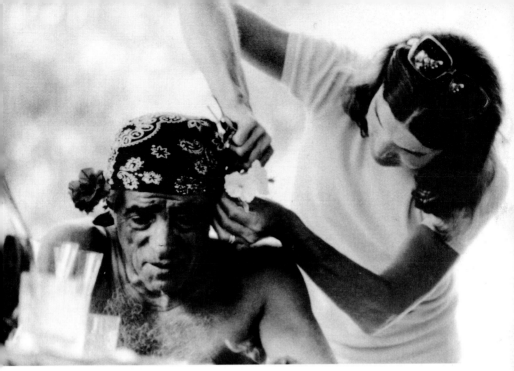

Jackie pins a flower behind Onassis's ear. When they were together, Jackie doted on her Greek husband, sketching his portrait, buying him modish neckties, and presenting him with a cigar cutter for his long Havannas. She filled a book with translations from Homer's Odyssey and illustrated it in the margins with photos she took of Onassis, depicting him as Ulysses. (Peter Beard/The Time Is Always Now Inc.)

On the beach in Skorpios. "Jackie is a little bird that needs its freedom as well as its security," Onassis said, "and she gets both from me. She can do exactly as she pleases." (Settimio Garritano/ Gamma Liaison)

Caroline paints a design on John Jr.'s back. As John grew older, his impulsive behavior, which first became noticeable after the assassination, developed into a serious problem. (Courtesy of Niki Goulandris)

Shopping in the Greek Isles with Niki Goulandris. In many ways, Niki was a Greek replica of Jackie's best American friend, Bunny Mellon. Both women embroidered life with flowers. (Courtesy of Niki Goulandris)

Jackie in Greece with Onassis's sister Artemis. "Jackie, you are so young and beautiful," Artemis told Jackie after the death of Onassis. "Now you need to find a man who will give you some happiness." (Gamma Liaison)

(Below) Jackie and Onassis seated far apart in the back of his limousine. They did not understand each other's world. She was Catholic, Anglo-Saxon. He was Eastern Orthodox, Mediterranean. (Gamma Liaison)

Jackie with her stepdaughter Christina on the way to Onassis's funeral. "Christina was angry as hell," said Onassis's attorney. "She thought that Jackie was behaving badly by asking for a bigger share of the estate." (Keystone/Sygma)

A windblown Jackie captured in an offguard moment in New York by paparazzo Ron Galella. She sought privacy by marrying Onassis, but was as exposed and vulnerable as she had been after Kennedy's assassination. (Ron Galella/Ron Galella Ltd.)

Paparazzo Ron Gallela snaps one of the 4,000 pictures he took of Jackie. She suffered an ordeal by the media such as no other woman in this century, with the possible exception of Britain's Princess Diana, has had to undergo. (Ron Galella Ltd.)

Jackie O with (from left) Liza Minelli, Irving "Swifty" Lazaar, and Bianca Jagger. Suddenly Jackie was the new "in" personality to invite and hope to be invited by. "More than anyone else in New York," wrote Liz Smith, "Jacqueline [typifies] the new society of the metropolitan Eastern Seaboard." (Sonia Moskowitz)

With Leonard Bernstein and Oliver Smith at Studio 54. Jackie's friendship with gay men had a profound effect on her outlook. She came to believe that no good would ever come from trying to sanitize or standardize behavior. (Corbis/Bettmann)

With journalist Pete Hamill at a 1977 movie premiere. Hamill embodied many of the bad-boy qualities that attracted Jackie to Kennedy and Onassis. But Hamill also represented a break with the past. He was both masculine and sensitive. (Ron Gallela/Ron Gallela Ltd.)

With constant companion Maurice Tempelsman on the way to a Kennedy Library fundraiser. They made no attempt to disguise their living arrangements, though visitors noticed that Tempelsman occupied the guest room, not Jackie's bedroom. (Brian Quigley/Outline)

The Bouvier sisters enjoy a reunion in Montauk, Long Island. Lee blamed Jackie for meddling in her life. The breach between the sisters became so great that it never completely healed. (Peter Beard/ The Time Is Always Now Inc.)

At a book store in Vineyard Haven in 1989, Carly Simon autographs her children's book Amy the Dancing Bear, which was edited by Jackie. After Jackie fell ill, Carly wrote Touched by the Sun for her good friend. (Stephen Rose/Gamma Liaison)

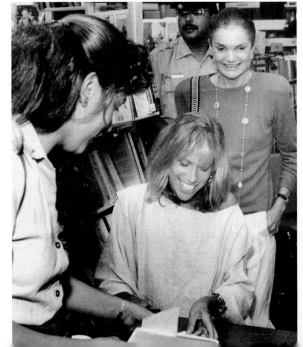

With Ted Kennedy and Caroline at a 1990 JFK Memorial dedication. Considering the snares and pitfalls of growing up a Kennedy, Caroline was amazingly well adjusted. (J. Bourg/Gamma Liaison)

(Below) With John Jr., Jackie summed up the difference between her children this way: "Caroline is focused and dedicated. John is spread out." (Ira Wyman/Sygma)

Jackie and Tempelsman return to her apartment after a stroll in April 1994, one month before her death. "He's a special person," a hospital aide said of Tempelsman. "Oh, yes," said Jackie, "he is." (Paul Adao/Sygma)

With granddaughter Rose. Jackie struggled to recapture her old life, with all the power and glory, only to discover that the key to her happiness lay where she least expected to find it—in the simple pleasures of family, friendship, work, and nature. (Keith Butler/Rex USA Ltd.)

Ari's love of Jackie was dangerous, and Gratsos did his best to turn Ari against her.

"To Onassis's face, Gratsos described her with a phrase in Greek that is not polite—it is obscene—but which meant that she was poisonous," said one of Ari's friends. "And he prophesied that [Jackie] would bring bad luck."

When Artemis arrived in St. Thomas, she found her brother in a state of acute anxiety. She had never seen him like this before. He was sweating even more profusely than usual. He had ordered the oil painting of Tina Onassis, his former wife and the mother of his children, to be removed from its place of honor over the fireplace in the yacht's salon. In its place he had hung a large, hand-tinted photograph of his beloved mother, Penelope, who had died when he was six. He had asked all but one of his passengers on the *Christina* to leave the ship at the previous port of call, St. John. Only Joan Thring remained on board.

"I thought that a very big deal must have been in the works," Thring said. "In the past, no matter how many important matters were on his mind, he had been able to shut off and concentrate on the most trifling thing when he was entertaining aboard the *Christina*."

The next day, Ari sent a delegation composed of Artemis, Captain Costa Anastassiadis, and the chief engineer of the *Christina*, Stefanos Daroussos, to the St. Thomas airport to pick up his guest. None of them was told in advance whom they were meeting. Artemis said a silent little prayer as the door of the first-class section swung open.

Out stepped Jackie, looking glorious in a brown Valentino dress. Her large sunglasses were pushed up into her hair to keep it from being blown by the wind. Artemis was so thrilled that she rushed forward in the busy terminal, threw her arms around Jackie, and kissed her on both cheeks. Jackie would make a far better wife for her brother than Maria Callas.

"As soon as Jackie came on board," Captain Anastassiadis said, "the crew started speculating that something would happen. A visit by a lone woman was not usual."

"For Chrissake, stick close," Ari told Joan Thring after they had weighed anchor and were out at sea. "Don't leave her side during the day. I don't want any sonofabitches getting any of those Peeping Tom pictures of just the two of us, making it look like we're horsing around alone out here."

———

Late one evening after dinner, Ari asked Jackie to join him for a night-cap on the deck. They stood in silence for several minutes, peering up at the vast shower of stars that spilled into the black expanse of the sea. Jackie always traveled with a portable record player and a collection of her favorite tunes, and the voice of O. C. Smith could be heard coming from the yacht's salon. He was singing "Little Green Apples."

> And she reached out an' takes my hand;
> Squeezes it, says "How you feel-in', Hon?"
> And I look a-cross at smil-ing lips
> That warm my heart and see my morn-ing sun. . . .

The air was warm and clear. For a change, Ari was not fouling it with one of his Cuban cigars. As he later confided to Costa Gratsos, he did not want to spoil the romantic moment. He recalled that he was feeling as nervous as a schoolboy about to steal his first kiss.

"Jackie," he said, "the time has come for us to discuss plans for marriage."

> And if that's not lov-in' me, then all I've got to say:
> God did-n't make Little Green Apples
> And it don't rain in In-dian-ap-lis
> In the sum-mer time.

"Oh, Telis," Jackie said, using her pet name for Ari, short for Aris-totelis, the Greek form of his name.

But that was all she said. She left the rest up to him.

"He made it clear to her," wrote his biographer, Frank Brady, "that if they married, she would be free to go wherever and whenever she pleased—with him or without him—and that she would enjoy the posi-tion of being among the richest women in the world."

Ari was deliberately drawing an equation between money and peace of mind. He was offering Jackie the chance to recapture the life she had with Jack Kennedy, a life with all the power and the glory.

"Jackie, like many Bouviers, especially her father and grandfather,

[was] highly susceptible to beauty, luxury, and great wealth," wrote her first cousin John H. Davis. "Who could put more beauty, luxury, and wealth into her life than Aristotle Onassis? A Greek island of her own. Apartments in all the capitals of Europe. One of the most luxurious yachts in the world. A fortune that made the money President Kennedy had left her seem modest in comparison."

Jackie knew that any woman who married Aristotle Onassis, the notorious Golden Greek, would be accused of doing it solely for the money. Even she would not escape the sting of that criticism. Some people would call her venal; others would accuse her of surrendering her integrity.

But Jackie believed she could handle it. Let them carp. She knew the truth. And the truth was that Ari's money was only part of the over-all picture.

"She didn't need *just* money," said Jackie's friend Vivian Crespi. "She needed to escape for sanity. I went out to a Martha Graham perfor-mance with her one night. Some strange woman came up to her and said Jackie killed her husband. It was ghastly, really a horrible way to live, putting up with this every day."

"She told me in the late spring, before she married, that she felt she could really count on Onassis to be there for her children," said Roswell Gilpatric. "That he was extremely protective of her, that he truly wor-ried about her well-being. He could afford to build the buffers she then needed to ensure some degree of privacy from the public eye."

For Jackie, feelings of attraction, affection, and sexual desire were roused when her emotional needs were fulfilled. This was probably more true of Jackie than it was of most women. After Dallas, she had an ur-gent need to feel safe.

"Onassis roamed the seas of the earth, a lord unto himself," said Pamela Harriman, who knew a thing or two about why women were at-tracted to men. "Imagine being able to slip into that, away from the real world after so much sadness."

But did Jackie *love* Ari?

The answer to that question depended in large part on whether Ari fulfilled another of Jackie's needs. Though no one could explain it, in-cluding Jackie herself, she had a compelling need to surrender herself to a man. William Manchester had noted this when he visited her in

Hyannis Port, and Jackie had automatically handed him the keys to her convertible. Men drive; women are driven. That was the logic of things to her.

No man since Jack had made as much sense to Jackie as Ari. Other people, including her own mother, might find Ari's features coarse and gangsterish, and wonder how Jackie could possibly sleep with such a hideous man. But Jackie saw Ari through her own prism. He appeared to her as a strong and masterful man. She had been searching since Jack's death for a man who could rescue her from her feelings of helplessness. In Ari, she had finally found the man. By affiliating herself with Ari, she would regain all her lost power.

If that was love, then Jacqueline Kennedy loved Aristotle Onassis.

"A FAMILY
WEAKNESS"

Jackie could hardly wait to call Bobby on the *Christina's* ship-to-shore radio the next morning and tell him about Ari's proposal of marriage.

"You're not serious," Bobby said.

For a stunning moment, Jackie did not know what to say.

"I've agreed to marry Ari," she said at last. Then she added: "In principle."

"You must be joking," Bobby said.

"We'll discuss it when I get back," Jackie said.

On the long flight back to New York, Jackie had time to consider the consequences of her decision. If she married Ari, a divorced man, she ran the risk of being excommunicated from the Catholic Church. She would tarnish the Kennedy image and damage Bobby's chances for the presidential nomination. And she would be asking an awful lot of Caroline and John, who were now eleven and eight years old.

"During the few times they met, Caroline was at best sullen and reserved toward Onassis, and on some occasions overtly hostile," wrote Frank Brady. "John was more open and friendly toward Onassis, but the question of whether he could ever consider this sixty-two-year-old man his father was one that disturbed Jackie. Each time Onassis met the children, he brought gifts and toys for them, but the role he seemed to be developing with them was less paternal than that of a rich uncle or kindly grandfather."

Once back in her apartment on Fifth Avenue, Jackie started to hear from all the people who had heard from Bobby. It was obvious that Ethel, Joan, and Ted had compared notes, because they used the same words in their effort to argue her out of marrying Ari:

"You'll destroy everything that Jack worked for before he was murdered."

Her financial guru, André Meyer, got into the act. Meyer had done business with Ari, and he knew the man's fundamental character.

"He's not good enough for you, Jackie," Meyer said. "If you marry Onassis, you will topple from your position at the pinnacle of society."

Then it was Robert McNamara on the phone. He believed that Onassis was beneath contempt. His message: "Don't marry him!"

Truman Capote filled her in on Lee's reaction.

"How could she do this to me!" Lee had screamed at Truman over the phone. "How COULD she! How could this HAPPEN!"

By the time Bobby arrived at Jackie's apartment, her resolve had begun to crumble. There was something about her relationship with Ari that always seemed to bring out the guilt in Jackie. This had happened when she came back from her first extended trip on the *Christina* in 1963. Jack had sensed her guilt, and got her to agree to accompany him on the trip to Texas. Now, Bobby played the same guilt card.

According to what he and Jackie told their friends later, their exchange was less like a conversation than an interrogation.

"Why Onassis?" Bobby asked. "Can you give me one good reason why him out of all the men you have to choose from?"

"You know I've always talked about going to the Mediterranean to stay," Jackie answered. "Ari is there. The moment is there."

"I guess he's a family weakness," Bobby said, alluding to Lee's earlier liaison with Ari. "He is a complete rogue on a grand scale."

Jackie protested. Bobby didn't know Ari. He was a kind and generous man. He was wonderful with her children.

"Even if that's true," Bobby said, "what's the big rush?"

"Who said there was a rush?" Jackie said.

"Couldn't you wait at least until after the election before making any public announcement about your future plans?" Bobby asked.

"Of course I can," Jackie said. "It's just something I have in mind."

"Good," said Bobby. "Then let it wait. Just let it wait."

"All right," Jackie said. "I'll just let it wait."

"And how about coming out of your retirement from public life to campaign for me?" Bobby asked.

"Sure, Bobby," Jackie said. "I'll go wherever you want."

"THE LAST LINK"

Shortly after ten o'clock on the morning of June 6, 1968, Ari received word in London that Robert Kennedy had been assassinated in the kitchen of the Ambassador Hotel in Los Angeles. Ari picked up the phone and called Costa Gratsos in New York.

"She's free of the Kennedys," Ari said. "The last link just broke."

"Ari had always taken what he wanted," recalled Gratsos, "and for the first time in his life he had come up against a younger man who was as tough, competitive, and determined as he was. And now that man was dead."

But Ari was a Greek, and Greeks did not believe in happy endings.

"Another assassination might just double their [the Kennedys'] right of veto over Jackie's life," he said.

There was no time to lose. Ari flew to Los Angeles to comfort Jackie, then flew back with her to New York to attend Robert Kennedy's funeral at St. Patrick's Cathedral.

"I called out her name and put out my hand," said Lady Bird Johnson of her encounter with Jackie at the conclusion of the mass at St. Patrick's. "She looked at me as if from a great distance, as though I were an apparition."

THE ONLY ONE WHO
COULD HAVE STOPPED HER

The funeral train that carried Bobby's remains from New York to Washington was packed with eleven hundred invited guests. Many of them got drunk during the eight-hour movable Irish wake. Only a select few were allowed into the hushed precincts of Jackie's private Pullman car. They went there to give her hand a gentle pat and say a few words of condolence. But they came away profoundly disturbed by the person they met.

Jackie was not the same brave young woman who had impressed the world with her flawless performance after the death of President Kennedy. She had lost her grip on reality. She rambled on incoherently, sounding as though she thought she was still the First Lady. She seemed unsure who was going to be buried today—Bobby or Jack.

Bobby's death had deranged her. She blamed herself for persuading Bobby to stay in public life and run for office. It was her idea that he put himself in harm's way. It was her fault that they had killed him.

One of the guests on the train, Frank Mankiewicz, Bobby's press secretary, recalled a conversation he had with Jackie at the Los Angeles hospital where Bobby died. Jackie could talk of nothing but death.

"The Church is . . . at its best only at the time of death," Jackie told him. "The rest of the time it's often rather silly little men running around in their black suits. But the Catholic Church understands death. I'll tell you who else understands death are the black churches. I remember at the funeral of Martin Luther King. I was looking at those faces, and I realized that they know death. They see it all the time, and they're ready for it . . . in the way in which a good Catholic is. . . . We know death. . . . As a matter of fact, if it weren't for the children, we'd welcome it."

Night had fallen by the time the funeral train arrived in Washington. The mourners, carrying twinkling candles, followed the coffin into Arlington National Cemetery.

"The cemetery itself was dark and shadowed," wrote the historian Arthur M. Schlesinger Jr. "The pallbearers, not sure where to place the coffin, walked on uncertainly in the night."

At the graveside, the priest picked up a handful of earth and began saying the prayers. A few minutes later, the sound of the earth striking the lid of Bobby's coffin snapped Jackie out of her delusional state. Suddenly she was no longer confused about whose corpse was in the coffin. It was the body of the one she had truly cared for. The one she had loved. It was Bobby. His death made her more angry than sad.

"If America ever had a claim on her after Jack's death," wrote Willi Frischauer, a friend of Aristotle Onassis's, "that claim was now forfeited. If she ever had any doubt or obligation to consider the impact of her action on the political prospects of the Kennedys, they were resolved by the shots that ended Bobby's life. For her, escape was the only way out. Jackie was shedding the Kennedy shackles . . . her decision to marry Onassis was made at the grave of Robert F. Kennedy."

SOME KIND
OF STATEMENT

On the morning of October 15, 1968, Pierre Salinger, the master political spin doctor who had served as JFK's press secretary, received a call in his Washington office from Steve Smith.

"I need to see you right away," Smith told Salinger.

Smart and ruthless, Smith was the Kennedy son-in-law who had been tapped to run the family business after Joe Kennedy's stroke. When Smith whistled, the Kennedys and their hangers-on came running. Salinger was on the next plane to New York City.

"Guess what's happened?" Smith said as Salinger walked through his door. "Jackie's going to marry Onassis."

He tossed a copy of that day's Boston *Herald-Traveler* on the desk in front of Salinger. There was a story on the front page reporting that John Kennedy's widow planned to marry Aristotle Onassis.

"We have to figure out some kind of a statement for the family to put out," Smith said.

Salinger lit up one of his famous cigars.

"Have you got any idea of what you want to say?" he asked.

"How about, 'Oh shit!' " Smith said.

THE PERFECT
MATCH

That very same day in Greece, Ari sent word to his children, Alexander and Christina, to meet him for dinner at the home of his sister Artemis. Her seaside villa in Glyfada was located on Vassileos Georgiou, a lovely street shaded by palm trees. The old house had large, well-proportioned rooms filled with shining new reproduction Napoleonic furniture in mahogany and gilt. An elegantly carved wooden staircase led to a set of airy bedrooms on the second floor. One of those rooms was now occupied by Jackie Kennedy.

Shortly after Alexander and Christina arrived, Artemis announced dinner, and Jackie appeared on the stairs wearing a simple sheath dress and a single strand of pearls. She joined the family in the dining room, whose walls were covered with old-master-style oil paintings in ornate gold frames. Alexander and Christina, who were just emerging from their teens, avoided looking at Jackie as they took their places at the long table. Each place was set with expensive silver, along with hand-painted china that matched the serving dishes that Panagotitis the butler used to dole out Artemis's specialty, meatballs with chili.

Ari looked across the table at Christina. There was not a hint of love or kindness in his eyes. He was perpetually upset with his daughter. He did not like her crazy moods. She was addicted to uppers and downers, and she suffered from bouts of suicidal depression. Ari did not like to watch Christina eat. It made him extremely nervous. She consumed vast amounts of chocolate and Coca-Cola, and at times ballooned to more than two hundred pounds. Sometimes Ari could not suppress his disgust, and he ranted and raved at his daughter in front of everyone in the house.

Alexander was another matter entirely. Ari often lost his temper at his son, but his rage was tempered by pride and love. Alexander was the apple of his father's eye. Like Christina, he had benefited from plastic surgery on his conspicuous Onassis nose. But unlike his overweight sister, Alexander was turning into a lean and attractive young adult.

For dessert there was *galaktoboureko*, a sort of crème caramel, after which Jackie excused herself and went upstairs to her room. Ari lit a long Cuban cigar. He told his children to follow him into the library. He closed the door.

Ari knew that Alexander did not like Jackie. His son had never liked any of his women, Maria Callas especially. Alexander and Christina wished that he would remarry their mother, even though that was impossible.

But Ari had made up his mind about Jackie, and he was not one to mince words.

"I plan to marry Jackie as soon as possible," he said.

Alexander bolted from his chair. "I will never sleep in the same house as that American woman!" he shouted.

He stormed out of the room. A few moments later, the whole neighborhood was shaken by the deep roar of an engine as Alexander took off in his Ferrari.

Ari was aware that Christina disliked Jackie even more than her brother did.

"Christina was jealous of Jackie," said Stelio Papadimitriou, Onassis's second-in-command. "Jackie was all that Christina was not—thin, composed, loved."

After Alexander had gone, Ari turned to his daughter.

"Well, what about you?" he said.

"It's a perfect match," she said, staring contemptuously at her father. "You like names, and Jackie likes money."

Christina got up from her chair, picked up one of Artemis's prized vases, and smashed it against the wall.

SKORPIOS

A s its name implied, the island of Skorpios was formed in the shape of a scorpion: short and thick on one side, long and slender on the other, with curving tendrils of land running out into the sea like a pair of large pincers. When Jackie arrived there in August, the island was bathed in that fuming, glaring light that she had come to love about Greece.

"The sun was everywhere, the setting sun, the rising sun, shining on the other islands in the distance," recalled Karl Katz, a friend of Jackie's, who visited Skorpios as her guest. "The warm water was a color that is often mentioned in Greek mythology as wine colored, a deep purple that wasn't blue, the clearest, most beautiful water. It was like a lake. There were various places on the island where you could swim or have tea or eat dinner or lunch. Each site was perfect at a different time of the day."

Brilliant butterflies came out into the blazing noonday sun to pollinate the flowers in the sprawling gardens. Lemons seemed to ripen to bright yellow in a matter of hours. An army of servants made up the beds, cleaned and cooked, and brought iced drinks to the swimming pool behind the Pink House. Everything was lush and fragrant, and Jackie began to feel as though she, too, was coming to life.

"Onassis was proud of Skorpios," said Stefanos Daroussos, who in addition to being the chief engineer on the *Christina* also functioned as the steward of the island. "Onassis personally supervised the construction of every single mile of road that was carved into the hillsides, the planting of every single tree, the building of every guest house. He had the sea dredged and two harbors built, one for the *Christina*, the other for the yachts of his wealthy guests. But I have to tell you that as much as he loved Skorpios, he never slept on the island. He always slept on the *Christina*. That was his real home."

The *Christina* sparkled in its dock. Four decks high, it was an immaculate white leviathan whose proportions seemed out of scale with the small island. Throughout the day, the ship's Piaggio seaplane ferried people and parcels back and forth from the mainland, which was visible across Nydri Bay. In Jackie's honor, Ari brought a bouzouki band from Athens, and in the evenings the ship's running lights twinkled over scenes of gay, boisterous parties.

"Two pretty girls, one blonde and the other dark and with her leg in a cast, are there," the journalist Nikos Mastorakis reported in *Life* magazine. "All, including Jackie and Telis, seemed pleased with their lives, and they ate black caviar and red tomatoes. Jackie, who is resplendent in a red blouse and long gypsy skirt, prefers the vodka. She leans close when Telis whispers in her ear. At dinner, Onassis eats his lamb like a youth. She eats little and nibbles white grapes. But at four A.M., with Mr. Moon above, the sweet Mrs. Kennedy sings with Telis when he starts *Adios Muchachos* and I feel they are close."

After the guests had departed, Ari pulled on a pair of bathing trunks, and lowered himself down a narrow ladder into the pitch-black waters of the Ionian Sea. For the next hour or so, he swam alone around the dark island, his powerful arms and shoulders pumping in a steady rhythm. When he got back, he ordered Captain Anastassiadis to disconnect the ship's telephones and radios, to cut off all communication with the outside world. Then he went to his cabin, and as the fuming, glaring light of a new day brightened the water, he slipped silently into bed, careful not to wake Jackie.

A CREATIVE
SOLUTION

Several days later, Senator Edward Kennedy was deposited by helicopter on Skorpios like a deus ex machina. The sudden appearance of Jackie's surviving brother-in-law gave rise to a number of rumors. According to one story, Kennedy had come all the way to Greece to prevent Jackie from being carried off by Onassis like a modern Helen of Troy. Another story portrayed Jackie as the instigator of Kennedy's visit. It was said that she had summoned Teddy to Skorpios to help her wheedle a huge prenuptial settlement from Ari.

That was the story that gained the widest circulation and made its way into subsequent magazine articles and books about the marriage. In this version of events, Teddy was acting as a spokesman for Jackie's team of lawyers in America, and spent several days on Skorpios haggling with Ari over the terms of the prenuptial agreement.

According to sources who were never named, Teddy argued that the marriage would cost Jackie her status as John Kennedy's widow, and with that loss, her $200,000-a-year income from JFK's trust. She needed to have money of her own. It was said that Teddy even threatened to take Jackie back to America unless Ari agreed to give her an obscene amount of money—$20 million was the figure most frequently mentioned—as well as lump-sum payments for each of her children, a monthly stipend for her of $30,000, and written assurances regarding their sleeping arrangements, the frequency of their sexual relations, and Jackie's right not to have a child.

Ari reportedly balked at the $20 million figure and the written assurances about sexual relations, or any other kind of relations, for that matter. Teddy returned to America a defeated man. All that he succeeding in extracting from Ari was a measly $3 million.

It was a gripping tale of suspense, starring Ari as the plucky underdog. The only trouble was, the story was made up of whole cloth by Ari, and did not contain a shred of truth.

Ari wanted the world to believe that he had made a fabulous deal when he married Jackie. As always, a deal meant an opponent, and Ari concocted the story of a confrontation between himself and Teddy Kennedy to prove that he had outwitted the Senator and the best legal minds in America.

The facts were quite different.

"There was nothing in any written prenuptial agreement about money for Jackie's children," said Stelio Papadimitriou. "And there was nothing about a monthly stipend for Jackie."

In fact, Kennedy had come to Skorpios more to lend moral support than to act as Jackie's financial adviser. Indeed, the idea of a prenuptial monetary settlement had not been Jackie's at all. It had originated with Ari, and was prompted by his concern over Greece's inheritance laws.

Under that country's laws, the spouse was entitled to 25 percent or at least to a compulsory 12.5 percent of the deceased spouse's estate. Since Ari was worth about $500 million at the time (or about $2 billion in today's money), Jackie would have been entitled for her minimum 12.5 percent, an amount of $62.5 million (or $250 million converted into current dollars) in the event of his death.

Ari had put his lawyers to work on the problem, and they came up with a creative solution. They had discovered that under *American* law, Jackie could renounce her inheritance rights as long as she received reasonable consideration for doing so.

"If I die," Ari told Jackie, according to Papadimitriou, "you will automatically inherit a large part of my estate under Greek law. That will put you in competition with my children. This is something I do not want. In order to keep my children satisfied in matters of inheritance, I want you to sign a document renouncing your rights to my estate."

"Jackie agreed to Onassis's request," Papadimitriou told the author. "Jackie was victimized by the press, which portrayed her as avaricious, but it was her behavior in this matter that made me dead certain that she was not marrying Onassis for his money.

"Just look at the facts," Papadimitriou continued. "First, Jackie agreed to renounce her inheritance rights under Greek law, thereby forfeiting a huge financial windfall in the event of the death of Onassis, who was sixty-two years old, and not in the best of health. She did not have to do that.

"Second, she did not demand any money. It was something that we in the Onassis camp insisted on giving her because it was required under American law for a valid renunciation.

"And third, the money she agreed to was ridiculously low given the size of Onassis's fortune. She got less than the $3 million that has been widely reported. Much less in fact. It was between $2 million and $3 million. And there was nothing in the prenuptial contract about any other payments, either for Jackie's monthly upkeep or for her children.

"It is true that, as the wife of Aristotle Onassis, Jackie expected to live a wealthy life. But she did not go into the marriage looking for money.

"The irony of this whole story is that it was all for nothing," Papadimitriou said. "In my view, that prenuptial agreement was not legally binding. I advised Onassis that it would not work. I told him, 'If you die twenty years from now, when you're eighty-two, maybe this prenuptial agreement will hold. And maybe it won't. But if you die any sooner, necessity will undo the agreement. We will not be able to send Jackie away without enough money to live according to her station in life as the widow of Aristotle Onassis.' "

It was a couple of years later that Stelio Papadimitriou advised Ari that notwithstanding the prenuptial agreement, Jackie, in the event of his death, would still be entitled to the compulsory minimum of 12.5 percent of his whole estate on the basis of the forced heirship provisions of Greek law.

Ari thought that it was unfair for a Greek national marrying a foreign national to be obliged to give part of his estate to his foreign spouse who could, however, totally exclude him from her estate. This was a matter which did not interest Ari alone, but could interest several thousands of Greeks married to foreign nationals.

On that basis, Ari convinced the government and the legal authorities of the country to change the Greek law to match the foreign law.

ESIAH'S DANCE

A fine drizzle began to fall on the morning of the wedding, October 20, 1968. In Greece, a rainy wedding day was considered an omen of good luck. However, Artemis Garofalidis, who was as superstitious as her brother, was taking no chances. She had once discovered a hairpin with braided hair under Aristo's pillow, placed there as a spell by Maria Callas. Concerned that Maria might be up to her old tricks, Artemis decided to slip a charm of her own beneath the mattress of the nuptial bed on the *Christina*.

When she arrived on the yacht, her brother was in the master cabin getting dressed, along with his son Alexander and the chief engineer, Stefanos Daroussos. The three men stood in front of a long mirror, inspecting themselves. Ari was very nervous, and kept adjusting the knot of his necktie. One of his wedding presents to Jackie, a gold cross made by the Greek jeweler Ilias Lalaounis, bulged in its box in the pocket of his suit. His other gifts, a pair of heart-shaped ruby earrings and a huge matching ring, which had been appraised at more than $1 million, were locked away in a safe behind the El Greco in the *Christina*'s book-lined library.

"What do you think?" Ari asked Alexander. "Do I make a good groom?"

His son was in a foul mood, and did not answer. He had agreed to attend the wedding only because his girlfriend, Fiona Thyssen, had insisted he go as a mark of respect to his father. But true to his word, Alexander had already moved all of his belongings out of the Onassis house in Glyfada and into a suite in the Athens Hilton.

So many guests had been invited to the wedding that there was not a single available bed on the island or the yacht. However, no one had thought about accommodations for Alexander and Christina. They did not have rooms to sleep in.

After he had dressed, Alexander went to find the ship's captain.

"Can my sister and I share your room tonight?" he asked Captain Costa Anastassiadis.

Costa was struck by the look of utter desolation on Alexander's face.

"I said yes," he recalled thirty years later. "But I was really helpless. Alexander and Christina felt pushed out."

Several hundred newsmen descended on Skorpios for the wedding. To control this ravenous horde, Jackie distributed a statement to the press.

We wish our wedding to be a private matter in the little chapel among the cypresses of Skorpios with only members of the family present, five of them little children. If you will give us those moments, we will so gladly give you all cooperation possible for you to take the photographs you need.

Ari hired his own small navy of patrol boats to keep away the press. In addition, the real Greek navy was called into service; it set up a blockade 1,100 yards from the island. Needless to say, none of this had the desired effect. As press helicopters swooped down over Skorpios, a flotilla of fishing boats carrying newsmen attempted an invasion on the beach. They were beaten back by more than two hundred security guards hired expressly for that purpose.

A little after five in the afternoon, Archimandrite Polykarpos Athanassiou, resplendent in a gold brocade robe, began the service in the chapel of Panayitsa, or the Little Virgin. Jackie stood a good three inches taller than the groom, noted Mario Modiano, the Athens correspondent of *The Times* of London, who was one of four newsmen allowed to witness the ceremony.

"Jackie looked drawn and concerned," he reported. "She wore a long-sleeved, two-piece ivory chiffon lace dress with pleated skirt. Her hair was secured with an ivory ribbon. The groom looked slightly off-key in a blue suit, white shirt, and white tie—the sort of thing Onassis loved to wear. Caroline and John flanked the couple, holding ceremonial candles, dazzled and serious. Jackie's glance kept turning anxiously toward Caroline. The Onassis children seemed grim."

Artemis had been given the honor of being the *koumbara*, or sponsor, of the marriage. She placed delicate leather wreaths shaped as branches with lemon buds on the heads of the bride and groom. The wreaths were connected with a white ribbon, and as the priest chanted, Artemis crossed them three times. Rings were exchanged three times. Then Jackie and Ari each kissed a silver-bound goblet and drank the red wine. The priest translated the service into English for Jackie's benefit:

"The servant of God, Jacqueline and I, in the name of the Father, the Son, and the Holy Spirit."

Then the priest took Jackie's hand and Ari's hand, and led the couple around the altar in the concluding ritual, which was called Esiah's Dance. Jackie looked stiff and uncomfortable, like an adult trying to imitate the latest teenage dance craze. When the dance was over, the priest declared them husband and wife. There was no kiss to mark the end of the ceremony. Not even a smile, or a clasping of hands.

Instead, Jackie took Caroline's hand, and mother and daughter emerged from the chapel into a steady autumn drizzle. A sullen Secret Service man with a PT-109 tie clip, commemorating JFK's World War Two heroism, fell into step beside them. The invited guests showered the newlyweds with flower petals as they got into an open-sided mini jeep. Jackie got into the front seat, put Caroline on her lap, and held her tightly. Her sister Lee and Lee's own daughter sat in the back with John, who had never smiled once during the entire ceremony. Ari took the wheel, and drove toward the *Christina* in the harbor one mile away.

A SPECIAL
SURPRISE

That evening, a sumptuous multicourse Greek wedding feast was prepared by the chefs of the *Christina* and served on board the yacht to the guests, including the Kennedy family, some close friends, and a few directors of Olympic Airways. Despite the music and the romantic setting, the atmosphere was surprisingly subdued, and everyone was aware of the nervous expressions on the faces of the bride and groom.

Arrangements had been made for Mr. and Mrs. Onassis to fly to New York on an Olympic Airways flight for their honeymoon. All the seats in the first-class cabin had been removed, and replaced by a large, comfortable bed. The flying bridal suite was separated from the rest of the cabin by specially designed curtains, and the nuptial bed was covered with expensive silk sheets.

Shortly after takeoff, a steward separated the curtains to the honeymoon suite by mistake, and was greeted by the sight of two naked bodies in the throes of energetic and creative lovemaking. When he realized exactly what he was viewing, he pushed the curtains back together and staggered out of the first-class section.

"I could not believe what I was seeing," he told a friend in Greece when he called from New York the next day. "But the fact that the two of them never even knew I was standing there, openmouthed, dumbfounded, and staring at them, amazed me even more."

"WOULD *YOU* SLEEP WITH ONASSIS?"

Joan Rivers was headlining in Las Vegas at the time, and like countless comedians, she worked material about the Onassis wedding into her act.

"Come on, be honest, would *you* sleep with Onassis?" she asked the women in her audience. "Do you believe *she* does? Well, she has to do *something*. I mean, you can't stay in Bergdorf's *shopping* all day."

The reaction around the world was just as unflattering to Jackie.

JACKIE, HOW COULD YOU? asked Stockholm's *Expressen*.

French political commentator André Fontaine wrote in *Le Monde*: "Jackie, whose staunch courage during John's funeral made such an impression, now chooses to shock by marrying a man who could be her father and whose career contradicts—rather strongly, to say the least—the liberal spirit that animated President Kennedy."

If Jackie was offended by these comments, Ari was more philosophical.

"She's got to learn to reconcile herself to being Mrs. Aristotle Onassis," he told his henchman Johnny Meyer, "because the only place she'll find sympathy from now on is in the dictionary between shit and syphilis."

A defense of Jackie came from a most unexpected source.

"Americans can't understand a man like Onassis," said Lee Radziwill. "If my sister's new husband had been blonde, young, rich, and Anglo-Saxon, most Americans would have been much happier. . . . He's an outstanding man. Not only as a financier, but also as a person . . . active, great vitality, very brilliant, up-to-date . . . amusing . . . a fascinating way with women. He surrounds them with attention. He makes sure that they feel admired and desired. He takes note of their slightest whim. He interests himself in them—exclusively and profoundly. . . .

"My sister needs a man . . . who can protect her from the curiosity of the world," Lee continued. "She's tired of having to exercise such enormous control over herself, not to be able to move without all of her gestures being judged and all her steps being traced. . . . Onassis is rich enough to offer her a good life and powerful enough to protect her privacy."

However, no one seemed ready to buy Lee's argument. This was especially true of the defenders of the faith in the Vatican, who considered excommunicating Jackie because she had married a divorced man. While they pondered that extreme step, a spokesman for the Vatican declared that Jackie was no longer eligible to receive the sacraments of the Holy Church. The whole thing struck Jackie as a supreme irony. She had tried so hard not to repeat her mother's mistakes, and yet she had ended up in the same predicament. Like her mother, Jackie felt herself to be a Catholic, but in the eyes of her church, she had lapsed irrevocably.

In the eyes of most ordinary Americans, Jackie was more than a lapsed Catholic. She was the Queen of Camelot, who had betrayed her martyred husband by prostituting herself with a swarthy, lascivious foreigner. Her marriage to Onassis was another jolt in the wild ride of the 1960s. As a shocking cultural phenomenon, it ranked up there with urban riots, campus rebellion, bra burning, and black separatism. Theodore White was right. America *was* passing through an invisible membrane that separated an era of hope and idealism from an era of disillusionment. This time, however, Jackie was on the dark side of the great divide.

TEN

THE PEONIES
OF GREECE

Spring—Summer 1970

THE PINK HOUSE

While Ari was away on business, the summit of Skorpios became Jackie's widow's walk. She spent long hours there, walking, meditating, reading, and painting watercolors of the sea. In the purplish, slate-colored water, the Ionian islands sprawled like green stepping stones along the west coast of Greece. On a clear day Jackie could see the silhouette of Ithaca, the legendary home of Odysseus, far off on the horizon.

By the spring of 1970, Jackie's life on Skorpios had settled into a comfortable routine. Each morning, she distributed a written schedule to Captain Anastassiadis, whose job it was to take Caroline and John fishing, waterskiing, and on day trips to neighboring islands.

John in particular needed looking after. As he grew older, his impulsive behavior, which had first become noticeable after the assassination, developed into a serious problem. He was restless, had a low threshold for boredom, and could not sit still for any length of time. He was disruptive in school and did poorly academically.

Jackie suffered a great deal of anguish over John. She tried to figure out how to help him do better in school. She passed up the more fashionable private schools in New York, Buckley and St. Bernard's, and enrolled John in the Collegiate School, which had a less pressured atmosphere. Though Jackie never spoke of it directly, she conveyed the impression to friends, including to this author, that she was concerned her son might have been born with a low IQ.

John was an exhibitionist like his stepfather, and he and Ari formed a special bond. Ari often took the boy to Athens in his Piaggio seaplane. While the tycoon conducted business, John, accompanied by his bodyguards, went off to the movies. Ari gave John and Caroline a twenty-eight-foot red sailboat, and when Caroline christened it the *Caroline*, Ari was concerned that John's feelings would be hurt. So he gave him his own red speedboat with JOHN stenciled on the stern.

From her vantage point at the very top of the island, Jackie peered out to sea. Off in the distance, so far away that it looked at first like another island, she could spot Ari's helicopter coming from the direction of Athens. It flew in low, stirring whirlpools in the calm surface of the water. When it got closer, it made such a racket that it scared away the flocks of imported finches that inhabited the island.

Jackie put away her brushes and paints, and waved to the helicopter. To a remarkable degree, she and Ari lived separate lives. Ari was constantly flitting from Athens to Paris to London. For her part, Jackie spent a good deal of time in New York, where her children went to school. During the first year of their marriage, the couple spent a total of 225 days together and 140 days apart. Their record of togetherness in the second year was even more dismal.

Yet if the truth be told, Jackie enjoyed her solitary life. She had always been more comfortable alone or in crowds than in one-to-one relationships, and she found it hard to be with anyone for a sustained period of time. All through her childhood, she had spent hours alone with books, spinning fantasies in which she was the heroine of her own romantic stories. Now she was living out one of those stories on Skorpios. In Ari she had found a man after her own heart; he was so absorbed in himself and his work that he left her mostly alone.

"Jackie is a little bird that needs its freedom as well as its security," Ari said, "and she gets both from me. She can do exactly as she pleases—visit international fashion shows, and travel, and go out with friends to the theater or anyplace. And I, of course, will do exactly as I please. I never question her, and she never questions me."

The arrangement was similar to the one that Ari had established with Ingeborg Dedichen, but it seemed to work for Jackie. When they were together, she doted on her Greek husband, sketching his portrait, buying him modish neckties to offset his somber suits, and presenting him with a cigar cutter so he would not bite off the tips of his long Havanas.

Ari gave Jackie expensive jewelry and lavished attention on her and her children. He also encouraged her to indulge her appetite for beautiful things. Once, in a published interview, he explained his tolerant attitude toward his wife's spending.

"God knows Jackie has had her years of sorrow," he said. "If she enjoys it, let her buy to her heart's content. . . . There is nothing strange that my wife spends large sums of money. It would be abnormal if she didn't. Think how people would react if Mrs. Onassis wore the same dresses for two years, or went to second-class beauty salons, or rode around in a family-type automobile. They would immediately say that I am on the verge of bankruptcy, and that soon my wife will be forced to work to earn a living. . . . If women didn't exist, all the money in the world would have no meaning."

Indulged by her husband, Jackie was happier than she had been since the last few months of her marriage to Jack Kennedy.

"One day we were relaxing at the beach," said Jackie's friend Vivian Crespi. "We were lying in the sun . . . drinking wine in our bikinis. And Jackie turned to me. 'Do you realize how lucky we are, Vivi?' she said. 'To have gotten out of that world we came from. That narrow world of Newport. All that horrible anti-Semitism and bigotry. Going every day to that club with the same kinds of people. Don't you feel sorry for them? You and I have taken such a big bite out of life.' "

The helicopter settled on the helipad, and a moment later a lone figure emerged from the swirling storm of dust. But instead of the short, stubby figure of her husband, Jackie saw the thin silhouette of a stylishly dressed woman.

This was Niki Goulandris, one of the richest women in all of Greece. Niki and her husband Angelos had founded the Goulandris Natural History Museum, the only private museum of its kind in the world. In addition to being a trained botanist and horticulturist, Niki was an accomplished botanical painter. She was presently engaged in an ambitious, years-long project of painting life-size pictures of the twelve different varieties of wild peony that were native to the hills and mountains of Greece.

Her interest in the study and portrayal of Greek peonies was a fitting project for a woman of Niki's Greekness. Myth and legend surrounded such plants in ancient Greece. Magical powers were attributed to them, and it was said that their black seeds, when drunk in wine, guarded against nightmares. In many ways, Niki was a Greek replica of Jackie's best American friend, Bunny Mellon. Both women embroidered life with flowers.

Jackie and Niki climbed into an open vehicle and began the bumpy ride down the steep side of the island. Below them they could see an excavation site swarming with workmen. Towering, full-grown trees, their roots wrapped in huge balls, were being unloaded by cranes from flatbed trucks and lowered into place.

For the most part, Ari ran Skorpios exactly as he saw fit. He hired all the help, set the menus for the meals, and made up the seating arrangements for the parties. The island was his domain. In a certain way, Jackie was as much a guest on her husband's island as were the many friends they invited to visit them each spring and summer.

To keep Jackie occupied, however, Ari ceded sovereignty over a part of the island to her. She had his permission to landscape the grounds and decorate one of the island's villas, the Pink House, where Maria Callas had once resided.

Ari suggested that Jackie use the Spanish architect Julio Fuentes to help her with the project. Fuentes was already drawing up plans for a gigantic villa that Ari was thinking of building on the crest of the island. Ari had in mind something like the Trianon at Versailles, or a kind of domesticated Acropolis, though Jackie vowed that she would never let him build such a house there.

Instead of Fuentes, however, Jackie summoned the American decorator Billy Baldwin, who had done residences for her and Bunny Mellon.

"This house I want to be a total surprise," Ari told Baldwin shortly after he arrived. "I trust you and I trust Jackie, and I don't want to know anything about it."

But as Baldwin soon discovered, that was not the way things worked in a Greek marriage.

"Onassis had made me responsible for the island," said Stefanos Daroussos, "and I was expected to know down to the last penny exactly what was being spent. Jackie was no exception. She could not spend Onassis's money without his prior knowledge and approval. She needed to discuss with him all her decorating and landscaping ideas. Then I would get orders directly from Onassis, not from her. Everything came from him. Everything had to be in writing, even Jackie's garden plan."

Before long, Ari grew fed up with Billy Baldwin's exorbitant fees, and Jackie had to let him go. She turned to the interior designer Renzo Mongiardino, who had done Lee's spectacular New York apartment. But Mongiardino's tastes were too grand for Jackie, who wanted the Pink House to be a simple cottage. In exasperation, she called Bunny Mellon for help. Bunny dispatched her own private decorator, Paul Leonard, to Skorpios to replace Mongiardino.

"I went there and helped her pull this cottage together," Leonard said. "One day, we were sitting there, and she looked out the window and said, 'Look at all those snapdragons. They shouldn't be on this island. It looks like a Burpee's catalogue.'

"She sounded just like Mrs. Mellon," Leonard continued. "I recalled that Mrs. Mellon had once written, 'Too much should not be explained about a garden. Its greatest reality is not a reality, for a garden, hovering always in a state of becoming, sums up its own past and its future.' Jackie had the same taste as Mrs. Mellon, so I knew exactly what she wanted. Nothing should be noticed."

Jackie intended to bring unity and order to Skorpios. She tackled the Pink House and the landscaping with the same zeal that she had brought to the restoration of the White House and Lafayette Square.

"Onassis had made Skorpios a garden of showy tropical plants," Niki Goulandris said. "The head gardener on Skorpios had planted cultivated roses at Ari's request. He had to be dealt with discreetly, so as not to hurt his feelings. Jackie and I were trying to repair and restore Skorpios to its original, natural state. Ari was not thrilled, but he didn't interfere.

"Jackie and I drew up plans," Niki continued. "She dedicated much of her time during the first couple of years of her marriage to this project.

We visited nurseries specializing in Greek plants and trees. We had hundreds of plants and shrubs, and thousands of fully grown trees hauled by trailer truck to Nydri, the small town across the bay, then shipped on barges to Skorpios. We landscaped the Pink House, the Hill House, and up the hill from the harbor. Jackie wanted to make it a Greek island again."

THE JOURNEY
TO ITHACA

In the early summer, Niki Goulandris fell ill, and had to go to the hospital. While she was recuperating, she received a letter from Jackie about her life on Skorpios. Written on the stationery of the *Christina*, the letter provided a unique glimpse of Jackie's state of almost childlike contentment in the second year of her marriage to Ari. She wrote of the delight she took in planning her garden and watching it slowly mature.

"I can't wait to talk to you about everything. I won't drag you around and tire you out—but how wonderful to have started a garden—and now to watch it develop each year like a child. . . ."

After Niki recovered from her illness, she and her husband joined Alexis Miotis, the director of the Greek National Theater, for a cruise of the Greek islands on board the *Christina*. Niki and Alexis took great pleasure in introducing Jackie to Greece. This was not the modern Greece of pollution and tourists, but the ancient Greece of poetry, and philosophy, and art.

They visited Delphi, the temple of the legendary oracle. They went to mass at Corfu's St. Francis Church. They searched for antiques and old books on Greek art. And they attended plays at Epidaurus, with its ancient Greek stage dating back to the fourth century B.C.

In Jackie's mind, Greece acquired some of the mythic attributes of Camelot. It had more to do with legend, saga, and story than with politics and history. In many ways, Jackie admired a past that had never existed. But it did not seem to matter.

"In the beginning," recalled Miotis, "Jackie and Ari seemed harmonious. Jackie is a sweet person, very noble. Her behavior sets a standard for those around her. Obviously many people thought the marriage a sham, but I saw nothing wrong with it.

"Ari had a sense of glory about everything," Miotis continued. "He paid a good deal of attention to the 'glorious' people. He admired Jackie because she was First Lady, not only in the White House but First Lady of the land. Ari wanted to be Emperor of the Seas, and wanted a Cleopatra to sit by his side.

"For Jackie, it was his charm combined with his money. He had money, yes, but he also had charisma. He was a domineering personality. He was the one man she could marry who would never become Mr. Jackie Kennedy."

For her part, Niki was impressed by how well Ari got along with ten-year-old John.

"Ari took him on his knee and explained the Greek myths to him," Niki said. "Especially the myth of Daedalus. He told John how Daedalus was a fabulously cunning artisan, and made a pair of wings of wax and feathers for himself and his son Icarus. And Icarus disobeyed his father's instructions, and flew too close to the sun, and his wings melted, and he fell to his death in the sea. And Ari told John, 'Never go beyond the prudent mean, or the gods will destroy you.'"

Jackie listened to Ari's stories of the Greek myths, and he became mixed up in her mind with her mythological view of John Kennedy, a man who had paid with his life for defying fate.

She wrote about all this in a letter to Arthur M. Schlesinger Jr., who had served in the Kennedy White House as the unofficial historian of the New Frontier.

There is a conflict in the hearts and minds of the Greeks. Greeks have esteem and respect for the gods; yet the Greek was the first to write and proclaim that Man was the measure of all things. This conflict with the gods is the essence of the Greek tragedy, and a key to the Greek character.

On the piano in the salon of the *Christina*, there was a huge red leather-bound book that Jackie had given to Ari as a present.

"In her own handwriting, Jackie had filled the book with English translations from Homer's *Odyssey*, and she had illustrated it in the margins with her own photos of Ari," Niki Goulandris said. "Part of Jackie's fascination with Ari was her search for a contemporary Greek hero, and this can be seen in her photos, particularly one of Ari on the bow of the boat with wind blowing in his hair. An image of the contemporary Ulysses."

One day during the cruise, Ari was standing on the bow of the *Christina*, looking very much like the photo in Jackie's leather-bound book.

"There, *there!*" he suddenly shouted. "You can see it! *Ithaca!*"

Jackie had just finished reading Homer's description of Ithaca—the fountains of Arethusa, the cave of the Naiads, the stalls of the swineherd Eumaeus, the orchard of Laertes. She was all fired up when the *Christina* weighed anchor and a launch took them ashore. Ari had arranged for a guide to give them a tour of the excavations of Heinrich Schliemann, the brilliant nineteenth-century German archaeologist, who had also discovered the remains of the Homeric cities of Troy and Mycenae.

Jackie was deeply moved by Schliemann's story, especially by how he had overcome an impoverished boyhood and poor health to master thirteen languages and restore to the world the glories of a heroic civilization. The ruins of Ithaca were like a giant stage set, and the place appealed to the art director in Jackie.

During a break in their tour, Jackie showed Ari a book of modern Greek poetry that had been given to her by Niki Goulandris. She especially liked C. P. Cavafy's poem "Ithaca."

> When you start on your journey to Ithaca,
> then pray that the road is long,
> full of adventure, full of knowledge. . . .
>
> That the summer mornings are many,
> that you will enter ports seen for the first time
> with such pleasure, with such joy! . . .
>
> Always keep Ithaca fixed in your mind.
> To arrive there is your ultimate goal.

But do not hurry the voyage at all.
It is better to let it last for long years. . . .

One of the *Christina*'s passengers overheard the following exchange between Ari and Jackie:

"What does it mean?" asked Ari, who did not go in much for poetry.

"It means that our dreams and goals are never completely realized," said Jackie. "They are always there before our eyes, but always just slightly out of reach. And so, as we strive to fulfill our vision, we must make the most of every living moment."

"Indeed we should, my lady," Ari said. "You and I are in complete accord."

THE CABAL

A s soon as they returned from Ithaca, however, Jackie began to pack her bags and prepare to leave for New York.

"Caroline and John need me to help them get ready for the new school year," she explained to Ari.

"Your husband needs you, too," he said.

"I know you do, Telis," she said. "But gosh, I'll only be gone a month."

After she was gone, Ari phoned his old friend Costa Gratsos.

"Aristo!" Gratsos said. "Where are you? What's up?"

"I'm in Athens," Ari said. "Alone. I just put Jackie on a plane to New York."

Gratsos knew how upset Ari became every time Jackie left Greece. "Shit on that!" Gratsos said. "Excuse me for saying so, but Jackie's never around any more."

"Don't call her Jackie," Ari said sharply. "Call her Mrs. Jacqueline, or Mrs. Onassis. Show some respect!"

"Okay, Mrs. Jacqueline," Gratsos said. "But still, I say a wife's place is beside her husband."

"I don't mind," Ari lied.

"Shit on that!" Gratsos repeated.

"Look," Ari said, "I'm free. I want to get the hell out of here. Let's go to Paris and have some fun."

Ari was only dimly aware of the connection between Jackie's absences and his bad moods. Introspection was not one of his strong points, and it did not occur to him that whenever a woman withdrew from him, either physically or emotionally, he suffered the pangs of abandonment that he had felt when he lost his mother.

He knew that he had no right to be annoyed with Jackie. After all, hadn't he said early in their marriage that they were both free to do exactly as they pleased? However, Ari was approaching his sixty-fifth birthday, and as he slowed down, he found that he valued the companionship of a wife more than before. The freedom to do as one pleased, he concluded, should apply to him, not to Jackie. Like most Greek husbands, he lived by a double standard.

"He was a Greek—that says it all, really—a Greek seaman who'd be home for a short while, then go away all over the world, then expect his wife and children to be waiting for him at home whenever he got back," said Costa Gratsos's executive secretary, Lynn Alpha Smith. "There was no way Jackie could give him that continuity. Nor did she understand his world. She was Catholic, Anglo-Saxon. He was an Eastern Orthodox, Mediterranean, and Jackie just didn't understand."

As far as Ari was concerned, only three women had ever completely understood him: his sainted mother Penelope, his sister Artemis, and Maria Callas. Of course, that was his narcissism and self-pity talking. But when he expressed this opinion to his friends, they were quick to agree.

It was all a matter of being Greek, they said. To be Greek, you had to grow up in Greece, speak the language, go to Greek schools, attend Orthodox services, eat Greek food, breathe the sun and air of Greece. You did not become Greek by reading books and visiting ancient ruins!

Ari was aware that, although his marriage was immensely popular among ordinary Greeks, none of his friends liked Jackie. They had banded together in a loose sort of cabal that had no use for Jackie. This cabal was composed of a half dozen people: Ari's children, Alexander and Christina, who hated Jackie with a passion; Costa Gratsos, who was Christina's honorary uncle, and had stayed close to Maria Callas after her breakup with Ari; Johnny Meyer; Maggie van Zuylen, a socialite who had introduced Maria to Ari; and Willi Frischauer, Ari's authorized biographer, who believed that Jackie's identity—and that of her children—had more to do with her dead husband than with her living spouse.

"JFK's ghost will always cast a dark shadow over your marriage," Frischauer warned Ari.

The members of the cabal seized every opportunity to bring up the subject of Maria Callas. *She* was Greek, they said. She would never leave Ari.

As the society columnist Taki wrote: "Gratsos loved Maria, stuck by her until the end, and, more important, told Ari that Jackie K. O. was a woman who not only would ruin his life, but would bring him bad luck."

Maggie van Zuylen played an important part in this drama, as well. She let Ari know that Maria was still madly in love with him, *sincerely* in love with him, unlike you-know-who. Maria was waiting for him to return to her.

"She had a mad passion for him," Maggie said. "They were like two wild beasts together. They got along well, but in the end she wasn't glamorous enough for him. Jackie Kennedy was glamorous. Maria learned of the marriage not from Onassis but by reading about it in the newspapers, like everybody else. She was totally devastated. It was dreadful, awful. She was so frightfully broken up, so disappointed, so profoundly hurt."

"Not Paris," Gratsos said in reply to Ari's suggestion that they go off and have some fun together. "I've got a better idea."

"What's that?" Ari asked.

"Didn't you hear?" Gratsos said. "Maria is on her way back to Greece."

Maria had been invited to Greece by Perry Embiricos, the scion of a prominent Greek shipping family. A confirmed bachelor in his fifties, whose passion was music, Perry had asked Maria to spend some time on Tragonisi, his private island in the Aegean. He had also invited Pier Paolo Pasolini, the notorious Italian homosexual writer and film director, who had directed Maria in the film version of *Medea*; Nadia Stancioff, Maria's half-American, half-Bulgarian private secretary and best friend; and Costa Gratsos and his wife Anastasia.

"Why don't you join us on Tragonisi?" Gratsos said to Ari. "Saturday is the Feast of the Holy Virgin. It's Maria's name day. You're allowed to give her a kiss."

On Saturday morning, August 15, Ari slipped a pair of antique diamond earrings into his pocket, climbed aboard an Olympic Airways helicopter, and took off for Tragonisi, which was located just south of Euboea, one of the largest islands of Greece.

From the air, Ari could see the wooden drop bridge at Chalkis, the capital of Euboea; the bridge spanned the narrow Euripos channel. Legend had it that in 322 B.C. Aristotle drowned himself in the Euripos because he could not explain the enigma of how its current changed direction from north-south to south-north as many as fourteen times a day.

A moment later, Ari spotted Perry Embiricos's marvelous gardens on Tragonisi.

The helicopter landed on the beach, and Ari got out. Maria was a hundred yards away, under a big beach umbrella with Djedda, the poodle Ari had given her. Her hard peasant skin had turned nut brown under the Aegean sun, and her black hair was pulled back in a sleek bun.

She looked up, and saw Ari coming toward her.

CHIPPED
INTO STONE

It was not the first time that Ari and Maria had met since his marriage to Jackie. Back in December 1968, shortly after Ari had celebrated his first Christmas with Jackie, he flew to Paris, where he dined with Maria at Maxim's, and then lunched with her the next day at Maggie van Zuylen's home. The face-to-face meetings between the two former lovers attracted the attention of the press, and spawned the first generation of rumors that Ari's marriage to Jackie was on the rocks.

However, these encounters were brief, and not the romantic trysts they appeared to be. In fact, they were about business. Ari was still handling some of Maria's financial affairs, as he was those of Lee Radziwill, and he needed to talk to Maria about her investments. In addition, he and the opera singer had to discuss business arrangements that had been left unresolved from their joint lawsuit against Panaghis Vergottis, an old friend with whom they had had a bitter falling out.

Despite rumors of a divorce, Costa Gratsos and the other members of the anti-Jackie cabal knew that Ari was still madly in love with his American wife. There was nothing they could do about it but bide their time. Their patience was rewarded when all the letters that Jackie had written to her former escort Roswell Gilpatric, the New Frontiersman, were stolen from his office safe, and published. One letter in particular, which Jackie had written from the *Christina* during her honeymoon, caught everybody's attention.

Dearest Ros

I would have told you before I left—but then everything happened so much more quickly than I'd planned. I saw somewhere what you had said and I was very touched—dear Ros—I hope you know all you were and are and will ever be to me—

With my love,
Jackie

The day after the letter was published, Gilpatric's third wife, Madeline, filed separation papers, leaving the impression that she, for one, suspected her husband had committed adultery with Jackie. Shortly thereafter, sensational stories began to appear in the press offering readers the inside scoop on Onassis's private reaction to the Gilpatric affair.

It was said that Jackie's letter was a blow to Ari's Greek manhood, and that he felt his American wife had emasculated him. He had suffered the very thing he feared the most—social humiliation. The whole world was laughing at him behind his back.

The stories had the ring of truth. And they were given added credibility by Ari's own bitter words, which ran between quotation marks in all the newspapers.

"My God, what a fool I have made of myself," he was quoted as saying. "What a fool. I'm afraid my wife is a calculating woman, cold-hearted and shallow."

Or another quote: "This woman is a bore. Why didn't I see that before I married her?"

Or yet another: "She is always reading."

There was only one problem with the press coverage of the Gilpatric affair. Through it all, Ari did not speak to a single reporter. Nor, for that matter, did he authorize his public relations man, Nigel Neilson, to issue any statements, on or off the record, on his behalf. Whatever Ari had to say, he said in private to Jackie, and of course no one but the two of them knew what that was. The entire press campaign—quotes and all—was the invention of Gratsos and the cabal.

Willi Frischauer, Ari's biographer, portrayed Jackie as a woman who did not know when to leave well enough alone. She found her husband's taste to be vulgar, and tried to get rid of the whale-scrotum upholstery and the Vertez murals on the *Christina*. She was dissatisfied with her surroundings, so she kept her homes in a constant state of upheaval.

"The syndrome seemed almost pathological," Frischauer said. "Find a place, rent it, buy it, decorate it, then leave it. Find another place, et cetera."

But it was Costa Gratsos who inflicted the most damage on Jackie's reputation.

"Gratsos had the bad habit of saying strange things about people just for the fun of it," Stelio Papadimitriou said. "It was a way of getting people to pay him attention and respect."

In his talks with reporters, Gratsos sought to create an image of Jackie as a selfish ingrate.

"[Ari] was very generous with Jackie's children," Gratsos said. "He bought John-John a speedboat and Caroline a sailboat for use at Skorpios. He bought John-John a jukebox and a mini jeep to ride around the island. He gave them Shetland ponies.

"But beyond presents, he tried to give himself, to be with them," Gratsos continued. "He attended their school plays in New York, and went out to Jackie's place in New Jersey to watch them ride. And the truth is, Ari hated it there. He didn't care for horses at all. But he'd go out anyway, when he was in New York, and most of the time he'd just stand around. He was always complaining that the mud and the horse dung ruined his shoes and pants.

"Once when he complained, Jackie told him off. 'You're so badly dressed, what difference does it make?' she said."

Costa Gratsos provided the river of sludge that spilled from the pages of the first book-length examination of the Onassis marriage. This book, which set the tone for dozens of others that were to come, was written by Fred Sparks, a Pulitzer Prize–winner who seemed to have forgotten everything he had ever learned about responsible journalism. In *The $20 Million Honeymoon: Jackie and Ari's First Year*, Sparks alleged that Ari managed to spend a mind-boggling $20 million during the first year of marriage, the great bulk of it on things for Jackie.

Since most people assumed that Jackie had married the aging, gnomelike shipping tycoon for his money, they were ready to accept almost anything that Sparks said.

"Probably Jackie is now spending more on herself than any other woman in the world," Sparks wrote, "and that includes such extravagant ladies as the wife of the Shah of Persia, Mrs. William Paley, and Elizabeth Taylor, whose husband, Richard Burton, recently said: 'Liz can spend $1,000 a minute, and I'm not joking.' "

But Sparks's $20 million figure (the equivalent in today's money of $120 million a year) was grossly misleading. The fact was that Ari's basic expenses—for his offices around the world, his far-flung residences, his yacht, his several hundred employees, and his own lavish lifestyle—did not change substantially after he married Jackie. At most, Jackie's upkeep may have added a million or two to his annual budget—at a time when financial publications estimated that his yearly income from shipping alone was $50 million.

Jackie herself did not help matters when she joked about a pair of fabulously expensive earrings that Ari had given her for her fortieth birthday. The earrings represented the earth and the moon joined by a miniature Apollo 11 spaceship.

"Ari was actually quite apologetic about them," she told Greek actress Katina Paxinou. "He felt they were such trifles. But he promised me that, if I'm good, next year he'll give me the moon itself."

Her self-mocking humor was lost on most people. Even *The New York Times* seemed to prefer the pathological Jackie to the real one. In a review of Sparks's book, the *Times* portrayed Jackie as an "emotionally malnourished" woman whose slow-motion nervous breakdown during perimenopause took the form of shopping.

Jackie's reputation as a compulsive shopper was being chipped into stone.

AN EVEN
DOZEN

John Fairchild, the editor of *Women's Wear Daily*, and the reigning arbiter of style and fashion, dubbed Onassis "Daddy O" in recognition of his sugar-daddy status. Jackie became known forever more as "Jackie O," a nickname that, among other things, was an allusion to the sex-slave heroine of the sadomasochistic French novel *The Story of O*. But even as the world's imagination was being inflamed by tales of Jackie's orgiastic shopping, Ari happily continued to indulge his wife's fancy.

One day he took her to the exclusive Park Avenue boutique owned by Hélène Arpels, an international fashion plate and the wife of the proprietor of Van Cleef & Arpels. Hélène had known Jackie for more than twenty years, and had been advising her on her wardrobe since before she married John Kennedy.

Hélène was waiting at the door when Jackie arrived with Ari. Her shop was decorated with tasteful Chinese furniture. A voluptuous antique Chinese rug, owned by Hélène's partner, André Azria, was laid on the wall-to-wall blue carpeting. Three Chinese salesgirls, hands clasped demurely at their waists, looked on as Madame Arpels bussed her friends French-style on both cheeks.

"I love your shoes," Jackie said as she looked around.

Everything in the shop was designed by Hélène herself. Each pair of shoes cost several hundred dollars.

"I'm glad you like them," Hélène said.

"Do you have something in my size?" Jackie asked. "Preferably low heels."

"I knew Jackie's taste very well," Hélène told the author of this book. "I had gone with her many times in Paris to the House of Givenchy. I helped her choose things. It was I who had lent her the jewels that she had worn in 1961 when she and President Kennedy visited de Gaulle at the Elysée Palace.

"Despite what the newspapers said about Jackie," Hélène continued, "I knew from first-hand experience that she was *not* a compulsive shopper. She was *not* extravagant, *not* at all like the acquisitive monster portrayed in the press. Yes, she liked to have money, but believe me, she was *not* a big spender. A good deal of what she bought, she sent back to the stores. Many of those stories about her spending came from Costa Gratsos. Ari's Greek associates didn't like Jackie. They believed she had married Ari for his money, and they resented it."

One of the salesgirls helped Jackie try on a pair of low-heeled shoes.

"Hélène," Ari said, "I like these better." He was holding a shoe with a very high heel. "A woman is exciting in high heels," he said.

"But I would prefer to have low heels," Jackie said. "I'm tall enough as it is."

"I'll tell you what," Ari said to Hélène. "Make it an even dozen. Give her six pair of low heels and six pair of high heels."

NO HOLDS
BARRED

No matter how hard he tried, however, Ari could not remain emotionally unaffected by the press's picture of him as a hapless victim of his own wife. Beneath his calloused exterior, there was a delicate personality that bruised easily. He believed that his mystique—not to mention his success in business—depended on his image of potency. He could not afford to look like a fool. And so he grew determined to show the world once and for all that he was the master of his fate.

In May, Henri Pessar, a French journalist who specialized in Ariwatching, reported that Ari spent four successive evenings at Maria Callas's apartment on Avenue George Mandel. Ari was seen leaving between twelve-thirty and one A.M. each night. On the evening of May 21, Ari tipped off the press that he and Maria would be at Maxim's with Maggie van Zuylen. The photograph of the radiant couple with their friend was flashed around the world.

When Jackie saw the photo in the New York Post, she phoned Ari and tearfully informed him that she was leaving for Paris immediately. The next night, she and Ari were seen at the same table in Maxim's where Ari and Maria had dined with Maggie van Zuylen. Once again, photographers had been tipped off, and they recorded the event. In the photo, Jackie did not look very happy, but she had made a public statement.

"Maria heard it all too clearly," wrote Arianna Stassinopoulos. "She knew that Aristo had opened his heart to her as to no one else. He had complained about Jackie, he had raged against Jackie, he had defied Jackie by appearing with Maria at Maxim's. But when Jackie instantly demanded a symbolic replay of his dinner with Maria, Aristo did what Jackie wanted."

Four days later, Maria was admitted to the American Hospital in Neuilly, on the outskirts of Paris, with a condition that was officially diagnosed as sinus trouble. However, one of the nurses leaked the true story to a reporter. In a fit of depression, Maria had taken an overdose of sleeping pills.

Maria was still in a depression in early August when she arrived at Tragonisi, Perry Embiricos's private island in the Aegean. She spent hours lying on the beach, pouring out her soul to her friend Nadia Stancioff.

"She seemed obsessed by death at the time," Nadia recalled. "In an instinctive, almost primitive way, she believed in reincarnation. 'I wonder what I'll be when I come back,' she said once. 'I don't want to be buried,' she told me at another time. 'I want to be burned. I don't want to become a worm.' Like many Greeks, she was superstitious about preparing a will, as if writing things down brought bad luck."

This was Maria's frame of mind when she looked up from her beach blanket and saw Ari coming toward her.

When he reached her, Ari leaned over and kissed her full on the mouth. Then he sat down beside her, and kissed her poodle.

"*Chronia polla,*" he said. "Happy birthday."

Maria was instantly his.

Once again, their meeting was recorded by a photographer.

"Responding like a dalmatian to the fire bell," *Time* magazine reported, "Jackie flew to Greece, to Onassis, to the yacht *Christina*, and to squelch rumors."

Jackie had been accustomed to prying reporters when she was in public life, but she was dismayed by the escalating coverage of her private life. There was something new about this kind of journalism, and it was not simply the fact that a reputable publication like *Time* was following the lurid details of the Ari-Jackie-Maria soap opera.

Since the turn of the century, serious publications had devoted space to scandals involving people prominent in society. The best publications had followed the trial and imprisonment of Oscar Wilde, the murder of Stanford White by Harry Thaw, and the Lindbergh kidnapping. But now, journalists had powerful new tools at their disposal to record and disseminate their stories—superfast 35 mm film, powerful telephoto lenses, miniature tape recorders, travel by jet airplane, telephone and TV communication via satellite. Nothing seemed beyond a reporter's reach. The most intimate details of a person's life could be communicated to vast audiences within a matter of hours, even minutes.

Jackie was one of the first victims of this technological revolution in mass communications. She had sought privacy and protection by marrying Ari, but now she was as exposed and vulnerable as she had been after John Kennedy's assassination.

Shortly after the *Time* story appeared, Niki Goulandris invited Jackie for tea. Niki expected that her friend would be an emotional wreck because of the press coverage of her husband's renewed relationship with Maria Callas. To her surprise, however, Niki found Jackie in a cheerful mood.

All of Jackie's old defense mechanisms, which she had developed as the child of an alcoholic, had come back into play. She did not hear things she did not want to hear, did not see things she did not want to see. She was in a state of complete denial about Maria Callas.

"You know, Niki," Jackie said, "since I've been married, I'm sure that Ari has never been with another woman."

ELEVEN

THE FALL
OF THE HOUSE
OF ATREUS

January 1973

PANICKED
OR STUNNED

War was still raging in Vietnam, and each week hundreds of American casualties were airlifted straight from the battlefield to veterans' hospitals all over America. Kitty Carlisle Hart, who had arranged a stage audition for Lee Radziwill nearly eight years before, was now on the board of the American Red Cross, and someone suggested that she bring a friend to the veterans' hospital in the borough of Queens in New York City to cheer up the wounded soldiers. She asked Jackie to come along.

"Well," said Kitty, "I had no idea that these very young men, teenagers, were just thirty-six hours away from the battlefield. I worried—you know how shy Jackie was. They were missing limbs, some of them. Row after row, panicked or stunned, in bandages. Some of them were dying—in fact, some of them were dying as we spoke to them.

"And Jackie just went from bed to bed, and she talked with them. I don't know how she did it, but, somehow, some way, Jackie seemed to calm them, and comfort them. No hanging back. I just followed in her wake, because she was doing it all herself.

"She just knew what to say, and what to do. No fear, hesitation, or anxiety. She cared a great deal about these poor souls."

RESUSI-ANNIE

On a frigid January evening in 1973, Jackie dined with Ari and an American friend at the Coach House, a Greenwich Village restaurant that was owned by a Greek and that specialized in fine American cuisine. The friend had heard tales of Jackie's troubled marriage, and as he dipped his spoon into a bowl of the Coach House's famous black bean soup, he was on the lookout for signs of marital discord.

There was none. Ari treated Jackie with a tenderness bordering on reverence. And she, in turn, seemed to be genuinely concerned about her husband's welfare. A good deal of champagne was consumed during the course of the meal, and by the time dessert came around—generous slabs of rich pecan pie topped with dollops of whipped cream—Jackie was in a light, playful mood.

"I've been keeping a secret from you," she teased Ari.

"A secret?" Ari said, feigning concern. "What kind of a secret?"

"A deep dark secret," Jackie went on. "And you'll never guess what it is."

"All right, let's have it," Ari said, playing along.

"Well," Jackie said, "I had a consultation with Doctor Rosenfeld."

Dr. Isadore Rosenfeld was an eminent heart specialist who treated Ari for minor cardiac symptoms.

"What on earth for?" Ari asked.

Suddenly, he was no longer playacting.

"I'm going to tell you," Jackie said.

She had phoned Dr. Rosenfeld and asked, "What would happen if Ari had a heart attack?"

"Someone would have to resuscitate him," the doctor replied.

"How?" Jackie asked.

"In the first instance, by chest compression and mouth-to-mouth re-suscitation," the doctor told her.

"I want you to show me how to do that," Jackie said.

A few days later, Rosenfeld showed up at Jackie's Fifth Avenue apartment. He was followed off the elevator by Dr. Michael Wolk, his bright young partner, who was carrying a four-foot-tall vinyl doll.

"What's that?" Jackie asked.

"It's called a Resusi-Annie," Rosenfeld explained, "and we use it in hospitals to teach CPR techniques."

Jackie ushered the doctors into her living room, where Wolk laid the Resusi-Annie on the floor.

"He's going to give you a demonstration," Rosenfeld told Jackie.

Wolk pressed down on the doll, whose chest swelled to suggest a woman's breasts. Then he performed mouth-to-mouth resuscitation.

"Okay," Rosenfeld said to Jackie, "now it's your turn."

Jackie got down on her hands and knees, and bent over the Resusi-Annie. She placed her lips over the doll's mouth, and pretended that she was breathing life into the lungs of Aristotle Onassis.

"Now, that is a very good secret," Ari said when Jackie had finished her story.

"You really like it?" Jackie asked.

"Of course I like it," Ari said.

Jackie basked in his approval.

"You see," Ari said, turning to the American friend sitting at their table. "People say Jackie and I don't get along. But does a wife who is not getting along with her husband take lessons on how to save him from a heart attack? No! She doesn't. She *gives* him a heart attack. And then she collects his money."

THE HEIR APPARENT

The day after Jackie and Ari dined at the Coach House in Greenwich Village, Alexander Onassis pulled up in front of the Olympic Airways office in Athens in his red Ferrari. Alexander was twenty-four years old, and his face and body were finally beginning to fill out. He had matured considerably since his father had anointed him the heir apparent of his vast shipping empire, whose worth had nearly doubled to a billion dollars in the past few years.

Father and son had a volatile relationship. They argued constantly, especially about Jackie. Still, Ari had begun to trust Alexander with day-to-day business affairs. Not that Ari was ready to retire. But as he approached his sixty-seventh birthday, and began to experience health problems, his future no longer seemed as limitless as before.

Ari did not find it easy to delegate authority to Alexander. He was never sure whether he approved or disapproved of his son. Depending on his mood, Ari's feelings toward Alexander alternated between a gushing sentimentality and a raging contempt. But he had named his son after Alexander the Great. Alexander represented Ari's bid for immortality.

Alexander normally showed up at the Olympic Airways office dressed in a dark navy suit, silk shirt, and conservative tie. The women there often remarked on how handsome he looked—especially for an Onassis—though they carefully avoided mentioning that they could detect a deep sadness in Alexander's eyes. He had not inherited his father's magnetic personality. He was more like his mother Tina—moody and mournful.

Today, however, Alexander appeared to be in better spirits than usual. He was an experienced pilot who had flown everything from Piper Cubs to big commercial jets, and his calendar was filled with appointments related to aviation, his great passion. He was booked to have lunch with two German pilots at his favorite fish restaurant in Athens, Antonopoulos. And right after lunch, he had made a date, at his father's urging, to train an American pilot in the operation of the family's Piaggio amphibian airplane.

It was rare to see the young man in a good mood. Over the past couple of years, the Onassis family had been battered by one crisis after another.

To begin with, Alexander's mother had divorced her second husband, the Marquess of Blandford, who was related to the Churchills, and married Ari's archrival, Stavros Niarchos. To her son, Tina's choice of a third mate seemed totally inexplicable, since Niarchos was widely suspected of having murdered his previous wife, Tina's own sister Eugenie.

Then, Christina Onassis, Alexander's sister, had run off and married an obscure American real estate man named Joseph Bolker. This had so enraged Ari that he began tapping the couple's phones, and had them followed by private detectives. Christina finally threw up her hands in surrender and started divorce proceedings.

Then, father and son had been engaged for months in a brutal argument over Alexander's mistress, Fiona Thyssen, a divorced baroness who was old enough to be his mother. Ari had more than once threatened to disinherit Alexander if he married Fiona.

And finally, there was the biggest problem of all—Jackie.

Alexander never called his stepmother by her proper name. To show his contempt, he referred to her as "the widow," or "the geisha," or "that woman."

One night at Maxim's, after Ari had berated Alexander for his romantic involvement with Fiona, the subject shifted to a showgirl who was taking an older man for everything he was worth. Alexander turned to Jackie, and said:

"You certainly don't think there's anything wrong in a girl marrying for money, do you?"

At the last moment, one of the Germans developed stomach problems, and Alexander's lunch was canceled. He left for the airport on an empty stomach. About an hour and a half later, a secretary at the Olympic office received a shocking phone call from Athens International Airport.

Alexander's SX-BDC Piaggio 136 had taken off from runway F, banked sharply, cartwheeled for 460 feet, and then crashed nosefirst into the ground. Rescue teams who rushed to the scene of the accident found the badly mangled body of a man whose face and skull were reduced to pulp. The only way they could identify him was by the monogram on his bloodstained handkerchief. It was AO—Alexander Onassis.

Before the secretary had a chance to digest this cataclysmic news, Aristotle Onassis's cousin, Costa Konialidas, arrived in the office. In tears, the secretary told him what had happened. For a long moment, Konialidas was speechless. Then he said:

"How can I find a way to tell Aristo?"

"ALL MY SHIPS, ALL MY PROPERTY, ALL MY PLANES . . ."

By the time Jackie and Ari arrived at the hospital on the outskirts of Athens, a team of neurosurgeons had performed two operations on Alexander's crushed skull. Under the white hospital sheets, the young man looked as though he had already been mummified. His head was wrapped in a bandage. There were two holes for his eyes, which were closed, and an opening for oxygen.

His aunts—Artemis, Kalliroi, and Merope—sat in a corner of the room, three Greek Furies dressed in black from head to toe, keening and moaning. In the corridor outside the room, family members spoke in hushed tones. Tina and her husband Stavros Niarchos had flown in from Switzerland. Christina had arrived from Brazil, Fiona Thyssen from Germany.

"Only a miracle will save him," a doctor told Ari.

Over the next two days, Ari brought in top physicians from around the world—a neurosurgeon from Boston, a heart specialist from Dallas, a brain specialist from London. While they worked feverishly to save his son, Ari summoned a fourth doctor—a plastic surgeon from Geneva by the name of Dr. Popen.

When Popen arrived the next day, Ari took him aside.

"You must fix his face," Ari said. "You must make him look like Alexander again so that I can remember his face as it was."

Alexander was slipping deeper and deeper into a coma, and the specialists objected to the operation by Popen. But Ari insisted that Popen go ahead even though, for all intents and purposes, Alexander was already dead.

At seven o'clock that evening, Ari returned to the Olympic Airways office. His black-and-silver hair had turned white.

"I have lost my boy," he said.

"No, I do not believe it," a secretary replied.

He asked her to call the hospital. When she reached the chief doctor, Ari took the phone.

"If I give you all my ships, all my property, all my planes, and all the money that I have," he said, "would there be any hope to save my boy?"

The doctor told Ari that his son had suffered irreversible brain damage. Alexander was neurologically dead. Only the machines were keeping him alive. There was nothing more that could be done for him.

"We can keep him alive through extraordinary measures for three or four days at the most," the doctor said.

"All right then," said Ari, "leave him be in calm."

The tubes were removed from Alexander's body, and within hours, he was gone.

"We decided it was in vain, so we gave the doctors the orders to stop," Ari said later. "We weren't killing him. We were just letting him die. There is no question of euthanasia here. If he had lived, he would have been dead as a human being. His brain was destroyed and his features completely disfigured. Nothing could be done for him."

HUBRIS

At first Ari wanted Alexander's body to be deep-frozen and kept in a cryonic state until medical science could find a way to rebuild his shattered brain and bring him back to life. To carry out his wishes, Ari instructed Johnny Meyer to get in touch with the Life Extension Society in Washington, which specialized in cryonics. But at the last moment, an old Onassis friend, Yanni Georgakis, who had debated theological issues with Ari and was not afraid to speak his mind, put a stop to these macabre arrangements.

"A father has no right to impede the journey of his son's soul," Georgakis said.

Ari accepted Georgakis's reasoning. But before he would agree to bury Alexander, he insisted that Dr. Popen perform one last plastic-surgery procedure on his son's face. Only then did Ari have Alexander's body embalmed, then airlifted to Skorpios.

There, Alexander's coffin was put into a truck and driven from the harbor up the road that Jackie, with Niki Goulandris, had lovingly landscaped. In a few minutes, the funeral procession reached the tiny chapel of Panayitsa, where Jackie and Ari had been married. Jackie stood in the dim, candle-lit chapel as the priest said his prayers. The workmen slid the heavy lid over Alexander's imposing tomb, which was cut from the same pure white marble used to build the Parthenon. The lid made a loud thud as it fell into place.

This was the second time in less than ten years that Jackie had stood beside a husband and watched him bury a son. John Kennedy had been staggered by the loss of Patrick Bouvier, and had collapsed in sobs and tears. But his behavior was restrained compared to the flood of anguish unloosed by Ari, who gnashed his teeth, and howled at God.

The display of raw emotion always terrified Jackie, though she probably could not have said why. Perhaps it was because she felt responsible, like Guinevere, for the death and destruction that always seemed to follow in her wake. Or perhaps it was because the suffering and misery of others reminded her of her own submerged feelings, which she was afraid to express. Whatever the reason, Ari's pain was too great for her to bear, and she managed to get through Alexander's funeral the way she had gotten through Jack's funeral—by becoming the detached observer, and watching everything from her art director's chair hanging in space.

For weeks after the funeral, Ari lived in a trancelike state. He stared off into space, his face a study in grief. He was a deeply superstitious man, and he could not believe that Alexander's death was a matter of pure chance. It must have been the result of cause and effect. There must have been a connection between Ari's own actions and the tragedy that had befallen his son.

As time went on, Ari came to the conclusion that the fatal accident was a punishment for his god-defying arrogance, the excessive pride that the ancient Greeks had called hubris. But what was the exact nature of his hubris?

It could only be one thing, he decided. His hubris had led him to marry Jackie. He had overreached himself. He had failed to take the advice he had given his own stepson, John Kennedy Jr. He had flown too close to the sun, and the gods had destroyed him.

"Onassis was conscience-stricken," said Stelio Papadimitriou. "First of all, he started feeling remorse for having let the relationship with his former wife deteriorate. He really loved Tina. He felt bad that she had married Niarchos. He felt bad that his children didn't like Jackie. He saw his life in a bad light. And the death of Alexander exacerbated his feelings that his life was not good."

Ari's personality underwent a dramatic alteration. Friends and associates said he was a different man. He seemed to lose all hope. His raison d'être had disappeared along with Alexander.

"In his own eyes, his life resembled the life of the ancient Greeks," said Papadimitriou. "He was guilty of the sin of hubris, overweening pride, and he had suffered the punishment of the gods. It was like something out of Aeschylus's great trilogy of tragedies, the *Oresteia*. It was like the fall of the House of Atreus."

TWELVE

LOVE, DEATH, AND MONEY

October 1973–September 1977

TO HELL AND BACK

"I have houses in Acapulco, Florida, Normandy, Lausanne, and Paris," Loel Guiness, the English banking magnate, was saying. "I have a yacht and a plane, and because of Gloria, I never have to worry about any of it."

It was a few minutes past noon, and Guiness was sitting by the side of the swimming pool at his home in Lantana, Florida, and talking to his guest, Aileen Mehle, better known to the readers of her society column as Suzy. He was extolling the domestic virtues of his wife, Gloria Rubio von Furstenberg Fahkry Guiness, a twice-divorced Mexican beauty who had the lithe figure and regal profile of a princess in an ancient Egyptian frieze.

"Just look at her," said Guiness, pointing to his wife. "Jackie and Ari decide at the very last minute that they would like to come for lunch, and Gloria has everything under control."

Before she snagged her rich husband, Gloria had been a manicurist. But like so many women who managed to scale the heights of society, her origins were of little importance. Born with equal amounts of brains, beauty, and style, she was one of those women Truman Capote lovingly referred to as "swans." She often made a bold-faced appearance in Aileen's "Suzy" column, usually a paragraph or two away from her sister swans: Babe Paley, Slim Keith, and C. Z. Guest.

No one knew more about the strange connubial habits of the swans and their superrich husbands than Aileen. Despite the evident pride Guiness took in his wife, he was away from home most of the time, and on those rare occasions when he and Gloria found themselves together without the company of others, he paid her scant attention. Like most men of wealth, he placed his wife in the same category as his houses, yacht, and plane. She was another pretty possession to impress his wealthy friends.

During her long hours of solitude, Gloria suffered from bouts of depression, as in fact did many of the swans. Still, her main goal in life was to please Loel, and she had outdone herself decorating the Guiness residence in Florida. Loel had bought the house from Bunny Mellon's father, Gerard Lambert, who had designed it himself. Called Gemini, it was built on a parcel of land that ran from the Atlantic Ocean to Lake Worth. The beach house on the ocean side was connected to the pool on the lake side by an underground music room, which was a marvel of engineering, and had a skylight, a working fireplace, and an electric organ.

Gloria was supervising the servants as they set a table under a large market umbrella by the pool. The terrace overlooked six hundred feet of manicured lawn, which was spotted with tall coconut palms, bayans, screw pines, gumbo limbos, and hibiscus plants. Gloria waved a note at Aileen. Written by Jackie in her precise handwriting, it announced that Jackie was bringing Ari and her children for lunch.

"We must try to cheer her up," Gloria told Aileen.

Gloria had heard that Jackie and Ari were not getting along. Ordinarily this would not have fazed her, for whatever her private demons, Gloria dealt with public occasions in a confident, down-to-earth manner. She had once told Noël Coward at a dinner party that she could not bear to sleep in the same bed as her husband because "he farts too much." But Gloria seemed unusually nervous today, perhaps because she had also heard that Ari had recently taken to airing his dissatisfaction with Jackie in public.

In fact, even as she rearranged the Christofle teaspoons so they were exactly parallel with the edge of the Pratesi place mats, Gloria was expecting the worst.

Jackie had tried everything she could think of to cheer up her husband after the death of Alexander. She neglected Caroline and John in order to spend more time with Ari. She accompanied Ari on long cruises. She gave dinner parties at her New York apartment, and invited friends, like the photographer Peter Beard and the feminist Gloria Steinem, who she knew would interest him. Nothing seemed to help. The style that Jackie had used all her life to camouflage unpleasant things was no longer working.

Ari was drinking more heavily than ever. He looked out-of-sorts and complained of headaches. His lifelong insomnia had grown worse. At night on Skorpios, he often took long walks, invariably ending up at the tomb of his son. He squatted there on his haunches like a peasant, staring at the large marble sarcophagus. One time, an American woman, unable to sleep herself, came upon him. He did not notice her presence.

"For a man to be that enclosed, it seemed to be a kind of happiness," she said later. "I had the feeling that if Alexander were alive and at his side, Ari would have been no nearer to the boy than he was at that moment."

Ari's crushing personal loss was compounded by devastating reversals in business. Several months after Alexander's death, the Arabs declared an oil embargo, and the bottom fell out of the world tanker market. In the past, Ari might have seen the crisis coming and taken steps to ward off the worst. But since the death of Alexander, he seemed to have lost his mental acuity. The Arab embargo caught him completely by surprise.

"More than a third of his tonnage was already laid up, none of the oil giants was interested in long-term charters, and he was forced to cancel the two French ULCCs [ultra-large cargo container ships], at a loss of $12.5 million," noted Peter Evans.

The skyrocketing price of oil put a terrible squeeze on Olympic Airways, which Ari had transformed from a dilapidated company into the jewel in the crown of his empire. Ari asked the government of Constantine Karamanlis, which had recently replaced the ruling military junta in Athens, to authorize an increase in ticket prices to help him cover the skyrocketing cost of fuel. Karamanlis, a friend of many years, turned Ari down flat.

At half past noon, Ari's limousine swung off the ocean road into the Guiness estate and headed down a winding gravel driveway that was planted with lush tropical specimens. The car came to a halt in a square courtyard in front of the imposing entrance of Gemini. Ari, Jackie, and her children entered the front hall, which was covered from floor to ceiling in milky white marble. A maid escorted them through the living loggia to the pool, where they were greeted warmly by the Guinesses.

"Gloria, black hair falling to her shoulders, golden bangles sliding up and down her arms, looked like a ravishing gypsy," Aileen Mehle recalled.

Gloria's superb sense of style was not the result of her husband's money. He was actually quite stingy with her, and her trademark Florida sun hat was a jaunty straw model from the local five-and-ten. Once, when a reporter for *Time* magazine asked Gloria what her favorite at-home costume was during the day, she answered: "Comfortable robes that I pick up for twelve ninety-five apiece in Manhattan."

"Loel, true Brit that he is, was as sartorially splendid as ever, blazer and ascot impeccable," Aileen continued. "I, too, had done my best. . . . The Greek tycoon, even at his nattiest, could never set Savile Row on fire, so his rumpled state was nothing new.

"It was Jackie who was the big surprise. Always before when I had seen her, she was marvelously pulled together, secure in that throwaway chic that was so much a part of her. But this day was another matter. One look and it was clear she had been to hell and back: no sign of makeup, an unbecoming cotton dress that didn't know where it began or ended. An odd cotton scarf, knotted at four corners, was tied on her head, covering her hair completely.

"While we took startled note, Ari took revenge—he had an audience.

" 'Look at you,' he said, pointing. 'How can you be seen looking like that? You don't see Gloria and Aileen in that kind of getup. What is your problem?'

"Her problem was doing the pointing. We could not believe what we were hearing. We cringed—but Jackie didn't.

"Just for a second, a look of hurt and sadness crossed her face, but then she smiled her brightest smile and said, 'Yes, don't they look great!'

And then without missing a beat, 'Loel, after lunch will you take John for a ride in your helicopter? He has been looking forward to it all day.'

"Her husband had humiliated her in front of her friends, and while another woman might have snapped back in anger, she handled this awkward moment with grace and charm, turning aside an ugly incident. . . .

"As was his way, [Ari] laughed boisterously and joked at lunch, drinking glass after glass of red wine. Now I watched as he stumbled out to the beach, curling on the sand in a fetal ball, falling into a deep, uneasy sleep. . . . He was no longer in love with [Jackie]—if he ever was—and nothing she could do was right."

ABANDONED

Late in the evening on Christmas Day in 1973, Onassis phoned Stelio Papadimitriou, his personal attorney and number-two man in Athens.

"Season's greetings," he said. "What're you up to?"

"I'm with my family celebrating the holiday," Papadimitriou said. "What are *you* doing?"

"Nothing," Onassis said. "Jackie's in New York with her children. I'm all alone."

Papadimitriou detected a note of self-pity in Onassis's voice, and he did not know how to respond.

"I'm going to the Olympic Airways office," Onassis said. "I've asked Paul Ioannides [general manager and chief pilot of Olympic Airways] to join me. Will you come?"

"Of course," Papadimitriou said. "I'll be right there."

When the short, dapper attorney arrived at the office, it was almost midnight. Nonetheless, the place was bustling with activity. The loyal members of Onassis's inner circle had left their homes and families to rally round the boss.

"Jackie is always away," Onassis complained to Papadimitriou. "I feel as though I don't have a wife. I'm alone. My son is dead. I need someone to rely on."

"It was natural for a sick man to feel that way," Papadimitriou said in recalling this episode. "He was angry that Jackie was away so much. He felt that she was not around as much as before. Whether that was true or not—and, in my view, it was not—he did not know what to do with himself. His mother had died when he was young, and he was feeling abandoned all over again. He was used to abandoning other people. Now, for the first time, he was the one abandoned."

"I STILL LOVE HER"

R ight after Christmas, Onassis visited Papadimitriou at the Olympic Airways office and informed him that he and Jackie planned to fly to Acapulco for a few days in the sun. Before they left, however, there were two pressing matters that he wanted Papadimitriou to take care of.

"Of course," said the attorney, removing a notepad from his desk drawer to jot down his orders.

Onassis seemed to sag, rather than sit, in his chair. As Papadimitriou knew, Onassis had just been shown the latest figures from the Petroleum Institute. Three months into the Arab oil embargo, world oil imports were still in a free-fall. Each day, more and more of his tankers were becoming idle. His cash flow was drying up.

Onassis leaned forward and tossed a set of papers on Papadimitriou's desk.

"Here," he said, "I've written out my will."

Under Greek law, a will, to be valid, had to be in a person's own handwriting. Papadimitriou flipped through the pages, and was satisfied that the document had been composed by Onassis in his precise penmanship. A quick glance also convinced him that he did not have to read what Onassis had written. Papadimitriou had done numerous drafts of the will for Onassis over the past year, and this was a handwritten copy of the most recent version.

"Having already taken care of my wife Jacqueline Bouvier," Onassis wrote, "and having obtained a written agreement notarized by a Notary Public in U.S.A., by which she gives up her hereditary rights on my inheritance, I limit [the] share for her and her two children."

Onassis bequeathed a lifetime income of $200,000 a year to Jackie, and $25,000 a year to Caroline and John each until they reached the age of twenty-one. In addition, Jackie was to be given a 25 percent share in both the *Christina* and Skorpios. It was the minimum Onassis could give her. If Jackie chose to dispute the will, she would immediately forfeit her annuity, and Onassis's executors and the rest of his heirs were instructed to fight her "through all possible legal means."

"I want you to hold this will for me," Onassis said. "And when I die, consult with my daughter and my advisers, and decide whether to make the will public or not."

"If you give me this will now," Papadimitriou said, "I have a legal duty as an attorney to post it with the court."

"I want you to withhold publication, but perform it," Onassis said firmly.

"I can't avoid publication," said Papadimitriou, who refused to play the role of a yes-man. "I must deposit it in the court."

"Then I'll give it to someone else," Onassis said.

"Fine," Papadimitriou said, handing him back the document.

Onassis let out a weary sigh, then continued. "Okay, I have something else I want to talk about," he said. "I hope we can make more progress on this matter."

"I hope so, too," Papadimitriou said.

"No matter what harsh words I may have used in the past about Jackie, you and I know that she is at heart a kind and good woman," Onassis said.

"That is true," Papadimitriou said. "She is a real lady."

"I adore her," Onassis said. "To tell the truth, I still love her. But I want to divorce her. Do you understand what I am saying?"

"No, I'm afraid I don't follow you," Papadimitriou said.

Onassis rolled his eyes. "It is simple," he said. "I want to divorce my wife in accordance with Greek law."

"It is not that simple," Papadimitriou told him. "As you know, there is no such thing as a consensual divorce in Greece. You have to prove the fault of the other party. You have to show the judge that the relationship is irreparably broken. But you're asking me to draw up divorce papers while you're praising your wife. That's unheard of. No court will consider starting divorce proceedings under those conditions. You need to give me some complaints about Jackie."

"I can't do that," Onassis said. "That's totally out of the question."

"Then there's no point in my drawing up divorce papers," Papadimitriou said.

"Just do what I tell you," Onassis said, his voice betraying mounting exasperation.

He got up from his chair and went to the door. Then he turned back to Papadimitriou, and said calmly:

"Remember, Stelio. Don't put in anything bad about Jackie."

PLAYING FAIR

Jackie was on her widow's walk on Skorpios, putting the finishing touches to yet another watercolor of the Ionian islands. As Oliver Smith had once said, there was a certain primitive charm to her style of painting. Her green islands zigzagged to the horizon, diminishing in size as they neared the point where the water met the sky. Yet she could not seem to get the farthest island right. The perspective of Ithaca still eluded her.

As she put away her paints and brushes, she became aware of the flutter of Ari's approaching helicopter. She was not looking forward to seeing her husband. Ever since their vacation in Acapulco several months before, Ari had become impossible to deal with.

It was as if he was a different man. He had once possessed almost superhuman stamina. He could negotiate for days without end, and make love two and three times a night. But in Acapulco, he had run out of steam. During the day, it was hard for him to keep up with Jackie, who was more than twenty years his junior. And at night, when she put on his favorite Halston gown and joined him in bed, he had trouble performing the sex act even once.

Jackie's vitality became an affront to him, and nothing she did or said pleased him. When she suggested that they look for a house to buy in Acapulco—an idea they had discussed many times before—he flew into an uncontrollable rage. His screaming went on for two or three days, and it continued on the flight back to America. He sat by himself in a corner of his Lear jet, took out his will, and signed and dated it. When he arrived in New York, he gave it to his American money manager Creon Broun for safekeeping.

Back in Greece, his health continued to deteriorate, and Jackie persuaded him to return to America and enter the New York Hospital for tests and observation. There, doctors informed him that he suffered from myasthenia gravis, an autoimmune disease in which the body turns against itself. The progressive and sometimes fatal neuromuscular disorder induced fatigue, depression, and loss of muscle tone, especially in the muscles that controlled the eyelids.

The doctors prescribed massive doses of cortisone, the same medicine that John Kennedy had used to control his secret illness, Addison's disease. There were dangers associated with the administration of cortisone. Doctors were unable to fine-tune the level of laboratory-produced cortisone in a patient's bloodstream, and excess cortisone led to Cushing's syndrome. Ari suffered from its symptoms: a full red face, headaches, back pain, and a feeling of vulnerability.

His face and body became bloated from the cortisone, but the myasthenia gravis progressed at an alarming rate. He could not hold his eyelids open. They had to be fastened to his forehead with transparent tape so that he could see. Before, he had been merely ugly; now he looked grotesque.

He was dying, and he knew it. He felt like the biblical Job, and he wondered why God had sent him so many afflictions in the final years of his life. He looked around for a scapegoat and found one in Jackie. He quarreled with her about her spending, her clothes, even the way she raised her children (he did not like their sloppy blue jeans). He grew more superstitious than before, and was certain that Jackie possessed supernatural powers and was responsible for the loss of his son. He called her "the witch."

Appalling stories of Ari's abuse began making the rounds.

"Onassis treated her so badly," said Jackie's friend, the photographer Peter Beard, who spent long stretches of time with Caroline and John on Skorpios. "I can't tell you how many meals I sat through on Skorpios when Onassis would scream at her, and she would just continue eating. She took a lot of shit from him. He used to make insulting comparisons between Jackie and Callas. Jackie was just interested in superficial gossip. Callas was a real artist."

Jackie sought advice from Ari's sister Artemis, who, having suffered the loss of her only child years before, looked upon Jackie as a surrogate daughter.

"I don't know what to tell you," Artemis said. "Despite my strenuous objections, Aristo has asked his lawyer to draw up divorce papers."

The helicopter settled on the landing pad on top of Skorpios, and Ari stepped off, followed by a surprise guest: Stelio Papadimitriou.

Jackie had always gotten along with Ari's attorney, and they greeted each other warmly. Then the three of them climbed into Jackie's open jeep, and Ari drove them down the steep side of the island. On the way down, Ari pointed out the work that Jackie had completed on the Pink House. He seemed proud of her accomplishment. Papadimitriou took this as a good sign; perhaps Onassis was coming to his senses. The attorney complimented Jackie on the way she and Niki Goulandris had transformed the island into a glorious arboretum of indigenous plants, shrubs, and trees.

"It was pleasant chitchat," Papadimitriou recalled, "but from the moment Jackie saw me get off the helicopter, I'm sure she knew why I had come to Skorpios."

That evening after dinner in the main house, an inebriated Onassis started berating Jackie again.

"Why do you continue to buy British paintings of Irish horses?" he asked. "You know I don't like those paintings. In any case, the art dealers in Britain always cheat you on the price."

Jackie ignored him and turned to Papadimitriou.

"If Ari dies," she said, "I know who my opponent will be. It will be you, Mr. Papadimitriou. You will carry out his final wishes. But I know something else. I can trust you. You are a fair man, and you will be fair to me when it comes to money."

"I try at all times to be as decent as possible," Papadimitriou said.

Then Jackie turned to Ari.

"I don't want to divorce you," she said. "But if that is your final decision, I accept it in sadness. I'll never forget the good life we had together."

Onassis sat there, and for once said nothing.

Then Jackie addressed Papadimitriou again.

"I know that you have been drafting writs of divorce," she said.

"I laughed like a fool, and did not know what to say," Papadimitriou recalled. "I felt sorry for Jackie. She was in a real bind. She could not satisfy her husband's requirements and, at the same time, the require-ments of her children. In her eyes, her children required her presence more than he did.

"Onassis wanted her around all the time. He wanted feminine com-pany. He wanted to be the centerpiece. But Jackie was never there when he needed her. That made him very angry. He had me drafting and re-drafting divorce papers for him.

"He always gave me the same instructions: 'Say that Jackie is very nice, very kind, very polite.'

"And I would tell him, 'No judge will grant you a divorce that way.'

"And he would say, 'I don't care. Do it the way I say.'

"And then, he would either tear up my draft, or put it in the shred-ding machine.

"This went on for two solid years. And all that time, from what I could tell, Onassis and Jackie continued to be intimate. And he never initiated divorce proceedings, which made me wonder what all the fuss was about.

"And I came to the only conclusion that made sense. In my view, Onassis never really wanted to divorce Jackie. All his talk about divorce was part of his deal-maker's psychology. It was a negotiating tactic. His goal was to bring Jackie back to him. The only thing is, I don't think Jackie realized that it was an empty threat."

A SWEEPING
INDICTMENT

Jack Anderson barreled through the door of the "21" Club, a New York restaurant favored by the barons of business. The hatcheck counter was three-deep with patrons shedding their bulky coats, but Anderson, a crack investigative journalist who wrote the syndicated column "Washington Merry-Go-Round," was traveling light. Despite the chill in the fall air, he was hatless and coatless. The only thing he carried was a small spiral notebook, which was jammed into the side pocket of his rumpled suit jacket.

He was recognized by the "21" Club's sharp-eyed greeter, Harry Lavin, who steered him to a table located just inside the entrance of the Bar Room. There, slumped over a half-empty tumbler of whisky, his dark glasses failing to hide the loose strips of Scotch tape that dangled from his eyelids, was Aristotle Onassis.

"Onassis had reserved the best table in the place," Anderson said. "As soon as I sat down, he began making a start on Jackie: 'What does she do with all those clothes? All I ever see her wearing is blue jeans,' and then he would stop, apparently out of tact, delicacy, or reticence.

"I didn't get much more out of him than that," Anderson continued. "However, after lunch, he invited me back to his office to meet several of his colleagues, including Costa Gratsos, a tall, smooth-talking fellow with a white mane of hair and a pipe. Before we got started, I asked if I could call my chief assistant and legman, Les Whitten, who was in New York, and have him join us at the office. Onassis and Gratsos had no problem with that."

"By the time I got there," said Whitten, picking up the story, "Onassis had disappeared, and Jack [Anderson] was huddled with Gratsos and Gratsos's secretary, a woman named Lynn Alpha Smith. They were showing Jack some confidential documents, one of which they claimed was a copy of Onassis's premarital agreement with Jackie.

"Gratsos was a tough guy," Whitten continued, "and it was clear that he wasn't fond of Jackie in the least. In fact, his sole purpose in meeting us was to discredit her. His real worry was who was going to get Onassis's millions after he died. He sure didn't want that money to go to Jackie."

Gratsos had been hatching plots against Jackie from the day she married Onassis. He had managed to convince most of the world that Jackie had a serious psychological flaw, and was a pathological spender. He made certain that Onassis got to see these negative stories, because he knew that Onassis, an avid consumer of gossip, was ready to believe the worst about people. Yet, for a long time, this strategy had failed. Gratsos, despite his best efforts, had not succeeded in hardening Onassis's heart against his wife.

Now, however, Onassis was staring death in the face, and Jackie, who had been so important to him before, no longer seemed as significant in the great scheme of things. It was not so much that he cared for her less. He still loved her, in his fashion, but he cared more about the survival of his shipping empire.

His sole living descendant was his daughter Christina. She was poised to inherit Onassis's fleet of ships, his banks, pier facilities, real estate (including the just-completed Olympic Towers on Fifth Avenue, and a quarter interest in New York's Pierre Hotel), his residences in Athens, Monte Carlo, Montevideo, and Paris, his yacht, the island of Skorpios, and tens of millions of dollars in stocks and bonds and other liquid assets.

Christina would soon be one of the richest women in the world. As her honorary uncle and trusted adviser, Gratsos had great expectations. After all, Christina had no experience in running a worldwide shipping business, while Gratsos was the son of a shipowner. After her father's death, Christina would lean on Gratsos even more than be-fore, and he would become the power behind the Onassis throne. Or so he hoped.

But the handover from Onassis to Christina was not going smoothly. Christina had recently botched another suicide attempt. What was more, her mother, Tina Niarchos, whom Onassis had named as chief executor of his will, had been found dead in the Hotel de Chanaleilles in Paris, the apparent victim of an edema of the lung, though some suspected her husband Stavros Niarchos of more foul play. Onassis was so distraught that he could not bring himself to attend Tina's funeral.

In the midst of these family catastrophes, Onassis's aides informed him that Olympic Airways faced imminent bankruptcy. He had no choice but to sell his beloved jewel. Negotiations with the Greek govern-ment could not have come at a worse time for him. With the downturn in the oil-tanker business, Onassis's net worth had plummeted from $1 billion to $500 million, and his financial condition worsened by the day.

The enforced sale of Olympic Airways represented the greatest set-back in Onassis's business career. The very thought of losing his airline drove him into a rage. Sick as he was, Onassis came into the office, and he bellowed at everyone. Where was Papadimitriou? Onassis wanted to see him immediately! Where was Konialidas? Where was Johnny Meyer?

Most important of all, where was Jackie?

"Jackie seemed determined to stand aside from Ari's problems," said an aide. "There was not a lot she could have done in Athens except be there. They were some of the worst weeks of his life. He could have used some wifely comforting, not to mention her public relations pull. . . . He was putting up the backs of the very people he needed to beguile. His language even to those whose help he needed most was either sullen or griping. He'd lost his touch completely, he was played out. His name had once acted like a spell in Athens; now his world had turned upside down."

"He had climbed to the top of the tree, and there was nothing there," said Gratsos. "I don't think he ever knew what he wanted. The difference was that in his last years he knew he would never get it."

Onassis had run out of luck. Desperately sick, and frightened of dying, he felt more alone than at any time since he was a little boy, and his beloved mother Penelope had abandoned him and gone to heaven. He thought a lot about the past—past loves, past triumphs, past *mistakes*. With so little time left, he did not want to make any more mistakes. He was ready to listen to his oldest friend, Costa Gratsos.

And Gratsos did not spare him. He told Onassis that if he died while he was still married to Jackie, his prenuptial agreement would probably not hold up in court, and Jackie would walk away with more than $60 million. On the other hand, if Onassis instituted divorce proceedings against Jackie while he was in his current weakened condition, Jackie might be emboldened to fight him in the courts of Greece and America.

As Gratsos saw it, there was only one solution to this dilemma. They must attack Jackie where she was the most vulnerable: they must do it through personal exposure in the press. They must reveal her faults, her frailties, her excesses, and her pretensions. And they must do all this in such a brutal way that Jackie would be struck with fear, and would cringe from the idea of fighting over Onassis's millions.

What better way for them to get started, Gratsos said, than for Onassis to call Roy M. Cohn, the Attila the Hun of divorce attorneys. Cohn had served in the 1950s on Senator Joseph R. McCarthy's Permanent Subcommittee on Investigations, and had been described by *Esquire* magazine as "the toughest, meanest, vilest, and one of the most brilliant lawyers in America." He had once come close to trading blows with his co-counsel Bobby Kennedy during the Army-McCarthy hearings in 1954. He was, in short, no friend of the Kennedys.

"Mr. Onassis had definitely concluded that he wanted to break the marriage," Cohn said, "and had been consulting Greek lawyers, and so on, and there were a lot of complications over there, and he wanted to know whether I would be prepared to handle the American end—because he had assets over here—and participate in the overall strategy. He anticipated that the matter would be settled, because he did not think that Jackie would want to make a big thing out of it, but he also viewed the possibility that her appetite for money would be such that it might not be amicably settled."

In addition to unleashing Roy Cohn, Gratsos also convinced Onassis to meet with the muckraking Washington journalist Jack Anderson. All

Onassis had to do, Gratsos assured Onassis, was have a pleasant lunch at the "21" Club with the reporter, then leave the dirty work to him.

Gratsos was savvy in the ways of the press. After Onassis left them, Gratsos spoke to Anderson "on background," which meant that the information from the interview was on the record, but that Anderson could not reveal his precise source. Gratsos would get his message across, but his name would not appear in print.

Over the course of several hours, Gratsos gave Anderson his version of the inner workings of Jackie's marriage to Onassis. No reporter had heard anything like this before, and every so often, Gratsos would ask Anderson if he realized how lucky he was to be the first to get the story. But Anderson was a seasoned journalist, and he was not easily impressed. He knew that it was going to be difficult to check out Gratsos's story and unravel his truths from his half truths and outright lies.

While Anderson asked probing questions, Les Whitten took down Gratsos's answers. Later, Whitten typed up his notes, using only lowercase letters to save himself time. His five-page summary of Anderson's interview amounted to a sweeping indictment of Jackie as an acquisitive monster who shamelessly exploited her husband. It formed the basis for Anderson's bombshell columns, as well as for each new Jackie biography that appeared at the rate of one a year for the next twenty years of her life.

Whitten wrote:

gratsos . . . says at first [Jackie] got $30,000 a month tax free. It was onassis' personal money and could be given tax free because onassis is a foreigner. (I suspect this oversimplifies it). . . .

from time to time, nancy tuckerman [Jackie's old school friend and personal secretary] would complain to creon broun [Onassis's money manager in New York] that they (she and jackie) had run out of money. the kindly creon advanced it to them, even though they had run short in the first 10 days and the money was sometimes given in mid-month instead of at the end.

gratsos ended this practice. about two years after the marriage, the payments were [reduced to $20,000 a month] and
commenced from onassis hq. in monte carlo. . . .

the advice of andre meyer, the senior partner of lazard freres
brokers, cost jackie about $300,000. ari had wanted the money
to stay in tax frees, but jackie heeded meyer's advice and put it
into the market. . . .

john john's pet rabbit was put in the care of an olympic
pilot in the cockpit so it could be delivered safely to its
destination. . . .

And that was just for starters. Whitten continued:

it was not just the extravagance but the total incompatibility of
jackie and ari. and jackie's faggoty friends. . . .

gradually, ari came to really resent her spending. not only
did he pay her the allowance, but many of the bills were paid
from monte carlo in addition to the $20,000–$30,000. . . .

ari resolved to divorce her. he had lawyers working on it
in greece and in the u.s. but he confided only in his friends. it
had been informally determined that the greek orthodox would
allow him to break it off on grounds of simply, but definite
incompatibility. . . .

ari by that time was "very unhappy" over the marriage.
"they weren't getting along at all." a major factor, [Gratsos] repeated, was the "odd people" around her.

The most damaging revelations, however, concerned Jackie's spending
on her wardrobe. According to Gratsos, after Jackie wore a costly garment once or twice, or sometimes not at all, she would resell it, and
then squirrel away the cash. Her favorite resale house, Encore on Madison Avenue at Eighty-fourth Street, did a steady business in Jackie's
slightly used and sometimes new clothes.

She peddled everything from coats, suits, and gowns to pocket-
books, blouses, and slacks. The labels were the best: Yves Saint Laurent,
Valentino of Rome, Halston. Generally she would demand a fixed price;

other times she would accept whatever the market would bear. Once, it took Encore six months to sell a white coat with a Valentino label at the price Jackie demanded.

"When it comes to Jackie's spending habits, you can believe anything, *anything*," Gratsos said. "She went on wild spending sprees. She was clocked at $3,000 a minute. Often, she didn't bother with cash. Her face was her charge plate. She was virtually laundering money by charging couture clothes to Onassis's account, and then reselling them to consignment stores in New York. She was embezzling money from Onassis. She was defrauding her own husband."

To check out the charges against Jackie of money laundering, embezzlement, and fraud, Anderson sent Whitten to interview the manager of Encore, as well as those of the other resale stores in Manhattan. Whitten reported back to Anderson that Jackie had started taking her clothes to Encore long before she met Onassis. In fact, she had been dealing with Encore ever since she was the wife of Senator John Kennedy.

encore, a busy fascinating place with clothes filling racks and women in minks or cloth seeking bargains even as their sisters lug stuff in in suitcases for appraisal. the store made an exception for jackie and sent over for the clothes to her flat. generally it was a maid who gave up the clothes, and tuckerman who talks the business. . . .

some women were, of course, attracted to jackie's old clothes. some refused to buy them because they disliked the kennedys. encore and the other second hand . . . shops patronized by jackie are in the fashionable east 60s and 80s.

Whitten had stumbled upon a little-known sideshow to the main three-ring circus that made up New York society in the 1970s. Many wealthy men gave their wives hefty allowances to buy couture clothes and expensive accessories like hats, belts, handbags, and shoes. But once a woman was seen in a $5,000 Yves Saint Laurent dress or a $10,000 Givenchy gown, it had served its purpose, which was to define her husband as a rich man, and her as an avatar of current fashion. To appear in society in the same garment more than once or twice would have been, in a manner of speaking, counterproductive.

But what was a society woman to do with her used garments after she was done with them? She could have donated them to charity, and taken a substantial tax deduction. But since few of these women filed individual tax returns, the savings would have accrued to their husbands, and the women did not find that an appealing notion.

Instead, virtually all rich women sold their slightly used clothes to stores like Encore. Sometimes this was done with the knowledge and consent of their husbands; sometimes, what their husbands did not know did not hurt them. In any case, it was a practical way for women to stretch the dollars in their clothing allowance. At the same time, they received a psychological bonus, since the money they got back helped them rationalize the astronomical sums they spent on their wardrobes.

This attitude was completely foreign to the middle class in America, where puritanical sumptuary laws against the wearing of extravagant garments had been common in Colonial-era New England. Even in modern-day America, most people still looked upon a woman who wore a dress only once or twice as not only wasteful, but sinful.

However, such high-minded middle-class values were not shared by the superrich. William Paley, the founder of CBS, set up a trust fund that provided his wife Babe with $160,000 a year (about $1 million in today's money) to spend exclusively on her clothes. Although Jackie received considerably more than that from Onassis—$360,000 a year for the first two years of their marriage, if Gratsos could be believed—she also had sizable expenses that were not part of Babe's budget. Jackie paid for the upkeep on her own apartment in New York and her weekend house in Peapack, New Jersey; her staff of servants; the feeding and grooming of her horses in New Jersey and Virginia; and private schools for Caroline and John.

Until Onassis lost his son, and his world began falling apart, he had encouraged Jackie to spend more, rather than less. He had operated by the rich man's philosophy that when his wife looked good, he looked good. However, toward the end of his life, Onassis no longer felt that way. Beset by problems on all sides, and bitter over his fate, he came to see Jackie's spendthrift ways as a symbol of her disregard for him and his generosity.

It was not hard to understand why he felt that way. Jackie's allowance was, by any standard, exceedingly lavish. Of course, it did not begin to compare with Bunny Mellon's outlay for clothing, which came to $1 million in 1974 dollars, or the equivalent of $6 million a year today.

A LAST
REQUEST

In addition to all his other diseases and disorders, Aristotle Onassis began the new year with a rampant case of influenza. He lost forty pounds in eight weeks. He slurred his words, had trouble chewing his food, and could not speak without supporting his chin with the heel of his hand. The pains in his abdomen became so severe he could not stand up straight. On Sunday, February 2, 1975, he called Jackie, who was in New York, and complained of being alone. The next day he collapsed, and had to be helped out of his clothes and into bed.

The members of his retinue converged on his villa in Glyfada, filling the downstairs rooms like a somber assemblage of knights awaiting the passing of their liege lord. The ladies-in-waiting—Christina, Artemis, Merope, and Kalliroi—kept vigil outside his bedroom door. Everyone seemed prepared for the worst, except Christina. The daughter who had been the bane of her father's existence for most of his life was the one who fought hardest to save him.

She made three telephone calls: to Professor Jean Caroli, a gastroenterologist in Paris; to Dr. Isadore Rosenfeld, the heart specialist in New York; and to her stepmother, Jackie.

Come quickly, Christina told them. My father is very ill. He needs you now!

"I flew over with Jackie," Rosenfeld said, "and when we arrived at Ari's house in Glyfada, I examined him, and immediately made my diagnosis. In addition to his myasthenia gravis, he was suffering from acute gall bladder disease. He was taking a lot of cortisone, and was terribly weak. I ordered some equipment—oxygen and an electrocardiograph machine— and recommended that he fly to New York and undergo a period of intensive treatment there. We had an Olympic Airways plane ready to fly him to the New York Hospital.

"But the French gastroenterologist, Doctor Caroli, disagreed with me," Rosenfeld continued. "He wanted to take Ari to Paris and operate at once to remove his gall bladder. He had Ari's private jet primed and ready to fly him to the American Hospital in Paris.

"The French doctor did not seem to understand that Ari was not a good operative risk. He had myasthenia gravis, and the drugs being used for that would interfere with a successful surgery. I said that he was far too weak to survive such an operation."

However, Christina and Onassis's sisters did not agree. They were more familiar with Caroli than with Rosenfeld, and sided with the Frenchman in the heated debate that developed between the doctors.

"The family was pressing Onassis to go to the American Hospital in Paris," Stelio Papadimitriou said. "He heard my cough, and called me upstairs, and just outside his bedroom I came upon Christina crying inconsolably. I asked her why, and she said, 'Because my father refuses to go to Paris.'

"I went inside," Papadimitriou continued. "It was a simple room with very few furnishings, and I found Onassis in a bad situation.

"I said, 'Mr. Onassis, why are you behaving like a child? You should go to Paris. Or have you decided to leave everyone behind in a mess?'

"And he said, 'Do you hear my daughter sobbing outside my door? Would you call her to enter the room?'

"I went and got Christina. The old man sat up in his bed and whispered to us in a weakened voice.

" 'I know that my daughter has serious shortcomings and will not be able to cope with life,' he said. 'And I know that you, Stelio, are a fiercely independent man who is always ready to resign his position, and that Christina will make you desperate. So if you wish me to go to Paris, let's make a deal. Do you promise that no matter what my daughter does to you, you will never abandon her?'

"I said yes.

"And he said, 'Bend to kiss me. From now on, Christina is your sister.' "

ROOM 217

Two days later, Onassis, accompanied by Christina and Jackie, left his Glyfada villa for the airport.

"He was clutching a book called *Supership*, in which author Noel Mostert reported that the first million-ton tanker, a ship so big that a cathedral could be lost in its bowels, would soon become a reality," wrote the London *Daily Mail* columnist Nigel Dempster. "Ari sat with the book unopened on his lap for most of the flight; memories of the *Ariston*, the 15,000-ton 'monster' they said was impossible when he built her in the 1930s, must have been in his mind."

In Paris, a whole clutch of journalists had assembled outside Onassis's apartment at 88 Avenue Foch. There were five television crews, and photographers from *Paris-Match*, *Stern*, *Oggi*, and many other magazines and newspapers.

"I want to walk from this car under my own steam," Onassis told Jackie and his daughter. "I don't want those sons of bitches to see me being held up by a couple of women."

Jackie and Christina watched him make his way through the gauntlet of shouting paparazzi.

"How do you feel, Ari?"

"This way, Ari!"

"Ari, over here!"

"Ari, are reports that you're dying true?"

He walked slowly, looking neither left nor right, his hands thrust deep into the pockets of his blue overcoat. Once inside, he went straight to bed.

"When he awoke, shortly after 10 P.M.," wrote Nigel Dempster, "he took a Pyridostigmine slow-release capsule to get him through the night; the capsule [which was prescribed for myasthenia gravis and increased muscle strength] released one-third (sixty milligrams) of its dosage immediately, and gave him a surge of energy into which he crammed as much business as he could manage, and saw the people he wanted to see.

"One of the people he sent for on this night was [his old henchman] Johnny Meyer. They talked about the past, swapped familiar anecdotes. After one long silence when Meyer thought he had fallen asleep, Ari said:

" 'Soon I shall be on Skorpios with Alexander.'

" 'You're crazy, Ari,' Meyer replied. 'Who ever heard of anybody dying from droopy eyelids.' "

"He was operated on on Sunday," Johnny Meyer told a press conference two days later in the American Hospital in Paris. "It was a small operation, and now he is feeling much better. He can stand up. That's all I can say."

In fact, Onassis was being kept alive by a respirator in room 217 of the Eisenhower wing of the hospital. He suffered from jaundice, heart problems, pneumonia, and complications from his myasthenia gravis. Just as Dr. Rosenfeld had predicted, the cortisone lowered his resistance to infection and made his pneumonia hard to control.

At times he was delirious, and rambled on incoherently about Skorpios, and his problems with the government in Athens over the sale of his beloved Olympic Airways. He spoke mainly in Greek, which, of course, excluded Jackie.

She knew that Ari had told Christina and his sisters of his plans to divorce her. She felt mortified and chagrined by her situation. In the eyes of these Greek women, Jackie had scant claim to the title of Onassis's wife. When she and Christina found themselves alone in Onassis's hospital room, they did not exchange a word.

"I was in Paris with Jackie at the time," said Niki Goulandris. "She visited him in the hospital daily, although her time with him was restricted because he was in the intensive care station. We went to Notre Dame together, and she got down on her knees and prayed for Ari, even though she knew his condition was hopeless. She knew it was the end.

"But the doctors advised her that Ari could hang on like that for weeks, perhaps even months," Niki continued. "Jackie felt that she could be of more use in New York to her children than she could in Paris to Ari. So she left."

As soon as Jackie arrived at her apartment on Fifth Avenue, she called her sister-in-law Artemis in Paris, who told her that Ari was doing as well as could be expected. Four days later, Artemis again assured her that Ari was fine. However, late that night, he took a turn for the worse, and Artemis woke Jackie and urged her to return to Paris immediately.

Jackie was packing to leave the next morning, when the phone rang again.

"He's dead," said Artemis. "Christina was with him when he left us."

"HE MEANT
A LOT TO ME"

A fusillade of flashbulbs greeted Jackie as she stepped off the Olympic Airways plane at Orly Airport. When the photographs of the frenzied crowds were printed the next day, they reminded people of the scene of pandemonium created by Charles Lindbergh's historic landing nearly fifty years before.

The crowds wanted to see for themselves how Jackie was bearing up under her loss. In their eyes, she had changed since her marriage to Onassis. She was no longer the same Jackie whose flawless performance at President Kennedy's funeral had transformed her into a paragon of virtue. But if Jackie was not that person, it was not clear who she was now.

Perhaps more than any other people on earth, the French adored Jackie. But they needed to hear from Jackie herself why she had not been at Onassis's side when he died. It was the behavior of a wife who did not love her husband, and it made them wonder if Jackie had become like the woman in John Keats's poem "La Belle Dame sans Merci": a beautiful woman who was incapable of feeling love.

Dressed in black, Jackie approached the bank of microphones and took out a piece of paper that contained a single paragraph. The prepared statement was notable for its clarity and lack of sentimentality.

"Aristotle Onassis rescued me at a moment when my life was engulfed with shadows," she said, as the salvo of flashbulbs began again. "He meant a lot to me. He brought me into a world where one could find both happiness and love. We lived through many beautiful experiences together which cannot be forgotten, and for which I will be eternally grateful."

"TIME TO
TAKE CARE OF JACKIE"

<hr>

E ven *The New York Times* sent a reporter to cover the funeral.
"The courtyard [of the chapel] was lined with hundreds of white
lilies, their pots draped in red velvet," the paper's Steven V. Roberts reported from Skorpios. "On the terraced hillside behind the chapel,
cherry trees blossomed pink. In the distance was anchored the *Christina*,
Mr. Onassis's 325-foot yacht. Its Liberian flag was at half-mast."

On the yacht itself, John Vinocur, who was then a correspondent for
the Associated Press, telephoned a dispatch from the dining room. He
held the receiver close to his mouth, and relayed a piece of color about
Jackie's mother, Janet Auchincloss. Suddenly, he was interrupted by
Janet herself.

"The Kennedy children's grandmother is not having breakfast at
ten-thirty in the morning," she said firmly. "She ate hours ago."

Thousands of words were filed that day from Skorpios, but one scene
stood out from all the others and was etched in the world's collective
memory. It was the scene of Jackie, wearing a new black Valentino dress
beneath a black, tightly cinched leather coat, walking beside a heavily
sedated Christina, and offering her an arm for support.

"Oh God," Christina moaned.

"Hang on," said Jackie, who had some experience with funerals.
"Take it easy now. It'll soon be over."

They stepped into a waiting limousine, and were joined by Jackie's former brother-in-law, Senator Edward Kennedy. The chauffeur shut the rear door, then slipped behind the wheel and started the engine.

Although no reporters were present, the world was later treated to a blow-by-blow description of what transpired among the grieving passengers in the sealed compartment of the limousine. Teddy Kennedy—bloated, perhaps drunk, certainly insensitive to Christina's feelings—leaned forward and began talking to her about money. The anonymous source for this story was the indefatigable Costa Gratsos.

"Now," Teddy Kennedy said to Christina—or so Gratsos claimed— "it's time to take care of Jackie."

"Stop the car!" shouted Christina.

She struggled with the door until she finally managed to get it open. Then she fled to another car in the cortege, and sat with her aunts.

Later, Gratsos explained to reporters why Christina had been so "cool" to her stepmother during the funeral. It was because Senator Kennedy had attempted to discuss "financial matters," he told them.

This story became part of the permanent lore of tabloid journalism. However, it was just as false as most of Gratsos's stories were.

"It's true that Teddy acted awkwardly," said Stelio Papadimitriou, "but that did not occur until after the burial. During a Greek funeral, there is a ritual where you offer fish, which has the mystical meaning of resurrection in Christianity. When that was over, Teddy approached me, and took me aside. He said he would like to talk to me about money.

"It was not the time or place to make such a suggestion, but we agreed to meet as soon as possible. Christina heard about this conversation, and got mad. But all that came later, quite a bit later, when we began to work out the financial arrangements."

THE RECKONING

In his will, Onassis established a German-style *Stiftung*, or foundation, in Lichtenstein in memory of his son. The foundation would award scholarships for Greeks to study abroad, grant prizes for cultural and humanitarian achievement, and help treat sick people. But the *Stiftung* differed from an American charitable foundation in that it also ran a business, one of the world's most modern fleets of tankers and dry-cargo ships. Onassis had stipulated that all of his money—about $500 million at the time—go to the *Stiftung*, with half of it held in trust for Christina.

"But she objected to the financial arrangements in her father's will," Stelio Papadimitriou told the author of this book.

"She told me, 'Stelio, I do not wish to be subject to the foundation. If you compel me, I will be forced to go to litigation.'

"So we reinterpreted the will. We divided the entire estate into two equal parts—so many ships, so much cash, shares, real estate, etcetera—and wrote it all down on two slips and labeled them 'Part A' and 'Part B.' We went to a notary public in Zurich, and Christina agreed in writing that the two slips were of equal value, about $250 million apiece. We put the slips of paper into a small box, and Christina reached in and picked out 'Part B.'

"She said, 'Gentlemen, now I give it to you to manage for me. Not because my father wanted it that way, but because I wanted it to happen.' "

The final reckoning with Jackie proved to be a far more difficult task. On April 18, 1975, a month after Onassis died, *The New York Times* ran a story reporting that he had been planning to divorce Jackie, and had retained the attorney Roy Cohn to handle the American end of the proceedings. The fingerprints of Costa Gratsos were all over the story.

"Several friends of the Onassis family have said that Mrs. Onassis wants more money," John Corry reported on the front page of the *Times*. "[Christina] is said to be bitterly hostile to Mrs. Onassis."

Jackie went through the roof when she read the story.

"According to what I was told by very reliable sources on the Christina side," Roy Cohn said, "Jackie was calling up Christina in Monte Carlo after the story had been printed, threatening that unless Christina put out a statement saying that everything had been all lovey-dovey and wonderful between her father and Jackie, she was going to make no end of trouble over the estate, and everything else."

Four days later, the *Times* ran a wire-service story from Paris head-lined: MISS ONASSIS DENIES HER FATHER PLANNED DIVORCE. But Christina's statement only fueled speculation that things were not right between Jackie and the Greek side of the family.

Shortly thereafter, Christina flew to New York and confronted Jackie in a face-to-face meeting.

"How much money do you want in return for giving up all further claims to my father's estate?" Christina asked.

When Jackie refused to be pinned down, Christina threatened her with the public humiliation of a lawsuit.

Jackie responded with a not-so-veiled threat of her own. She told Christina that her attorney, Simon Rifkind, a distinguished former federal judge, doubted that Onassis's will was legally binding. If it came to a lawsuit, Jackie said, she was prepared to challenge the validity of the will.

Under Greek law, a last will and testament had to be composed "in a single sitting in a single location." But according to Onassis's own hand-writing, he had written his will on an airplane as it winged its way over international borders from Mexico to America. If Rifkind could prove that Onassis had died intestate, or without an enforceable will, Jackie would be entitled to receive 12.5 percent of his estate, or more than $60 million. That was a whopping three hundred times more than Onassis had bequeathed her (and was the equivalent of about $300 million in today's dollars).

Money aside, Jackie also wanted to keep her 25 percent share in the *Christina* and Skorpios, as well as her seat on the board of directors of the Alexander S. Onassis Foundation. In a letter, she asked Niki Goulandris to act as her proxy on the board of the foundation because of her fear that the other members of the board would give away money to any hospital or orphanage coming along.

She wrote, "Ari's thought was beautiful—but he didn't have time to complete his gesture—If we could complete it for him—in a way that will truly do good. . . ."

But Jackie was deluding herself if she believed that Christina would allow her to continue to participate in the affairs of the Onassis family. As always, Christina's attitude was reflected—and considerably exaggerated—by Costa Gratsos, who was interviewed by Kitty Kelley for her book *Jackie Oh!*

"Please don't talk to me about that woman," Gratsos told Kelley about Jackie. "She's despicable. I can't bring myself to even think about her. If it was something else I'd try to help you, but on this I can't. And don't even try to see Christina, because she can't bear the thought of that woman. She will turn you down flat. She never wants to see her again, or even hear her name."

"I represented Christina, assisted by Nicolas Cokkinis, the first managing director of the Onassis companies, in negotiations with Jackie," said Papadimitriou. "She was represented by Alexander Forger of the American law firm Millbank, Tweed, Hadley and McCloy. The negotiations took place at the Olympic Maritime headquarters in Monte Carlo.

"We met several times," Papadimitriou continued. "Christina was angry as hell. She thought that Jackie was behaving badly by asking for a bigger share of the estate. Costa Gratsos was egging Christina on, urging her to resist Jackie's demands. But I thought Jackie was entitled to a piece of the cake, and that she was being reasonable about what she asked for. I had to fight very hard with Christina, who wanted to give Jackie nothing.

"We finally settled on a reasonable cash figure, which was a fraction of what Jackie would have obtained by application of the forced heirship provisions of Greek law before the amendment of the law, but much more than what Onassis had contemplated under his will pursuant to the application of the amendment of the law. We thought that Jackie, as the widow of Aristotle Onassis, was entitled to a comfortable life to the end."

Jackie received $25.5 million, of which $6 million went for estate taxes, and $500,000 was for Jackie's lawyers. That left Jackie with $19 million. In addition, she received an annuity of $150,000 for the remainder of her life. John and Caroline received yearly payments of $50,000 apiece until they reached the age of twenty-one, after which their payments went to Jackie. All of the payments were tied to the inflation rate.

"In return for this, Jackie agreed to give up Skorpios, the *Christina*, and her position on the board of the foundation," said Papadimitriou. "She would have been entitled to one fifteenth of two percent of the profits of the foundation, as I was, plus a reasonable retirement plan, and medical expenses. If you deduct all the benefits that she renounced, Jackie ended up with a comfortable amount considering her status as the widow of a wealthy person."

"I COULDN'T
SAVE EITHER ONE"

All through the long and bitter struggle with Christina over Aristotle Onassis's money, Jackie continued to be friends with Ari's sister Artemis. The two women talked on the phone two or three times a week. And when Jackie was in Greece, she made it a point to visit Artemis in Glyfada.

The spacious seaside villa was full of memories for Jackie of her early days in Greece, when life seemed to be full of light, and there was an endless supply of laughter. She and Artemis took long walks before dinner. They reminisced about Ari and the old days, before the death of Alexander changed everything. The stories made them sad, and they often fell silent as they strolled through Glyfada's streets that ran down to the sea.

Artemis knew that it was not only the memories of former gaiety that haunted Jackie. In the months following Onassis's death, Jackie suffered one humiliating public blow after another. In August 1975, *Hustler* magazine ran a five-page picture spread of Jackie sunbathing nude on Skorpios. In September, the Senate Select Committee on Intelligence Operations, chaired by Frank Church, an Idaho Democrat, subpoenaed Judith Campbell Exner, who testified that she had a close personal relationship with President Kennedy and with Sam Giancana, the Chicago crime boss, who had been hired by the CIA to assassinate Fidel Castro. In December, Judith Campbell Exner appeared at a press conference in San Diego. Her tanned face partly hidden behind saucer-shaped sunglasses, she said that she had visited Kennedy twenty-three times in the White House, lunched with him in his office, joined him on road trips, and phoned in frequently—at least seventy times, according to official logs.

Caroline was eighteen, John fifteen, when the heroic legend of their father began to sink into the sludge of gossip and innuendo. The towers of Camelot, so painstakingly constructed by Jackie in her famous interview with Teddy White, were beginning to fall into ruins.

Desperate, Jackie tried to fight the campaign of desanctification by inviting friends who had worked closely with Kennedy to come to her home and speak to her children about their father. Arthur Schlesinger Jr., Theodore Sorensen, and Robert McNamara were among those she invited to give Caroline and John informal private seminars on the authentic legacy of President Kennedy. But the damage had been done, and the lights seemed to go out on the one brief shining moment that was Camelot.

Artemis invited Jackie's old friends to dinner in an effort to cheer her up. One evening, when all the guests had departed, Jackie turned to Artemis, and said:

"I am feeling so fragile. Sometimes I think that I am responsible for my misfortune. My first husband died in my arms. I was always telling him that he should be protected, but he would not listen to me. Before my second husband died, I was always telling him to take care of himself, but he wouldn't listen to me. He wouldn't visit the doctor. He could have [died] at any moment during our marriage. No matter what I did, I couldn't save either one of the two men I loved."

As Jackie wept, Artemis put a comforting arm around her shoulders.

"That was God's will," Artemis told Jackie. "Now you have to take care of your children, and make a new life for yourself. Jackie, you are so young and beautiful. Now you need to find a man who will give you some happiness."

THIRTEEN

THE
MYSTERIOUS
M.T.

Winter 1977–Fall 1978

"IN TRUST FOR
JACQUELINE ONASSIS"

M aurice Tempelsman came out of his office and waved a long Dunhill cigar at the three men waiting in his all-beige anteroom.

"Gentlemen," he said, "forgive me for having kept you like this.
Please, come in."

He led the way into his inner sanctum. It was filled with maps,
heavy tomes on international relations and Oriental religions, a photograph or two, and some mementos. His desk was on one side, a long mahogany conference table on the other. The room looked more like the
study of a university don than the office of a CEO who ran a multimillion-
dollar diamond-trading corporation.

Tempelsman was as plain as his office; five feet eight inches tall,
baldish, with a long, sharp nose, and a potbelly that bulged beneath his
dark, double-breasted suit. When he smiled, his moon-shaped face became suffused with a radiant glow, giving him the look of a picturesque
character in a Dickens novel.

His outward appearance gave no hint of the extraordinary man
within. He was, to begin with, one of only one hundred and sixty
"sightholders" throughout the world, which allowed him to make direct
purchases of diamonds from the De Beers cartel. He was also a powerful
behind-the-scenes figure in the Democratic Party, a mover in the world
of Jewish philanthropy, an important collector of museum-quality Roman and Greek antiquities, an active New York clubman (Century,

Council on Foreign Relations, African-American Institute), a legendary wheeler-dealer throughout black Africa, and, it had been long rumored, an elusive player at the fringes of the American intelligence community.

He took a seat at the head of the conference table and, using his cigar as a baton, orchestrated the seating arrangements of his guests. On his right he placed Alexander Forger, Jackie's patrician private attorney.

Once seated, Forger introduced Ken Starr, a man who was as out-going and hearty as Forger was stiff and formal. Starr was New York's preeminent tax accountant. His roster of clients included famous show-business personalities, Morgan Guaranty banking executives, and Paul and Bunny Mellon.

Starr, in turn, said a few words about the man sitting next to him, Sheldon Streisand. The older brother of Barbra Streisand, Shelly (as he was known to all) was a successful real-estate entrepreneur who special-ized in tax shelters for rich people.

"If I may begin," Forger said.

"By all means," Tempelsman said.

As everyone in the room agreed, said Forger, Jacqueline Onassis faced a new set of opportunities as well as new challenges now that she was in possession of her Onassis inheritance. The task of her advisers was to help her conserve her wealth, and at the same time, make her money grow.

Shelly Streisand had put together an interesting real-estate deal, which sounded like just the thing for Jackie. She would take the entire limited partnership in the deal, which included the net leases on three Safeway stores in western Utah and two in North Carolina. Her part of the investment would come to under $1 million—say somewhere be-tween $700,000 and $800,000—which represented less than 5 percent of the money she had inherited from Aristotle Onassis. She would get a very big loss, which would function for years as a profitable tax shelter.

From time to time, Tempelsman interrupted to ask a question. He had exquisite European-style manners, and there was not a misplaced word in what he said. But it was clear from the way he cut to the heart of things that he was made of stern stuff, and was not someone to be trifled with.

Forger concluded his presentation by saying that he, Starr, and Streisand were confident that the tax shelter made eminent sense for Jackie. They had drawn up all the necessary papers, but of course they could not proceed without the approval of Tempelsman, who had known Jackie for some twenty years, and was closer to her than any of the other men in the room. Indeed, at Jackie's request, the documents for the deal were titled "Maurice Tempelsman in Trust for Jacqueline Onassis."

Tempelsman was not involved in the actual hands-on management of Jackie's money. He left that task to others. But since Onassis's death, Tempelsman had taken complete control of Jackie's finances, and had become the chief strategist behind all her investments.

He had already made brilliant use of Jackie's millions. When inflation was at a low ebb, and the price of gold had sunk to about $100 an ounce, Tempelsman had ordered Jackie's money managers to invest a substantial portion of her funds in gold futures. And when inflation took off like a rocket, just as Tempelsman had anticipated, and the price of gold soared to more than $800 an ounce, he had told the money managers to sell Jackie's options. Overnight, Jackie's nice little inheritance had grown into an impressive fortune.

Tempelsman got up from the table, signaling to the three men that the meeting was over. They rose from their chairs, and looked at him.

He waved his cigar one last time, and said, "Let's do it."

And Jackie had her first tax shelter.

A CLANDESTINE
LIFE

Not long after this meeting, Tempelsman boarded a plane for Belgium. There, he was scheduled to make a connecting flight to Zaire, the former Belgian Congo, which was the biggest producer of diamonds in the world. He had been invited to attend the funeral of President Mobutu Sese Seko's wife, Marie Antoinette, who was known to her adoring countrymen as Mama Mobutu.

There were rumors that Mama Mobutu had been the victim of her husband's wrath. It was said that she had been brutally beaten by his secret police while she was pregnant, and that she had been sent for medical treatment to Switzerland, where she died in a private clinic. The official cause of death was given as a heart attack.

Whatever the truth, Mama Mobutu had become a national heroine since her death, a kind of Congolese Eva Perón. As a friend of her husband, the man who controlled the world's chief source of diamonds, Tempelsman did not think it would be wise to skip her funeral.

It was not a convenient time for him to leave Jackie. His involvement in her financial life had required that the two of them be in touch on a daily basis. Little by little since Onassis's death, she had come to depend on Tempelsman for more than financial advice. He had become her chief confidant, friend, companion, escort, and traveling companion. When Prince Stanislas Radziwill, now divorced from Lee, died suddenly of a heart attack, Tempelsman accompanied Jackie, Caroline, and

Lee to London for the funeral, which was held at St. Anna's Chapel, a church that Stas had built and donated in memory of his mother. Tempelsman did not leave Jackie's side during the entire time they were in London.

At first, they were hardly ever seen together in public in New York. However, Tempelsman was a frequent visitor to Jackie's apartment, where they spent hours conversing in French about poetry, literature, and Mediterranean and Mideastern history.

Jackie and Tempelsman struck many people as an unlikely pair. She was a living legend, athletic, outdoorsy, fun-loving, a Roman Catholic who had been reared in aristocratic surroundings. He was an obscure diamond merchant, overweight, physically unfit, intellectual, a Jew who had grown up in modest circumstances. Her friends found it hard to grasp how someone from Jackie's class, with its ferocious anti-Semitism and hatred of the lower orders, could embrace a Jewish refugee from Hitler's Europe as her significant other. They found it even harder to imagine that she slept with him.

"My gut tells me they were not intimate," said one of her closest friends.

What these friends failed to appreciate, however, was that in many ways Jackie had risen above her narrow-minded class. What was more, she had always been attracted to men like Tempelsman, paternal figures who fulfilled her emotional needs. She needed a man to lean on, or as William Manchester had once put it, a man to do the driving.

"I think Maurice certainly represented an ideal father figure for her," the *New Yorker* writer Brendan Gill, a friend of Jackie's, said in an interview shortly before his death. "The search for the father goes on forever, whoever you are. Women suffer more in the search for a father because they expose themselves to disappointing men so often while seeking a father. This may have been especially true in the case of Jackie."

After she was widowed for the second time, Jackie grew aware of her tendency to abdicate power over her life to men. This discovery—that all her adult life she had been a willing pawn in the hands of men—came as a humiliating shock to her. She was almost fifty years old, an age at which most women want to direct, guide, and plan their own lives. She wondered if it was too late for her to change.

Strangely enough, however, it was Tempelsman's secret business dealings in Africa that gave him his special allure to Jackie. Throughout her life, Jackie had always had a fascination with pirates, and had chosen two of them for husbands. Like John Kennedy and Aristotle Onassis, Maurice Tempelsman possessed that distinctive aura that surrounds men who conduct clandestine lives. It required a man with a certain kind of nervy courage to deal in diamonds in the darkest corners of Africa.

Tempelsman was met at the airport in Kinshasa, the steamy capital of Zaire, by a limousine sent by President Mobutu. He was whisked off to the presidential guest house, where he was served a sumptuous French meal that had been flown in that same day from Paris. Before he turned in for the night, he was told to be ready the next morning for the long flight to Gbadolite, Mobutu's ancestral village.

Seven hundred miles of impenetrable rain forest lay between Kinshasa and Gbadolite. The flight took Tempelsman over the equator and the Congo River basin, where some of the trees rose to a height of 180 feet. Except for Mbandaka, the chief town of Équateur Province, there was nothing but forests of oak, mahogany, red cedar, and walnut. The only living creatures were leopards, elephants, and chimpanzees.

Tempelsman had been coming to Africa since he was little more than a boy. He had been born in the Belgian port city of Antwerp in August 1929, which made him one month younger than Jackie. His father, who owned flour mills and traded commodities, spoke Galician Yiddish at home. He fled from the Nazis with his family, and eventually became a diamond broker in New York.

"His father was a trader in industrial diamonds, an unsophisticated man, very hardworking, somewhat on the crude side," said an old-timer in the diamond business. "Maurice's mother was a traditional Jewish mother. Maurice himself had enormous drive. From an early age, he sought to fulfill himself and his destiny. He was simply determined."

Maurice's father worked for several important diamond merchants in America, including the renowned Sydney Lamon. An elegant, well-educated Dutchman who decorated the lobby of his office with Mogul paintings, Lamon left a lasting impression on Maurice, who sought to emulate Lamon's refinement and understated style.

When Maurice was sixteen, he dropped out of school and went into the business. A couple of years later, he traveled alone to South Africa, and managed to wangle a private meeting with Sir Ernest Oppenheimer, then the uncrowned king of the Central Selling Organization, the secretive De Beers diamond empire. Sir Ernest was duly impressed and christened him "the boy wonder," and from then on, Tempelsman enjoyed a direct pipeline to the world's chief source of diamonds.

"Maurice never bought or sold a diamond himself as a trader," said a knowledgeable source in the business. "That wasn't his forte, to be a diamond dealer. He was a diamond *thinker!*"

Though Tempelsman was never as rich or famous as Onassis, the two men had much in common. Both had a compelling desire to break with their fathers and their pasts, to better themselves, and to be accepted by people of quality. And both had a psychological need to prove themselves by making huge deals.

"The Tempelsmans are a trading family," said someone who worked with Maurice. "They understand the art of the deal better than most businesspeople. What's more, they can see opportunity, and go after it."

In the mid 1950s, while Tempelsman was still in his twenties and a budding millionaire, he retained Adlai Stevenson as his lawyer. The former Democratic presidential candidate was viewed sympathetically in the soon-to-be-liberated colonies of black Africa, and Tempelsman asked him to accompany him on a get-acquainted tour of the Dark Continent.

"We visited several countries," said someone who was on the trip, "and stayed on in Ghana, trying to get a diamond license for Mr. Tempelsman. I finally hired a local lawyer, and we got the license."

By then, various heads of state were indebted to Tempelsman, who had better connections in black Africa than most of their ambassadors. In addition, Tempelsman was a heavy hitter among Democratic Party contributors, and in the late 1950s another one of his lawyers, Ted Sorensen, arranged a meeting with the skinny presidential hopeful John Kennedy, who wanted to get to know Sir Ernest Oppenheimer. Tempelsman set up the meeting, and Kennedy brought along his exotic-looking wife, Jacqueline. She was the personification of everything that Tempelsman had always dreamed of.

Building on his special relationships with Oppenheimer and Kennedy, Tempelsman devised a daring commodities scheme. This required some heavy lobbying in Washington to get a bill passed by

Congress, for it involved the barter of several hundred million dollars' worth of American surplus wheat and other agricultural produce for industrial diamonds, cobalt, and uranium to replenish the strategic materials stockpiled by the United States in case of emergency.

"Maurice stood to make in the neighborhood of $50 million on the deal," said a member of the Kennedy Administration who dealt with him. "He went to Jackie, and Jackie went to Jack and said, in effect, 'Here's a guy you ought to see.' JFK asked me to see him, and Maurice met me in my office.

"I said, 'We'll never get your scheme past Congress. There are thirty-five members of the Joint Committee on Atomic Energy, which is headed by Senator Anderson of New Mexico.'

"Maurice said, 'Who's going to raise objections?'

"I said, 'Every member of the committee.'

"He said, 'Let me talk to them.'

"I said, 'I can't prevent you from doing that. You can talk to anyone you want.'

"He went to every member of the committee, and somehow managed to get their approval, and then he came back to me.

"And I told him, 'Well, you've taken care of one problem, but there's still the press. They're not going to like it.'

"Maurice said, 'What would it take for the press to like it?'

"I said, 'If you'd cut your fee, then no one would object.'

"Maurice said, 'I might be willing to do that, but I've worked on this for two years, and I think I deserve something.'

"I said, 'I guess one percent or half of one percent would not be objectionable to anybody in view of all the time and money and travel you've spent on it.'

"And he agreed to cut his fee from $50 million to under $5 million. We approved the deal, and it went through Congress, and it was done."

Tempelsman's plane touched down at the airport in Gbadolite. The runway had been carved out of the bush to accommodate Mobutu's private Concorde, which Zaire leased from Air France to ferry the president and his family to shopping sprees in Europe. Gbadolite had once been a modest market town on the banks of the Ubangi River. But Mobutu had transformed it into a thriving jungle city with its own Coca-Cola bottling plant, modern telephone system, luxury hotel, and presidential palace.

This gaudy white marble retreat was often called "the Versailles of the Jungle," though in fact it was modeled after the Belgian royal family's Laeken Palace. It had its own casino, and it was surrounded by lawns where lions and elephants roamed freely. There was also a moat, which Mobutu had stocked with crocodiles.

The funeral took place in a crypt of white marble that evoked the royal crypt of Laeken. A priest bid the mourners bow their heads in prayerful silence in memory of Mama Mobutu (whose husband, after mistreating her during her lifetime, was now eager to see her beatified).

One of those mourners, Maurice Tempelsman, was described in secret State Department cables as a key intermediary between the Oppenheimers and President Mobutu. Although Tempelsman always denied the charge that he functioned as an Oppenheimer agent, he was regarded by his business competitors—who referred to him by his initials M.T.—as an important "link man" in black Africa for the De Beers cartel.

"M.T. always tried to be an intermediary to the rulers in black Africa," said one competitor. "After he succeeded in setting up the connection, he would go to De Beers and say, 'I've done this thing. Now, what's my cut?'"

In particular, the farsighted Tempelsman established personal ties with the "Binza Boys," the powerful, informal caucus of high-ranking officials who lived in the exclusive Binza residential area of Kinshasa and dominated politics in Zaire. As his man in Kinshasa, Tempelsman hired Larry Devlin, a former CIA station chief, whose office had been implicated in the plot to assassinate Patrice Lumumba, the democratically elected prime minister, and who helped install President Mobutu Sese Seko, who was one of the most rapacious and bloodthirsty dictators in Africa.

"This is a chapter in M.T.'s life that is a big question mark," said a major player in the international diamond business, who agreed to speak to the author on condition of anonymity. "The CIA wanted to have an invisible presence in Kinshasa, and that presence, as far as most of us could tell, was M.T.'s office. It was supposed to be a diamond buying and export office, but during those years not one diamond was bought or sold. It was entirely a front."

It was a well-established fact that the CIA made payments to Mobutu, who had created a cult of personality called Mobutisme, and that the size of those payments depended on the level of his activity against the Russian presence in central Africa. Less well known was the exact nature of Tempelsman's arrangements with Mobutu on behalf of De Beers. Each month, the Zairian government's mine sold diamonds to De Beers, and it was thought that Mobutu received an overriding commission, and that Tempelsman got a percentage as well for handling the Mobutu account.

"In any case," said the anonymous source, "M.T.'s fortunes took a sudden turn for the worse in the 1970s. I was summoned by Mobutu out of the blue. I flew to Kinshasa, and was taken in one of Mobutu's private planes to Gbadolite. There, I was shown to my room in the palace. Eventually I was called into Mobutu's presence.

"He received me in a large state room, very gaudy, all marble and gilt brought from Italy, phony trappings. We spoke French.

" 'I'm fed up with my arrangement with De Beers,' Mobutu told me. 'I'll take the diamond business away from De Beers and give one third of the shares to each of three people, one of whom will be you.'

" 'To what do I owe this honor?' I asked.

" 'We have a mutual friend,' said Mobutu. 'And his name is Kebe.'

"Kebe was Mobutu's witch doctor, a religious leader from Senegal, who was a trustee of lots of Mobutu's assets. Mobutu trusted him implicitly. I knew Kebe through my past activities in Sierra Leone and Guinea. I accepted Mobutu's offer.

"It was a terrible embarrassment to De Beers, whose shares plummeted. De Beers summoned M.T. and told him that he had to go and negotiate with Mobutu, and get the concession back. And that is exactly what he did. It is my understanding that, on behalf of De Beers, he offered Mobutu $5 million for starters, plus $1 million a month. Mobutu asked me if I could match the offer, and I said no, it didn't make any economic sense. I dropped out. And that was how M.T. got back into business with Mobutu."*

---

*In a letter to the author, Maurice Tempelsman declined to participate in the research for this book, or to comment on any matter relating to his business or his relationship with Jacqueline Onassis.

Even by black Africa's standards, the extent of Mobutu's corruption was breathtaking. He shamelessly looted his country and amassed a personal fortune that was estimated at $5 billion. But although Tempelsman was the foreigner who knew the Zairian dictator best, he always denied any firsthand knowledge of Mobutu's venality.

In fact, Tempelsman did everything he could to distance himself from the rough-and-ready world of the diamond business. As a man who had admired the elegant Sydney Lamon, Tempelsman preferred to think of himself as a lofty financier rather than a lowly trader.

He held luncheons in his office, and invited politicians, artists, editorialists, and academicians as his guests. They sat around his mahogany table and enjoyed the excellent food prepared by his private chef. While they ate, Tempelsman held forth, impressing everyone with the breadth and scope of his knowledge.

"The very qualities that caused us to rave about Maurice are the qualities that made him valuable to De Beers in Africa," said Brendan Gill. "The charm, the attractiveness, the many languages, the suavity— all this made him indispensable. When it comes to Maurice's relationship with some of the worst dictators in black Africa, I think we're treading on the territory of Balzac. I mean, *The Human Condition*. There's a huge novel about good and evil in Maurice's story."

ON THE STREET
WHERE SHE LIVED

Tempelsman's relationship with Jackie was complicated by the fact that he already had a wife. Back in the late 1940s, when he was barely out of his teens, he had married a seventeen-year-old girl by the name of Lilly Bucholz. She was an observant Jew of Polish extraction, and, like Maurice, a refugee from Hitler's Europe. Her father, like Maurice's, had dealt in diamonds in Antwerp before the war; he was a minor player in the diamond business in America.

Maurice and Lilly were the products of the close-knit Jewish immigrant community that flourished after the war in Washington Heights on New York's Upper West Side. It was a culture that made Lilly feel comfortable and secure. But it was one which Tempelsman was increasingly eager to leave behind.

Over the years, while he traveled around the world on business, expanding his horizons, Lilly stayed at home, close to her roots. She gave birth to three children—Rena, Leon, and Marcy—and the family moved into a fourteen-room apartment in the Normandy, a prewar building at Eighty-sixth Street and Riverside Drive in Manhattan. Though the marriage soon soured, Maurice and Lilly agreed to stay together while the children grew up.

"My wife and I traveled with Maurice and his wife to Israel after the Six Day War," said a close Tempelsman friend. "This was 1967, and Maurice and Lilly weren't showing any signs of affection for each other even back then. I was surprised that Lilly just picked up one day, and went off to France all by herself. Later, when I visited them at their apartment, I could tell that they didn't have a marriage made in heaven."

"Maurice was very young when he married," said another acquaintance, "and probably somewhat naïve. He simply outgrew his wife. He had immense success early in life when he met Sir Ernest Oppenheimer, and when he was accepted into that level of society, he was confronted with the problem of what on earth to do with his wife. He could not bring her along."

Trapped in a sterile marriage, Tempelsman began looking around for female companionship. He was attracted to well-groomed, well-spoken, well-off women who moved gracefully in the highest levels of society. When it came to winning women, Tempelsman was not the equal of John Kennedy or Aristotle Onassis, but according to the testimony of several of his conquests, his old-world charm worked wonders.

"He was doing it in the sixties, and he continued to do it right through the seventies and eighties," said one woman who spoke from personal experience. "It is simply part of Maurice's nature to run after women."

Jackie was the most desirable woman in the world, and Tempelsman made it a point to see a good deal of her when she was First Lady. During her White House years, she frequently made private, unannounced trips to New York to be with Adlai Stevenson, who was America's ambassador to the United Nations. Whenever Tempelsman heard that she was coming to town, he called up his former lawyer, and asked if he could come along when Adlai took Jackie out to dinner.

"Jackie was not a Kennedy," said Stevenson's son, Adlai Jr. "She didn't play touch football. She was a wonderful, sensitive woman who needed to escape. Maurice was an elegant, cultivated, sophisticated worldly type, very gentle, in some respects like my father. And I think Jackie really needed company to go to the theater and other cultural events, to escape the Kennedy tribe."

Tempelsman continued to see Jackie as a friend during the years she was married to Onassis. His sympathetic nature was stirred by Jackie's tales of marital woe. After Onassis died, and Jackie returned to New York, Tempelsman decided the time was ripe to leave Lilly, who, ironically enough, had become a marriage counselor with the Jewish Board of Family and Child Services. He moved out of his family's sprawling Normandy apartment on the West Side, and into a suite at the Pierre Hotel on Jackie's side of town. He was on the street where she lived.

FOURTEEN

SINGLE WORKING WOMAN

April 1979–Fall 1985

"AN UNHEALTHY BOND"

Maurice Tempelsman made Jackie a rich woman. During the decade of the 1980s, the Dow-Jones industrial average saw a fivefold increase in value, but under Tempelsman's expert guidance, Jackie's investments easily outperformed the Dow, and rose eight- to tenfold. This meant that her original $19 million inheritance from Onassis grew to at least $150 million, not including the $35 million to $40 million that she had in jewelry, art, antiques, and real estate. All this put Jackie's fortune at very close to the $200 million mark. Just as she began to lose her craving for material things, she stopped having to worry about money.

"People have this mania of interest about Jackie and money," said a friend. "But her real concern was not for herself; it was always for her family, for Caroline and John. The money evened out their place in the Kennedy family. They were not the poor relations anymore."

The dramatic change in Jackie's financial circumstances also had a direct bearing on her relationship with Lee Radziwill, who always seemed to be scrambling to catch up with her older sister. In April 1979, Lee told Jackie that she planned to marry Newton Cope, a carefree, easygoing San Francisco millionaire who owned restaurants, vineyards, and hotels in northern California.

Jackie professed to be both surprised and relieved by the news, since in recent months her sister had seemed desperately unhappy. Following the death of Stas Radziwill, Lee had taken up with Peter Tufo, a hand-some, ambitious, tightly wound New York attorney. Their affair had flared brightly, then just as quickly petered out, and Lee had gone back to heavy drinking. Her alcoholism became progressively worse; it started to consume her life and the lives of those around her. She became so dif-ficult to live with that her daughter Tina left home and took refuge with her aunt Jackie at 1040 Fifth Avenue.

"Lee grew bitterly resentful toward Jackie, and told her that what-ever had happened, she had no right to usurp her position and steal her daughter away like that," wrote Diana DuBois in her biography of Lee. "And for a time they even stopped speaking."

"They must have had quite a row," Newton Cope told DuBois. "Lee said to me, 'Tina and I aren't getting along and she is staying over at Jackie's.' And every time I saw or spoke with her after that, she'd say, 'Tina is still over at Jackie's.' It must have cooled things off between them for a while, because Lee never mentioned much about Jackie after that. I think she was hurt. She didn't say much about it, and I didn't want to pry."

As the time for Lee's wedding approached, the sisters began speak-ing again, and Jackie gave a dinner party in honor of the couple at her apartment.

"Why the hell are you so afraid of your sister?" Newton asked Lee as they walked back to her apartment after the party.

"I told her I sat there all night at dinner and I saw it," Newton said. "Her reaction every time Jackie spoke was like her mother was about to spank her. It was as if Jackie controlled her. I could feel the tension, the vibes going between them—it was Lee, not Jackie. It was quite obvious that Jackie intimidated her. It's too bad Lee couldn't get away from that sister of hers. Being just a few blocks away, it was like an unhealthy bond she couldn't escape from—like Devil's Island or something. When she was out in California, she seemed to be happy. Back in New York, she tightened up."

Before Newton left New York for his wedding in California, he received a call from Alexander Forger, Jackie's attorney.

"He told me that Jackie had asked him to look in on her sister be-cause Lee did not have an attorney, and he asked me if I would sign a prenuptial agreement," said Newton. "I said, 'Absolutely.' But when he came over to my hotel, he asked me what kind of deal I was going to make for Lee.

"I told him, 'I am not making any deal.'

" 'Well,' he said, 'how much are you going to give her each month?'

"I told him, 'That's none of your business.'

" 'Well,' he said, 'I think we should have something in writing of how much maintenance a month. What would happen if you die?'

"I said, 'I'll put it in my will that she gets a million bucks, how's that?'

" 'Well, I think we should have it in writing how much Lee gets a month.'

"I told him, 'I am not buying a cow or a celebrity the way Onassis did! I am in love with this woman!'

"And then he started apologizing. 'Now don't be upset,' he said, 'because I don't want to interfere in your love life, but why don't you just put it in writing that Lee will get $15,000 a month?'

"I said to him, 'Would you sign something like that?'

"He said, 'No.'

"Finally, I told him, 'Sorry, no deal,' and we parted company."

On the day of the wedding, Newton received a call from Lee, who was staying at the San Francisco hotel where they were to get married.

"I just got a call from Alexander Forger, and he said that you didn't sign anything," Lee said to Newton. "What's this all about?"

"Tell him to call my lawyer," said Newton.

But the lawyers could not reach agreement, and with less than an hour to go before the ceremony, Newton phoned Stanley Bass, the Supreme Court justice who planned to marry them, and called off the wedding. It was a devastating blow to Lee, who blamed Jackie for having once again meddled ruinously in her life. The breach between the sisters was now so great that it never completely healed.

LIFE

IN THE CITY

"Jackie's relationship with the Municipal Art Society began when we were trying to save Grand Central Station from having the Marcel Breuer building put on top of it," said the writer Brendan Gill. "I was president of the Municipal Art Society at the time, and Jackie phoned us. She was exercised by what she had read in the paper: Grand Central was in jeopardy, and was going to be altered.

"Jackie said she would do anything she could to help us in the fight. So she became our great symbol of the struggle, and by far the most powerful person. She was joined on the ramparts by Philip Johnson, who was also very important, because he was a modernist architect, who nevertheless wanted to save the past, which is what we were dealing with. We had everybody with us.

"But Jackie was 'It.' And she went down with us to Washington on a chartered train called the Landmark Express to lobby the Supreme Court to uphold the landmarks preservation law. Hundreds of people got on the train, and Jackie went through the cars and shook hands with every single person."

"This kind of thing kept coming up over and over," Brendan Gill continued. "Take, for example, the question of St. Bartholomew's Church. The idea that just because the church had the good fortune to have a garden on Park Avenue, which it wanted to sell for $50 million tax free so some developer could build a skyscraper on it—that was a scandal. So Jackie was out there on the vigil. And the rector of the church, the Reverend Thomas Bowers, denounced Jackie and me from his pulpit as 'architectural idolaters.'

"In our fight against St. Bartholomew's, if we were able to tell the media that Jackie was going to come at eight o'clock in the morning or whatever hour, the media would gush, and a couple of local politicians would even dare to kiss her for the cameras. She subjected herself to that kind of soiling and abuse for our sake."

"Within a year of her involvement, I invited Jackie to join the board of the Municipal Art Society," Gill went on. "I told her, 'If you miss more than two consecutive meetings, it will be taken as a resignation, and you will automatically have resigned.' Well, of course, that was the most idle threat that was ever made in history. Jackie was not going to go to every meeting of the Municipal Art Society. She had her own life out in the world. She wasn't going to keep any regular hours for anybody.

"But she was desperately important to us, and she did come to meetings, and she did make friends, and she did gain a total understanding of what it was that the landmarks preservation law meant in terms of the emotional quality of life in the city. It was, in a way, the coming-out of Jacqueline Onassis in New York.

"She had some understanding of this, of course, from her days of refurbishing the White House. Moreover, way back, one of the greatest influences on her life was her grandfather, her mother's father, who was a builder here in New York, and who actually was a partner of Raol Fleischmann, the owner of *The New Yorker* magazine.

"His name was Lee, but he was thought to have changed his name, and to be Jewish. There was a very nice painting of him at 25 West Forty-third Street, in the lunette over the Forty-first Street door, until they remodeled the building a few years ago. In the painting, Mr. Lee was portrayed as a white-haired, nice-looking man, with all the blueprints spread out on his desk. He was quite a good builder, and he was a very important influence on Jackie's life. Whether consciously or unconsciously, she imbibed some notion of this idea of building, what it meant, even as an adolescent."

"At almost all our Municipal Art Society benefits, we would be in the reception line," Gill recalled. "She was our star, and I was the old cannon they brought forward for that purpose. And of course the reception line was always entertaining to me from a novelistic point of view. I enjoyed watching all the people getting ready to come up there just to shake hands with Jackie.

"I would have to say, over and over, 'This is Mrs. Onassis,' to somebody who had been waiting an hour in line for this woman, who had no need to be identified by me. But that was the protocol. But, boy, could she pass them on! Again, I think this was her White House training. The Trumps and people like that would come, and she would get them through the line.

"We had an entertaining time at those things, in part because she had a perfectly lively sense of the degree to which she was being used. And she was prepared to consent to be made use of."

"The only time Jackie was ever angry with me was when I did an exposé of Joseph Campbell [author of *The Power of Myth*] in *The New York Review of Books*," Gill said. "This man was like a monster, whom Jackie had admired very much.

"Campbell was a guru for a lot of people of Jackie's generation, but his book was very bad scholarship. He was not a great scholar. He was radically anti-Semitic . . . and in that respect he was like Jackie's father-in-law Joseph Kennedy.

"Did Jackie see through these people? She may have, but it remains an intriguing question how much she saw through people like Campbell and Onassis and Joe Kennedy. In fact, it is the central question of her life: How does one live publicly in a world where one has to lie?

"Jackie was pitched headlong into the midst of such a world. And all her life, she had to make decisions to lie, or not to lie, and to go on living."

"THAT'S JACKIE. . . .
THAT'S JACKIE. . . ."

One evening in March 1980, Jackie stepped off a freight elevator into a crowded Soho loft, where an Academy Awards party was in full swing. Two men followed her off the elevator into the noisy, smoke-filled room. One was her escort for the evening, Pete Hamill, the ruggedly handsome, Brooklyn-born columnist for the New York *Daily News*. The other was a slightly built young man who was wrapped in the saffron robes of a Buddhist monk and carried a photo of the Sri Rajneesh on a leather thong around his neck.

"Hi, Pete," said Julienne Scanlon, a Broadway musical star and the wife of the party's host, public-relations man John Scanlon. "What would you like to drink?"

"I'll just have a Coke," said Hamill, who had lived the life of a sober alcoholic for the past eight years. "Oh, by the way," he added nonchalantly, "this is Jackie."

Julienne stared in disbelief at Hamill's date, who was dressed in a floral blouse, black trousers, and patent-leather pumps.

"And what would *you* like to drink, Jackie?" Julienne managed to stammer.

"I'll have what Pete's having," Jackie said.

The bartender, a young woman, took one look at Jackie, and dropped the glass she was holding in her hand. It smashed on the floor, and when she bent to pick it up, she cut herself so badly that her hand would not stop bleeding.

In all the confusion, Julienne had barely had time to deal with the young man in the saffron robes.

"And who are *you?*" she finally asked the follower of Sri Rajneesh, who had wandered in from the little Neeshie ashram located on Franklin Street across from the Scanlon loft.

"I'm with Jackie," he said.

"Jackie, do you know him?" Julienne asked her.

Jackie looked at the monk, and shook her head.

"Pete!" Julienne called after Hamill, who had begun to disappear into the crowd. "This fellow says he's with Jackie."

Hamill ran back to the entrance, grabbed the confused Neeshie by his homespun robe, and hustled him into the freight elevator.

"I'm with Jackie!" the young man yelled as he disappeared. "This is a sign! We were meant to be together!"

"I think I should go to the hospital to get some stitches," said the bartender.

Jackie followed Hamill into the jam-packed loft, which consisted of one large living area with windows all around, and a big bedroom, where three or four television sets were blaring at the same time. Edward Koch, the mayor of New York, and a bevy of journalists and writers were watching Jane Fonda hand Dustin Hoffman an Oscar for his performance as a beleaguered father in *Kramer vs. Kramer.*

Hamill knew a thing or two about the problems of fatherhood. He was still trying to repair some of the damage he had inflicted on his daughters Adrienne and Deirdre when they were growing up and he was drunk a lot of the time. After he stopped drinking, Hamill lived for a number of years with Shirley MacLaine, but she had always made it clear that she did not want to have anything to do with his daughters. Faced with a choice, Hamill dumped his kids, rather than Shirley, which made him feel doubly guilty.

Jackie did not know what to make of Hamill's struggles with his conscience and his rebellious daughters, who were now eighteen and sixteen, and were showing signs of being troubled kids. Jackie was touched by Hamill's confessions of guilt, but parenthood meant a great deal to her, and she found it hard to forgive Hamill for having been such a bad father. His candor did not evoke her sympathy; it only made her realize how angry she must have been at her own father for letting her down as a child.

For his part, Hamill was a writer who had fashioned himself as a voice of the workingman. He had once written a scathing denunciation of Jackie for selling herself to Onassis for a few pieces of gold. He eventually thought better of publishing his intemperate words, and had put the column away in a drawer. But when he started dating Jackie, the column resurfaced and was printed by his rivals at the New York *Post* as a way of embarrassing him.

He was surprised to learn that Jackie was very different from Shirley MacLaine, Faye Dunaway, and his other self-absorbed celebrity girlfriends. Jackie was much more open, and seemed genuinely interested in him and his work. All of Hamill's writer buddies assumed that he was sleeping with Jackie, but he was always too much of a gentleman to confirm their suspicions.

Jackie sat down on a bed next to a journalist who was so smashed that at first he did not recognize her. He offered her a toke, which she politely refused.

"A couple of people were ripped to the tits, they were so drunk," said Patsy Denk Powers, an actress and producer who was co-hosting the party with the Scanlons. "And I thought, please, God, don't let them go back there into the bedroom and say anything to Jackie."

By now, however, people had heard that Jackie was in the bedroom, and they were wandering back to take a look.

On the TV screen, Dustin Hoffman leaned over the shoulder of the Oscar statuette, paused, then observed wryly to the billion people who were watching: "He has no genitalia, and he's holding a sword."

The loft exploded in rowdy laughter. When it subsided, two words could be heard repeated over and over again: "That's Jackie. . . . That's Jackie. . . ."

"SOMETHING
TO THINK ABOUT"

Pete Hamill embodied many of the bad-boy qualities that had attracted Jackie to John Kennedy and Aristotle Onassis. But Hamill also represented a break with Jackie's past. He was both masculine *and* sensitive, a bang-it-out-on-the-typewriter kind of reporter *and* an accomplished novelist and painter. He was a liberal New Yorker whose consciousness had been raised by the women's movement. He was not threatened by strong, independent women, and he had no qualms about treating Jackie as an equal.

As a working journalist, Hamill lived a hand-to-mouth existence. He had neither the money nor the desire to insulate Jackie from the real world, where he got the material for his columns and novels. His love affair with Jackie, who was notoriously press shy, surprised a number of people, who could not understand her attraction to a poor, ink-stained wretch.

But it did not surprise the author of this book, who had the chance to observe firsthand Jackie's fascination with members of the fourth estate. In 1981, I was the editor in chief of *The New York Times Magazine* and was bringing out a new novel at Doubleday, where Jackie had recently taken a job as a part-time editor. She liked my novel well enough to make one of her rare public appearances at my book party. She wrote me a note shortly after the party, praising my book, and I called her a few days later for lunch. We became friendly, and that Christmas she invited me to a party at her home on Fifth Avenue.

"Oh, Ed," she told me at one point during the party, "I'm so glad you could come. Journalists are the most interesting people in the whole world!"

Given her ambivalence toward journalism and true confessions, it was fascinating to see what Jackie had chosen as her life's work. She spent three days a week—Tuesdays, Wednesdays, and Thursdays—at Doubleday, where she attended editorial meetings and gained the respect of her fellow editors as someone who knew how to shepherd her projects through the editorial bureaucracy, and get her books approved.

"She telephoned me one day from Doubleday," said John Loring, the former design director of Tiffany & Company, who worked with Jackie on a series of six Tiffany lifestyle books. "Some people had called an editorial meeting to get us to do certain things that she and I did not want to do with the book we were working on. And she said, 'We have to psych them out on this one. You know, we're not going to argue. We're just going to psych them out.'

"She did her homework thoroughly before the meeting," Loring continued, "and she knew what every man and woman was up to, and what they were trying to put over, and who was siding with who and who wasn't. And she knew how to tip the balance at the right moment in a meeting to get it the way she knew it should be done.

"And we were sitting across the table from these people who were proposing these unacceptable things, and she leaned over and whispered to me, 'Look at them! Look at them! They're all so vile, so vile! They think of things every minute that we couldn't imagine in a lifetime.' "

At Doubleday, Jackie occupied a cramped, nondescript corner office on the twentieth floor.

"There were a lot of books and paintings around her office," Loring said. "But there was no decoration, no personal touches of anything whatsoever. Well, maybe a photograph or two, the children or something. But there was nothing that would have told you that this was in fact her office. She was not being Jacqueline Kennedy Onassis. She was being an editor at Doubleday.

"And for the first number of years, she did not want to go out to a restaurant," Loring went on. "So we would end up with a brown paper bag full of Styrofoam containers—iced tea, cole slaw, potato salad, and some kind of sandwich—sitting on the floor of Jackie's office, eating out of these containers. We rather liked the floor because you could spread out a great many photographs, and just make this great accretion of paper and stuff all around you in every direction. We could crawl across the floor, and grab a photo and put it there, and I would have this photograph, and Jackie would have that one, and we had a lot of fun. And one time Jackie turned to me on the floor and said, 'Robin Leach's *Lifestyles of the Rich and Famous* should cover this event. That would give people out there something to think about.' "

At the beginning of a project, Jackie and Loring would each make a list of about fifty stylish people they thought should be included in the book.

"About fifty percent of our lists were identical, so there was no discussion," Loring said. "If there was someone who I didn't know but who Jackie particularly wanted, she'd just say, 'Believe me, John, this is the right person to put there.'

"And then I would make most of the phone calls. Jackie would say, 'If you need me to step in, I will, and make it happen.' And one time she said about someone, 'If I have to go and beat them up, I will, because with their social pretensions, they wouldn't dare say no to me.'

"Once, we wanted to do a cookbook, but the marketing department at Doubleday said, no, you're not going to do that until you write a book on American weddings. Thank God, that was about the time that Caroline was getting married, so Jackie was suddenly interested in weddings. She said, 'Let's just get all the books we can on weddings.' So we got all these books, including Martha Stewart's, and decided that it was too dogmatic, because it attempted to tell people exactly how to do the checklist and countdown to the terrifying event. Jackie's attitude was, 'Let's try to liberate the American girl from this nightmare.'

"While we were doing this wedding book, we came across a photograph of asparagus from a market with red rubber bands around it, and it was just beautiful. And Jackie said, 'Asparagus is so beautiful. It's more beautiful than the pictures of flowers. I don't see why American girls don't just carry bunches of asparagus at their weddings. But I guess that would be too close to the truth.' "

Much of Jackie's time at Doubleday was spent alone in her office, whispering intently into the telephone, trying to persuade famous people to tell all in their autobiographies.

"I remember Jackie's presentation of a book to be written by a fellow named Michael Jackson," said an old publishing hand who had watched Jackie in action. "She'd done all the financial projections, but what was impressive about it was that she was explaining to a roomful of older people why this book could be immensely successful and why it was worth paying a lot of money to get it. And she was right: it became an immense bestseller. She was not someone who backed down when she thought she was on the right track."

A number of other celebrities, including ballerina Gelsey Kirkland, succumbed to Jackie's persuasive editorial charms. But the biggest prize of all, Frank Sinatra, continued to elude her. This made Jackie all the more eager to snag Sinatra for a Doubleday autobiography. In her dogged pursuit of the famous crooner, she went so far as to invite him to have dinner with her in New York. They were photographed leaving the restaurant together, looking as though they were out on a date, which gave rise to the inevitable tabloid rumors of a hot romance.

Nothing could have been further from the truth. Jackie had never liked Sinatra, and had discouraged John Kennedy from having anything to do with him when he was President. "Jackie hates Frank," Kennedy told his brother-in-law Peter Lawford, "and won't have him in the house." Sinatra might be the greatest entertainer of his generation—and a sure-fire bestseller as an author—but Jackie considered him to be tacky and low class. He was not a candidate to share her bed.

"THE DEFINITION OF
HAPPINESS"

As a single working mother and a woman of a certain age (she was now in her early fifties), Jackie became increasingly confident of her ability to make decisions on her own. But maturity also brought with it some unwanted changes. She was buffeted by the hormonal storms of menopause, which in her case seemed to be more severe than in most women. Her gynecologist prescribed Premarin, an estrogen replacement made from the urine of mares, and Provera, a progesterone replacement. Although these drugs were also supposed to help a woman maintain her youthful appearance, Jackie's face began to sharpen and show signs of age. In the mid 1980s, she had the first of three face-lifts. And she started seeing a psychotherapist.

Jackie had always believed strongly in psychotherapy, and was open to ideas that could help people cope with their lives. She was responsible for Doubleday's publishing *Out in Inner Space: A Psychoanalyst Explores New Therapies*, by Dr. Stephen Appelbaum, the Erik Erikson Scholar at the Austin Riggs Center, one of the best psychiatric hospitals in the country.

"Jackie and I had a sort of friendship," Dr. Appelbaum said, "and met a time or two in New York for social reasons, and corresponded and talked on the phone. She had an interest in just about everything, but how deep it went was hard to tell. I don't want to call her deceptive exactly. She was quite open and receptive. But she was also strangely opaque and unrevealing. Free as she was up to a point, beyond that point you did not learn anything.

"There was, of course, some special circumstance in her relationship with her father that made her have relationships with various powerful men," Appelbaum continued. "But leaving it at that would be selling her short, and be one-dimensional. She had an independent, managerial, controlling streak. Her sibling position—she was the firstborn and the older of two sisters—made her by nature controlling, a person who took the initiative.

"She was the kind of person who would say to me when I was discussing a manuscript, 'Use my house as a drop,' as though she was a gun moll. I detected a certain tensile strength there. So it would be a disservice to call her overall a dependent person. She wasn't. She was no clinging vine. If a woman has, as women do, something missing in the sense of power, they can get it by affiliating themselves with powerful men. They are adopting for themselves the power they are close to. It's a method of being strong and independent. You can live through men, like Jackie, and have a lot of iron."

She had always lived through men—her father, JFK, Bobby, Onassis. Now she was trying to break the habit of a lifetime, and define herself. She was not certain where she was going, or how she was going to get there, but she was determined not to travel in the old grooves of the past.

After Dallas, she had tried to recapture a life of power and glory, but her marriage to Onassis had turned into a disaster. Now she was beginning to wonder if the key to her happiness might lie somewhere else—in the simple pleasures of family, friendship, and work.

"What has been sad for many women of my generation is that they weren't supposed to work if they had families," she said. "There they were, with the highest education, and what were they to do when the children were grown—watch the raindrops coming down the windowpane? Leave their fine minds unexercised?

"Of course women should work if they want to," she went on. "You have to do something you enjoy. That is the definition of happiness: 'complete use of one's faculties along the lines leading to excellence in a life affording them scope.' "

Since her days in the White House, Jackie had always had a great influence on the way women looked at themselves. Because she was such a private person, and allowed the public to know so little about her, she acted as a kind of tabula rasa on which women could project their fantasies.

In the 1980s, not many women were sure that they wanted to emulate Gloria Steinem and other politicized feminists, who were often portrayed by the media as man-hating, childless fanatics. By contrast, Jackie seemed to have it all. Not only was she lovely, stylish, and clearly attractive to men; she was also smart, capable, and a very good mother. Women who wanted to have a measure of independence and a profession of their own, without sacrificing the benefits of womanhood, looked to Jackie's example. They thought to themselves: If Jackie can do it, so can I.

"Jackie was tradition and modernity, the old femininity and the new womanhood, seemingly sustained in a perfect suspension," wrote the feminist author Susan J. Douglas. "Jackie had these traditionally 'masculine' qualities—she was smart and loved intellectual pursuits, she was knowledgeable about history and the arts, she wore pants, and she had big feet—yet she was still completely feminine, a princess, a queen."

"When she was alone again after Onassis's death," said Gloria Steinem, "the speculation about her future plans only seemed to split in two. Would she become a Kennedy again (that is, more political, American, and serious) or remain an Onassis (more social, international, and simply rich)? What no one predicted was her return to the publishing world she had entered briefly after college—to the kind of job she could have had years ago, completely on her own. And that's exactly what she did. . . .

"Her example poses interesting questions for each of us," Steinem continued. "Given the options of using Kennedy power or living the international lifestyle of an Onassis, how many of us would have chosen to return to our own talents, and less spectacular careers? In the long run, her insistence on work that was her own [was] more helpful to other women than any use of the conventional power she declined."

THE POWER
BEHIND THE THRONE

One day in the fall of 1985, Jackie was in her office, employing her irresistible powers of persuasion on some helpless celebrity, when the Doubleday operator interrupted the phone call. Maurice Tempelsman's doctor was holding on the other line.

"Yes, Doctor, what is it?" Jackie asked.

"I've just admitted Maurice to the coronary care unit of Lenox Hill Hospital," the doctor said. "He's complaining of chest pains."

As Jackie later told friends, the instant she heard the word "hospital," everything went blank. It was the same old nightmare: Jack and Parkland Memorial Hospital, Ari and the American Hospital in Paris. Now it was Maurice and Lenox Hill Hospital. The most important man in her life was seriously hurt, and had been rushed to the hospital.

She ran out into the street in front of the Doubleday building, hailed a taxi, and told the driver to step on it. As the cab sped off in the direction of the hospital on the Upper East Side, Jackie recalled that she was filled with a sense of dread. Was Maurice dying? Would she get there in time? Was she about to lose a third husband, which Maurice had become in all but name?

For the first few years after he left Lilly, Tempelsman had maintained his suite at the Pierre Hotel, even though he began spending one, then two, then three nights a week at Jackie's apartment. In 1982, he and Jackie decided it was pointless for them to maintain separate residences. His children were all grown up, and hers were out of the house: Caroline was twenty-five and married; John was twenty-two and a senior at Brown University.

Tempelsman moved out of his hotel and into 1040 Fifth Avenue. He gave out one of Jackie's phone numbers to his business associates. Messengers came and went with important documents for him. The doorman at 1040 accepted Tempelsman's drugstore prescriptions and dry cleaning, and delivered them to Jackie's apartment. The penthouse apartment was Tempelsman's home, and would remain that for the next twelve years, until Jackie succumbed to cancer.

They made no attempt to disguise their living arrangements, though visitors noticed that Tempelsman occupied the guest room, not Jackie's bedroom, leading them to wonder whether he and Jackie cohabited as lovers or were merely cozy companions. In either case, people thought it was courageous of Jackie to take up with Tempelsman, and a triumph of public relations how she managed to avoid being criticized in the press for living with a married man.

But it was not so much courage or public relations as it was Jackie's shrewd instincts that led her to make Tempelsman her spouse. She always had a natural feel for the zeitgeist—the spirit of the time, the "in" thing of the moment. And she apparently sensed that the culture in America had become so permissive that people did not even blink when famous couples lived together without benefit of a marriage license.

Whenever Jackie gave a dinner party for ten or twelve people in her red-lacquered library, Tempelsman not only presided at the head of the table, but he stayed back when everyone else left for home.

"I noticed that Jackie deferred to Maurice all the time," said a dinner guest who sat next to him. "I mean, he didn't try to dominate her; she does it to herself. She'd say to him across the table, sotto voce, 'Maurice, don't you think it's time for them to remove the dishes?' She could have had a bell or a buzzer to summon the butler herself. 'Maurice,' she'd say, 'should we have coffee here or in the living room?' Those kinds of things, and he would answer assertively in a loud voice, 'We'll have coffee here.'

"There's no doubt about it," the woman added, "Maurice was absolutely crazy about her. He seemed to relish looking after her. I remembered an article that appeared ages ago, I think in *The Saturday Evening Post*, in which Jackie complained that President Kennedy wouldn't help her decide what dress to wear. Well, you just knew that Maurice would pick out the dress for her every time she asked."

"She found security with Maurice," explained Hélène Arpels, who had known Jackie when she was married both to Kennedy and to Onassis. "She had finally found a man who, she believed, was not running around with other women. True or not, that's what she believed. Maurice wasn't a famous public figure like Kennedy or Onassis. Jackie could be herself with him. He was a gently domineering figure. Jackie might be the queen, but Maurice was the power behind the throne."

At the hospital, Jackie went directly to the coronary-care unit and found Maurice's doctor, who told her that Maurice had suffered a mild heart attack.

She was devastated. She should have known something like this was going to happen. It was her fault. She had been trying to get Maurice to do something about his weight, but she had not tried hard enough. She had not been able to persuade him to go on a diet, or to take up a regimen of regular exercise.

What could be done for Maurice now, she asked the doctor.

Maurice's coronary arteries were clogged, the doctor told her. There were only two alternatives: open-heart surgery and a bypass, or a PTCA.

A PTCA? What was that?

A percutaneous transluminal coronary angioplasty, the doctor explained. Otherwise known as balloon angioplasty. During the procedure, a long, flexible tube, or catheter, was inserted into the artery in the upper thigh and snaked to the aorta. From the aorta, the catheter was threaded into the opening of a coronary artery that was narrowed or blocked by cholesterol plaque. The goal in angioplasty was to open the artery with a tiny balloon at the end of the catheter by squashing the plaque against the artery's wall.

Was it safe, Jackie asked.

It had been used on only about three thousand patients in the United States since it was first performed in 1976, and was still in the trial stage. It had yet to be approved by the Food and Drug Administration. But Maurice would remain awake throughout the procedure, which was a lot safer than open-heart surgery.

Jackie gave the doctor permission to go ahead.

For three days following the angioplasty, Jackie did not leave Tempelsman's side.

"She moved into the hospital to be with him," said one of Tempelsman's oldest friends. "I was there, and saw how she behaved. She was very much in love with Maurice. And he with her. You could tell by the way they talked to each other, and looked at each other, and deferred to each other. In all respects, you could see the love. It really was a great love affair. They were two mature people with a lot of experience, and they felt lucky they had found each other."

Yet most of Jackie's friends did not see it that way. They knew that Tempelsman doted on Jackie, and attended to her in an almost obsequious manner. But they still failed to understand Jackie's fascination with him. As one of these friends said:

"He was not like John Kennedy or like Ari, a bad-boy archetype, the man who always got away, the black pirate. There seemed to be just enough in Maurice to keep her interested. He was a pillar of stability, a financial and personal adviser. But I had a hard time stringing together Maurice's syntax. He indulged in linguistic gymnastics, and inserted German terms in the middle of his sentences.

"And he wasn't around that much," this friend continued. "He was always traveling to Africa on business. What business? Don't ask me. 'Maurice is going to Botswana,' Jackie would say, 'so let's go to the movies!' It was like she was let out of jail."

"I think she found him an amusing conversationalist," said another friend. "He helped with investments. Their relationship was just cozy. It was predictable and not demanding on her. She'd talk about what pleased her—friends, work. But Maurice wasn't singled out. She'd say, 'I love my work, my writing, my editing, my grandkids'—when they finally came along—all the things that she had to be grateful for. But she did not mention Maurice."

Nonetheless, while Tempelsman was recovering from his angioplasty, he and Jackie discussed the idea of getting married. Tempelsman gave Jackie a gold eternity ring encrusted with emeralds and sapphires. The inscription inside was in French. It was addressed to "Jacks," the nickname that Black Jack Bouvier had given Jackie as a child. She wore it along with the wedding ring that had been given to her by Jack Kennedy.

"It was the only time they came close to getting married," said a Tempelsman intimate. "And it was Jackie who raised the idea of marriage."

For years, stories had persisted that Tempelsman was prevented from marrying Jackie by his wife Lilly. According to these tales, the strictly Orthodox Lilly refused to grant her husband a "get," or Jewish divorce. Her position, if true, seemed to present an almost insurmountable obstacle, since according to Jewish tradition, only a rabbinical court could overrule her wish to stay married.

"But I never believed any of those stories," said a diamond dealer who knew both Maurice and Lilly well. "He might have needed Lilly's consent to obtain a religiously sanctioned divorce, but he certainly didn't need her approval to get a civil divorce. You can't keep someone a prisoner in a marriage if he doesn't want to stay in it. In my view, it was convenient for Maurice to have the protection of being a married man. He was not ready for another marriage."

Others had a different interpretation of why Jackie and Maurice never married.

"There were simply too many things in the way of their getting married," said one of his friends. "The children were not a problem. His kids and hers saw each other and liked each other. But they had different religions. And a legal bond would have made things very complicated financially for both of them, and for their heirs. What's more—and this point cannot be stressed too strongly—Jackie had come to like her independence. She was no longer the woman she had been before. She did not need or want to be married. She was happy the way things were. Why change it?"

FIFTEEN

THE TIME OF
HER LIFE

Spring 1989–Fall 1993

THE BEST
DISGUISE

One day in the spring of 1989, John Loring, who was working on yet another Tiffany lifestyle book for Jackie, called her and said, "Where do you want to meet? Your office floor or my office floor?"

"Oh, could we just go to a restaurant?" Jackie said. "Couldn't we just go out?"

"You're joking," Loring said. "You don't really want to do that."

"Yes, I really want to do that," Jackie said. "Could we just go out and have lunch?"

"Where are we going to go?" Loring said. "I've got an idea. How about Le Cirque? It's the only safe place to go."

"Yes," she said. "Sirio [Maccioni, the owner of Le Cirque] knows how to handle these things. This is perfect! That's exactly where we are going to go. You get there well ahead of time, and get it all organized so I know when I come in where to go."

"I already know where you're going," Loring said. "You're going to a table in the corner by the door, so you don't even have to walk more than three paces into the restaurant before you're sitting down."

"Great," said Jackie. "I'll be there."

Just as they planned, Loring was waiting when Jackie came through the door of Le Cirque, the fashionable eatery in the East Sixties. Three waiters rushed forward to create a human shield and escort Jackie to a chair facing Loring, who was seated on the banquette at the corner table. Before anyone in the restaurant had noticed, Jackie was leaning toward Loring, her hand slightly up to her face.

"It wasn't because she didn't want to be seen by the people in the room," Loring explained. "It was so she didn't have to see the people in the room staring at her."

After a while, Sirio Maccioni came over to their table. He had known Jackie since the 1950s, when he was the maître d' at the Colony Club, and she dropped in with Senator John Kennedy. Sirio asked if he could bring his three sons over to meet her.

"Oh, yes, please send the boys over," Jackie said.

By a great coincidence, the columnist Liz Smith happened to be having lunch at Le Cirque that day. She devoted half her column the next day to the fact that Jacqueline Kennedy Onassis had lunched at Le Cirque, and had paid rapt attention to the man she was having lunch with.

"Well, Jackie's rapt attention to the person she was having lunch with," explained Loring, "was to avoid seeing everyone else in the room whispering to each other and doing things that would make her uncomfortable. But once she decided to eat lunch out, she loved going to Le Cirque for what she began calling her festive lunches."

Loring always arrived well in advance. One time, before Jackie made her appearance, Ivana Trump came over to ask Loring if he would introduce her to Jackie after she was seated.

"Let me ask her first," Loring said.

During lunch, Loring turned to Jackie and said, "Ivana would really like to meet you. She's a very sweet person."

"Okay," said Jackie, "tell her it's fine."

Loring got up and went over to Ivana's table, and brought her back.

"Oh, I've always wanted to meet you," Ivana gushed.

They chatted for a while, and Ivana left.

"She's really very sweet," Jackie said.

"Yes, Jackie, she is," said Loring. "She is nothing like what the press says about her. I think we all know a thing or two about that, don't we?"

"She changed a great deal over the years," said Loring. "In the beginning, she still seemed very haunted by things. She still seemed to be pursued by her own demons. And if anyone in the world had a right to be, she did. On occasion, she seemed very upset and troubled. But all that changed as the years went on, and one can suspect a lot had to do with Maurice Tempelsman, and finally having a very satisfying and good relationship with someone who was a very strong and very brilliant and quiet and charming and companionable person to be with. That undoubtedly was a tremendous influence on bringing her back to the happy person again.

"And the great change that was wonderful to me was that she became a very happy camper. She was very happy with everything. I think also she was delighted with her children, that as they grew up she was beginning to be so proud of them and so happy with them, and everything to do with them made her happy. And her enthusiasm was boundless all the time.

"And so all those haunted looks completely disappeared. It was like a scene change from one period, when we were hiding in her office, sitting on the floor, eating junk out of a paper bag, to, 'No, I'm a perfectly normal person and I can get all dressed up and go to Le Cirque for lunch and have a good time.'

"And it was astonishing. I mean that change just came like that. Bingo! At one point she was very much into trench coats and a scarf over her head and large sunglasses and things. Then suddenly, there she was, no trench coat, no scarf, just herself, walking straight down Fifth Avenue, leaving me at Tiffany and walking on down to Doubleday.

"It was amazing watching the passersby's faces. There was this look of astonishment, and then there was a look of total denial, and you could see them saying to themselves, 'Oh, it couldn't possibly be. . . .' And so, the best disguise in the world was to walk straight through the crowds on Fifth Avenue, because nobody believed it. They would sort of get a jolt, and then they would think, 'Oh, I'm crazy, that can't possibly be Jackie Onassis walking down the street.' So they'd pay no attention, and she learned that a disguise was not necessary, and that she could do whatever she wanted to."

SACRED
GROUND

The sun was rising over Martha's Vineyard, burning off the fog that had blanketed the island during the night. As Jackie pedaled her bike through Gay Head, a damp chill clung to the morning air. The town had three ramshackle buildings—the town hall, the library, and the fire station—and none of the understated glitz of neighboring Chilmark, where barefoot New Yorkers in self-consciously aging Volvos lunched on designer pizza at the country store owned by James Taylor's brother Hugh.

Jackie had spent her adolescence in the tony resort of Newport just a few miles away across Massachusetts Bay. But in its simplicity and unpretentiousness, Gay Head was about as far from Newport as she could get.

On this particular summer morning, she was dressed in her usual Gay Head getup—a pair of jeans, a windbreaker, and a scarf over her ponytail. She rode west on South Road, passing tumbledown fieldstone walls and wild, low-lying bayberry bushes, scrub oak, beach plum, roses, and poison ivy. Beyond these knotty masses, she could glimpse moors, beach grass, and the Atlantic Ocean. On the right in some places were small, sheltered inlets, and at one scenic turnout, a spectacular view of Menemsha Harbor, where Maurice Templesman kept his thirty-seven-foot schooner, the *Relemar*.

Moshup Trail was the last turn before the Gay Head cliffs and the end of the island. The first driveway on the left was Red Gate Farm, which belonged to Jackie. The rustic wooden gate was open, but her caretaker, Albert Fischer, had posted a NO TRESPASSING sign to keep out intruders. If anyone happened to wander in, Tempelsman usually took care of them himself, without bothering to tell Jackie.

She pedaled up a long, meandering gravel road, which passed over a creek, and came to a large forecourt in front of a cluster of three gray-shingled, white-trimmed buildings. Off to the side, there was a tall osprey pole for nesting that had been erected by Gus Ben David, director of the Audubon sanctuary at nearby Felix Neck. On the path leading to the main house, one of Jackie's grandchildren had abandoned an old red wagon.

The breathtaking wetlands site had once belonged to the Hornblower family of the Hornblower & Weeks stock exchange firm. In the late 1970s, Robert McNamara and a group of friends, including *Washington Post* publisher Katharine Graham, put together a syndicate to buy the property, but before they could close on it, some local Wampanoag Indians complained that part of the land was the sacred burial ground of Chief Moshup and his wife Squant. McNamara tried to settle the legal dispute, but while he dithered with the Indians, Jackie came along in the person of her attorney Alexander Forger and stole the land from under McNamara's nose.

Jackie took the Indians to court and eventually won the legal battle. However, her well-publicized victory inflicted some damage to her reputation as a dedicated preservationist. The property, which was assembled by Forger piece by piece over a period of years for about $3.5 million, constituted 464 acres, one third of the entire town of Gay Head. By the early 1990s, it was estimated to be worth more than $25 million.

"I worked with Jackie for two years on the purchase," said David Flanders, the real-estate broker who sold her the land. "The first time she flew into the airport on Martha's Vineyard, she came on Bunny Mellon's private plane. Bunny Mellon was her chief adviser, and she and Jackie came frequently together, walking the property, looking at it from different angles. Jackie was very impressed by what Mrs. Mellon had to say."

Bunny not only was involved in the purchase of the land itself, she also helped Jackie select the architect, Hugh Newell Jacobsen, who designed the traditional saltbox house. Bunny showed up on weekends with Jackie to check on the progress of the construction, and to plan the landscaping. Bunny influenced the interior décor, and she lent Jackie her private jet to fly in the furniture that Jackie selected to fill the house's nineteen rooms. And, finally, Bunny designed an apple orchard on the property. She left intentional gaps between some of the trees, explaining that she wanted it to look "as if a few old trees had died."

Jackie leaned her bike on its kickstand and went inside the house. Even with the door closed, she could hear the ocean roaring. She entered the living room, whose large picture window afforded a spectacular view of Squibnocket Pond and the Atlantic. Toys were strewn all over the bleached oak floor. Grandjackie, as she was called, was a permissive grandmother, and she let Caroline's three children—Rose, Tatiana, and the baby, Jack—have free rein in the house.

Jackie took justifiable pride in the way Caroline had turned out. Considering the snares and pitfalls of growing up a Kennedy, Caroline was amazingly well adjusted. She was thirty-six years old, and married to Edwin Schlossberg, a teddy-bearish man thirteen years her senior. Schlossberg, the scion of a wealthy Jewish textile manufacturer, was a former acolyte of Buckminster Fuller's and an avant-garde artist in his own right.

"Exactly what Ed Schlossberg does," the writer George Plimpton once confessed, "is obscure."

Apparently what Schlossberg did best was to look after Caroline, who had put her career as a lawyer on hold in order to take care of her children. Jackie never really warmed up to the humorless Schlossberg, who guarded Caroline as though he were her Secret Service agent, rather than her husband. But Jackie knew that Schlossberg functioned as a kind of protective screen around Caroline, who harbored a suspicious attitude toward strangers, and assumed that most people were trying to exploit her.

"Ed has taken Caroline out of the world of publicity and made her feel as though he has saved her," said one of Jackie's friends.

"When they were in the city, Caroline and Jackie saw each other a couple of times a week," said one of Caroline's best friends. "Being the daughter of a famous mother made it hard for Caroline to understand that her problems with her mother were the average person's problems with their mother. On the other hand, I think that Jackie was a woman who knew that she was thin and attractive, and it may not always have been easy for her to relinquish the spotlight to her daughter. Mother-daughter relationships are always complicated, and that could really be the case when it was carried to the grandeur of this particular family."

Caroline's close friend Alexandra Styron, daughter of writers William and Rose Styron, added:

"Caroline seemed to have come into her own in the last few years. I'd never seen her happier than she was now. She looked beautiful. She was stick-thin. Her skin was glowing. She and Ed were as much in love as any married people I had ever seen. They had a very quiet social life. They went out to an occasional dinner party given by a friend. They faithfully went to see friends who were actors in plays. They stuck pretty close to home. Caroline was really an extremely unassuming, down-to-earth person."

The same could not be said of John Jr., who at age thirty-three had movie-star looks that were a devastating blend of the Bouviers and the Kennedys. Like his sister, John struggled to be as normal as possible, but he had to contend with the invidious comparisons that people often made between him and his famous namesake. It was not easy being the son of a man who was associated with so much power—sexual as well as political—and who still came out on top in the polls of Americans' favorite presidents.

When John was growing up, Jackie sent him to see Dr. Ted Becker, a well-known adolescent psychiatrist. And when it was time for him to go away to college, Jackie passed up Harvard, JFK's alma mater, and enrolled John in Brown University, an Ivy League school that had no core requirements for graduation (John had flunked math at Andover), and where each student was allowed to design his own learning program. Brown was an innovative school.

For example, the year after John arrived at Brown, Harriet Sheridan, the dean of the college, created a special program for learning-disabled students.

After graduating from New York University Law School, John embarrassed himself (and his family) by twice failing the New York State bar exam. In the presence of friends, Jackie sought to make light of John's failure, pointing out that he had not prepared adequately for the tough exams. In private, however, she was furious, and demanded that John hire a tutor, which he did. He passed on the third try. John also had to pay $2,300 in parking tickets to clear himself of all outstanding legal judgments in order to qualify for a job as an assistant district attorney in Manhattan.

"Compared to his sister, John had a more open personality," said one of Jackie's friends. "He was more open to stimulation and to being led in wrong directions. In that regard, John was more a person after Jackie's own heart, more a loose cannon, unpredictable. John was always leaving crazy messages on his answering machine. And he always concerned Jackie, because she was worried that he could do something that could darken the family name."

Jackie summed up the difference between her children this way: "Caroline is focused and dedicated. John is spread out."

Once, while Jackie was away on a Memorial Day weekend, John threw a wild party for sixteen friends, including actress Daryl Hannah, at his mother's Martha's Vineyard house. When the maid later discovered marijuana in the mess left behind by the guests, Jackie banished John to the silo section of the detached guest cottage, which was two hundred feet away from the main house.

Jackie was less than thrilled about John's relationship with Daryl Hannah, a spacey five-foot-ten blonde from a broken home.

"Jackie called me one time, and asked me to look at that week's TV section of the Sunday New York Times," said a friend. "There was a photo of Daryl Hannah in her role as a twenty-foot-tall woman in some kind of silly science-fiction movie. It made her look like a giant amazon, or a cavewoman, and Jackie was appalled.

"Jackie told me that she would often stay in her bedroom and have dinner on a tray while John and Daryl were eating in the dining room," the friend continued. "There was a lot of tension between John and Jackie. There was something in him where he just resisted any authority.

He liked to play with fire. He was a pretty explosive guy. He went out and slammed doors. It was a very volatile relationship between mother and son in the last few years. She'd tell him, 'You can't be in acting.' She wanted him to do something of substance, something worthwhile. She worried about him, what he would do. He had never had a job except in the district attorney's office, and Jackie sure didn't get his magazine idea."

THE MAN WHO
WON ART BUCHWALD

O n Martha's Vineyard, Jackie took care of her grandchildren one afternoon a week. She liked to play with them on the beach, tossing a Frisbee back and forth. Sometimes she would let the children play by themselves while she did her yoga exercises.

She spent most of her evenings alone with Maurice Tempelsman and her family. Every so often, she would invite a special friend to come and visit her on the Vineyard. Joe Armstrong, the magazine publisher, spent a whole week with her one summer. Occasionally she dined with her son and friends at the Ocean Club. It was there that she met the singer-songwriter Carly Simon, who became one of her closest friends, and who wrote a series of four children's books for Jackie at Doubleday.

Once, when Jackie was still new to the Vineyard, and had not become quite such a loner, she agreed to go to lunch at Katharine Graham's house. Kay felt the need to gather some interesting people to entertain Jackie, so she invited the playwright Lillian Hellman; the novelist William Styron and his wife, the poet Rose Styron; and humorist Art Buchwald.

"Art called Kay back and asked her if she planned to organize a tennis game before lunch," said someone who attended the lunch. "Kay inquired why Art wanted to know. Well, it just so happened that a tennis

game with Art Buchwald had been auctioned off as a prize at the He-
brew Home for the Aged in Boston, and Art wanted to bring along the
guy who had won.

"Naturally, Kay was cool to the idea, and said, 'You know, Art, I've
invited Jackie to lunch.'

"And Art said, 'Oh, she'll like this guy who won me.'

"On the morning of the lunch, Art called Kay again, and told her
that the guy wanted to bring his daughter, too. The idea of Jackie facing
this situation folded Kay up, but there was nothing to do but proceed.
She called Jackie and told her.

"Jackie showed up alone in her car. And at lunch, the guy who had
won the tennis game with Art turned out to be atrocious. He kept bel-
lowing at his daughter. Worse, he sat down with this dazzling array of
people and acted as if it was only his just due.

"At one point, Jackie turned to the guy and said, 'Now tell me
again. How did you win Art?'

"And he said, 'I won him in an auction.'

"And you know what? Jackie thought it was funny. She was very
equal to this kind of thing. She was equal to just about anything."

A REAL
TROOPER

"Tillie's here!" Jackie called to Maurice as she passed his room on her way to answer the doorbell of her apartment. It was five in the afternoon, and she was wearing a pair of old black tights with holes in them. She swung open the door and greeted Tillie Weitzner, her tall, stately yoga teacher.

They went into Caroline's old room, whose dominant color was orange. It had been left exactly as it was when Caroline lived there before she got married. The walls were hung with fading black-and-white photos of Caroline as a young girl. Her schoolwork still filled the bookcases.

Tillie took off her jacket and began leading Jackie through a series of yoga postures. Jackie had just maneuvered a leg around her neck when Maurice suddenly poked his head in the room, said something to Tillie in her native Dutch, then disappeared.

"The yoga was quite intensive," Tillie said, "and Jackie was very good. She was incredibly disciplined, and eager to do it well. We had been working out together twice a week for sixteen years, since 1977, and I used to say, 'It's boring—always the same.' And she said, 'Oh, no, Tillie, it's never boring.'

"We worked straight for an hour, and sometimes we would talk," Tillie continued. "Once, Jackie mentioned Onassis, and said, 'We had a good time together. My kids had a good time. It was fun.' She never made any negative reference to Onassis. But she felt that she had to please Jack Kennedy and Aristotle Onassis, while she did not have to please Maurice Tempelsman. It was maybe the only relationship where she was totally herself.

"The purpose of our yoga was to work out the spine and keep it flexible. Jackie was incredibly limber. She had youthful movements, and was hardly ever sick. She was stoic, not a sissy. We did yoga at times when there was no air conditioning in the room and it was one hundred degrees, and it was unbelievably uncomfortable, and she was a real trooper.

"She was a horsewoman, which gave her strong legs. She had made several falls over the years. They could have been deadly, but she was so limber she didn't hurt herself. We talked about old-ladyhood, and she said that the only thing she wanted to be able to continue to do was ride."

SIXTEEN

TOUCHED BY THE SUN

November 1993–May 1994

A DUET
WITH DEATH

The nation was about to commemorate another anniversary of John Kennedy's assassination, an event still filled with trauma for Jackie. She had once sent John Jr. out of the country to India for the occasion, then followed close behind. This November marked the thirtieth anniversary, and Jackie decided to avoid the dreaded klieg lights of attention and escape to the horse country of Middleburg, Virginia.

"We teased each other about being fit," said Charles Whitehouse, one of her oldest friends and a man with whom she rode in Middleburg.

"I said to her, 'I get fairly out of breath, going around this course.'

"And she said, 'Well, I never get out of breath. I jog around the reservoir, as you know.'

"But when we finished, there she was at the finish line, her tongue hanging out.

"And I joked, 'Jackie, I don't think you're doing as much jogging as you pretend!'

"During one of our team point-to-point races, I entered our group for the 'best older team.' She pretended to be outraged. And I said, 'But, Jackie, we weren't born yesterday, you know.'

"In fact, she didn't think of herself as 'older,' and it was hard to believe that she had been First Lady thirty years before."

———

That same weekend, Jackie fell off Clown, her show jumper. She had taken many spills before, but this was a particularly nasty one, and she lay on the ground unconscious for thirty minutes.

"Oh my God, she must have broken her neck!" screamed a spectator.

"I'm perfectly fine," Jackie said when she finally came to.

But the emergency medics who responded to the call for help insisted on taking Jackie by ambulance to nearby Loudon Hospital Center. There, she was examined by Bunny Mellon's personal physician, who noticed that Jackie had a slight swelling in her right groin. The doctor diagnosed it as a swollen lymph node. He suspected that she had an infection, and administered antibiotics. The next morning, the swelling in her groin had diminished, and she was released from the hospital.

"She was in some pain," said Jerry Embrey, captain of the Middleburg Rescue Squad, "but I think she was in shock more than anything else. For a lady of her years to have taken such a fall and come through pretty much unscathed is almost a miracle."

A couple of weeks later, Jackie felt well enough to spend Christmas with Maurice Tempelsman and her family at her country retreat in Peapack, New Jersey. As she drove along in her BMW, she slipped a CD into the player and listened to her friend Carly Simon accompany Frank Sinatra in a selection from his latest album, *Duets*. As Sinatra crooned "Guess I'll Hang My Tears Out to Dry," Simon joined in on some of the verses of that song, then interwove part of the song "In the Wee Small Hours of the Morning."

Jackie sang along.

Over the holidays, while sailing in the Caribbean with Tempelsman, Jackie developed a persistent cough. She thought she had the flu, and asked a local doctor to prescribe antibiotics. But then she developed painful swelling in the lymph nodes in her neck, and she began to feel stabbing pains in her stomach. She cut the vacation short and flew back to New York.

There, she consulted Dr. Carolyn Agresti, a head and neck surgeon at the New York Hospital–Cornell Medical Center, who found enlarged lymph nodes in her neck and her armpit. A computerized axial tomography examination, commonly known as a CAT scan, showed that there were swollen lymph nodes in Jackie's chest and in an area deep in her abdomen known as the retroperitoneal area.

Dr. Agresti ordered a biopsy of one of the neck nodes. It revealed that Jackie had non-Hodgkin's lymphoma. A pathologist told Lawrence Altman, a medical expert who wrote for *The New York Times*, that the cells were anaplastic—that is, they were undeveloped, what doctors call "embryonic" or "primitive," indicating that the disease was highly malignant, and could spread to other parts of Jackie's body.

Maurice Tempelsman was at Jackie's side in the living room of her apartment when she broke the news to Caroline and John. Her children were devastated. They hugged her, and then they and their mother wept.

"She said, 'I feel it is a kind of hubris,' " Arthur Schlesinger recalled of his conversation with Jackie shortly after she learned of her cancer. "I have always been proud of keeping fit. I swim, and I jog, and I do my push-ups, and walk around the reservoir—and now this suddenly happens.'

"She was laughing when she said it," Schlesinger continued. "She seemed cheery and hopeful, perhaps to keep up the spirits of her friends, and her own. Chemotherapy, she added, was not too bad; she could read a book while it was administered. The doctors said that in fifty percent of cases lymphoma could be stabilized. Maybe she knew it was fatal. Maybe she didn't know at all, but even if she did, she still had hope for some other future."

Jackie may have been laughing when she spoke with Schlesinger. But she also must have been thinking of the tragic trail of destruction that had followed her for so much of her life. She had once demanded that a clergyman explain her husband's assassination. "Why, why? How could God do something like that?" she had asked. No one had an answer then. And no one had one now.

HOPE

"She came in early in January under an assumed name, and swore us to secrecy," said one of her doctors at the New York Hospital, where Jackie began receiving the first course in chemotherapy and steroid drugs. "It was a cloak-and-dagger operation. She wanted anonymity."

The same secrecy was employed when Jackie went to the Stich Radiation Therapy Center for periodic CAT scans. She arrived at seven o'clock in the morning wearing a hooded cape. While she waited outside in the car, Maurice made sure that no one was in the waiting room. When all was clear, he brought her in on his arm.

Maurice carried a small bag containing Jackie's breakfast, which she ate after the CAT scan. However, one morning she could barely wait.

"I'm really hungry," she told one of the doctor's assistants. "Would you bring Mr. Tempelsman here?"

"Gee, I hope he hasn't eaten your breakfast," the aide teased. "But I'm sure he wouldn't. He's a special person."

"Oh, yes," said Jackie, "he is."

Jackie was soon displaying the side effects of her chemo-and-drug treatment—hair loss, blotchy skin, and bloating. She was forced to wear a wig, and people noticed that there was something wrong with her. She knew that it would not be possible to hide the nature of her illness much longer, and so she instructed her old friend Nancy Tuckerman to release the news to *The New York Times*. In the story, which appeared on February 11, 1994, Nancy confirmed that Jackie was being treated for non-Hodgkin's lymphoma, but pointed out that her doctors were very optimistic.

"She's fine," Nancy said. "She goes in for routine visits, routine treatment. That's what it is."

This was no exaggeration. As Jackie's treatment progressed through four standard courses of chemotherapy, her doctors gave her consistently optimistic reports. The cancer, they said, appeared to be in remission. She was greatly encouraged by their outlook, and continued to go to her office at Doubleday three days a week.

"She enjoyed doing these books," said John Loring. "We'd laugh about it, and talk about all these titles of books we were going to do, and what the next one was.

"And one day she said, 'Oh, yes, isn't that wonderful. When we're eighty we can write *Tiffany Mushrooms*. We can just do this forever.'

"And this may sound naïve, but I honestly did not believe she was going to die. She seemed invincible. And if you knew her well, you just couldn't believe that this was a hopeless case. You believed that she would get over this, too. That she'd gotten over everything else, and she'd get over this. That this was not going to do her in."

In February, Jackie had lunch in her apartment with her friend Peter Duchin, who had just begun to write his memoirs. Duchin asked Jackie what she remembered about his father, bandleader Eddy Duchin, and his mother, Marjorie, who had died in childbirth. His question elicited a poignant recollection from Jackie, whose illness had obviously stirred some deep feelings from the past.

"I remember your parents only indirectly," Jackie told Peter Duchin. "But I'll never forget the night my mother and father both came into my bedroom all dressed up to go out. I can still smell the scent my mother wore and feel the softness of her fur coat as she leaned over to

kiss me good night. In such an excited voice she said, 'Darling, your father and I are going dancing tonight at the Central Park Casino to hear
Eddy Duchin.' I don't know why the moment has stayed with me all
these years. Perhaps because it was one of the few times I remember
seeing my parents together. It was so romantic. So hopeful."

PREPARING
FOR THE WORST

B ut the cure proved almost as bad as the disease, and Jackie aged
considerably in a matter of a few weeks. Her face grew sallow, and
more hair fell out. She wore a beret to cover her wig. Throughout the
harsh, stormy winter of 1994, she was too weak to continue her yoga ses-
sions with Tillie Weitzner. Instead, she took strolls in Central Park with
Maurice. She was familiar with the park's paths from years of jogging,
but now she was unable to venture very far before she became utterly
exhausted. She leaned on Maurice's arm for support. When she got back
to her apartment, she went to bed and took a nap.

She was puzzled. If the cancer was in remission, why didn't she feel
better? She refused to think about her own mortality. She could not believe she was going to die. Not yet, anyway. She was only sixty-four
years old. As her favorite Greek poet, Cavafy, wrote in "Ithaca,"

> But do not hurry the voyage at all.
> It is better to let it last for long years.

She encouraged Nancy Tuckerman to feed the press optimistic as-
sessments of her progress.

"She's doing so well," said Nancy. "She was coming in to a focus
group meeting today [at Doubleday], but it was called off because of the
snow. She had her grandchildren come over to see her yesterday."

Jackie was the one who did the most to promote the image of herself as a woman on the mend. She wrote dozens of sunny letters to friends, like this one to Brooke Astor:

... being with you would make me laugh. The greatest healer. This is your gift. . . . I shall look forward to our doing something together in a little while when all this first part is over. . . .

And to John Loring:

... Everything is fine. Soon we can have another festive lunch. . . .

One day in March, she experienced an alarming spell of mental confusion. She went to see an eminent neurologist at the New York Hospital, who told her that the cerebellum portion of her brain had been affected. Another type of scan, an MRI (magnetic resonance imaging), showed that the lymphoma had disappeared from her neck, chest, and abdomen, but that it had spread to the membranes that cover the brain and spinal cord.

"I can't believe this has happened," Dr. Anne Moore, Jackie's cancer specialist, said.

"Of all her doctors, no one saw this coming," said someone who was close to the case. "Her doctors were all totally shocked. They thought they had beaten the disease. The whole team was stunned when they got the results of the CAT."

A specialist in neurological diseases informed her that once cancer got into the brain it was very difficult to kill with chemotherapy. The brain had a natural barrier that kept out most chemotherapy drugs.

"Your best hope of survival is a very sophisticated procedure," the specialist told her. "We drill a hole in the skull, open a shunt, and insert a tube for feeding an anticancer drug directly into the brain. We combine that with radiation therapy to the brain and to the lower spinal cord for about a month."

It sounded horrific. But Jackie told the doctor that she was ready to try anything.

As a result of this radical treatment, she began to lose weight. Her speech slowed. And she was less alert.

"The moment I realized there was really something wrong with her was the last time we ate lunch at Le Cirque," said John Loring. "Sirio loved to send over a sampling of desserts after lunch. Jackie would never touch them. She might stick her fork in and eat two crumbs and say, 'Isn't that wonderful,' and that was the end of that.

"She was obviously not looking terribly well, but she was in a wonderful mood, and we were having a good time. And at the end of lunch, the usual four or five desserts appeared, covering the whole table.

"And she said, 'You start that one. I'm going to start this one.'

"And she actually started to eat this dessert. And I thought, Well, that's remarkable.

"So I said, 'You're not going to finish that, are you? I'm going to have the waiter take this away right this minute.'

"She said, 'If anyone tries to touch one of those, I'm going to stab them in the hand with my fork. I'm going to eat every single one of them.'

"And she did. We sat there and plowed through every single dessert on the table. It was astonishing, but it was also terrifying, because it was like she had decided that this was not going to work out, and so why not eat all the desserts on the table. She might as well eat everything if she wanted to."

On April 13, Jackie had lunch at Carly Simon's sprawling apartment on Central Park West. Carly invited three of Jackie's friends: Joe Armstrong, the publisher; Peter Duchin, the band leader; and Duchin's wife, Brooke Hayward. As an added attraction, she invited the talented documentary maker Ken Burns, who was in the process of editing his Public Broadcasting System series on the history of baseball. Carly was featured on Burns's sound track singing "Take Me Out to the Ball Game."

Jackie was fascinated by Burns's project, and she asked him a lot of questions. But he could only stay for a part of the lunch. After he left, someone asked Jackie how she was feeling.

"Only four more weeks and I'll get my life back," Jackie said, referring to what she expected to be the last course of radiation treatment.

"But," she added, reverting to the third person, "one does not look forward to a summer on the Vineyard with a bad wig."

Someone else then asked Jackie about her sister Lee.

"She stopped by for tea," Jackie said.

"Do you see her often?"

"We've only seen each other once this whole year," Jackie said. "I guess she called me so she could say that she saw me. I never could understand why Lee is so full of animosity."

On Jackie's way out, Carly handed her a big folded piece of paper.

"I wanted to give this to you," Carly said. "I wrote this for you."

It was the lyrics to a new song called "Touched by the Sun."

> Often I want to walk
> The safe side of the street
> And lull myself to sleep
> And dull my pain
> But deep down inside I know
> I've got to learn from the greats,
> Earn my right to be living
> Let my wings of desire
> Soar over the night
> I need to let them say
> "she must've been mad"
> And I, I want to get there
> I, I want to be one
> One who is touched by the sun, one who is
> touched by the sun.

The next day, Jackie collapsed with a perforated ulcer in her stomach, a complication of the steroid therapy. She was rushed to the hospital, where surgeons sewed up the hole.

When she came out of the hospital, her whole mental outlook had changed. She now seemed prepared for the worst. She reviewed her living will, which stated that doctors were not to use aggressive medical treatment to keep her alive if her condition was hopeless. She had one final discussion with her attorney Alexander Forger about her last will and testament, in which she left the bulk of her estate to her two children, and asked that they help maintain in death the privacy that she so fiercely guarded while alive. She went through the books in her library, picking out a few as gifts for friends and her doctors. And she summoned Nancy Tuckerman to her apartment.

A roaring blaze was going in the fireplace when Nancy entered the library. Jackie was sitting before the fire, an astrakhan thrown over her lap. On the table beside her were bunches of letters, all neatly bound with ribbons. These were letters that Jackie had received from famous people over the years.

Jackie unbound the letters, and read some of them to Nancy. Then, when she was finished, she tied them together again with the ribbon, and tossed them into the crackling fire.

PART OF HISTORY

"Caroline says you should come over now." The voice on the other end of the phone belonged to Marta Sgubin, the Italian housekeeper who had worked for Jackie for twenty-five years. Marta was calling Carly Simon, and she did not have to explain the reason for her urgent tone of voice.

Three days before, on Monday, May 16, Jackie had developed shaking chills, and had become disoriented. She was admitted to the New York Hospital, where she was diagnosed with pneumonia. The doctors told her that the cancer had spread to her liver and throughout the rest of her body.

"Let's try more chemotherapy," Dr. Anne Moore said.

"No," Jackie said, "I want to go home to die."

On Wednesday, she discharged herself from the hospital and returned to 1040 Fifth Avenue.

As soon as Carly Simon got the call on Thursday from Marta, she and Jackie's other great friend, Joe Armstrong, headed over to Jackie's building. There were thousands of people out on the street on Fifth Avenue, throngs, some hysterical, newsmen and ordinary people. The police were taken by surprise, and they did not have their barricades up, and people spilled off the sidewalks on both sides of Fifth Avenue into the street.

Traffic was brought to a virtual standstill. Rubberneckers were trying to see what was going on. TV was capturing the whole thing via huge satellite transmitters on the tops of trucks, and beaming it around the world.

Upstairs in Jackie's apartment, John Kennedy Jr., dressed in an impeccably tailored navy-blue suit, greeted those who had been summoned to say a last farewell to his mother. In the front hall, Caroline was sitting on a bench and softly crying. Her husband Ed Schlossberg was by her side, consoling her. In the library and roaming around the apartment were family members—Lawfords, Kennedys, and Shrivers. The guests could hear a Gregorian chant dimly coming from Jackie's bedroom.

Members of the family and a few close friends were led singly back to Jackie's bedroom, which was done in coral and peach tones, and had a fabric canopy over the bed. Except for Maurice Tempelsman and John and some other male members of the family, only women were being allowed in the bedroom. One of Jackie's last wishes had been that none but a few women friends outside the family be permitted to see her at her time of dying.

As Carly Simon entered the room, Bunny Mellon was sitting on a chair by the bed holding Jackie's hand. No one in the room seemed to be as comfortable with what was going on as Bunny. She was in her spiritual element. She had a smile of acceptance and serenity.

"You sit with her now," Bunny said to Carly.

Carly exchanged places with Bunny, and looked at Jackie.

Jackie was unconscious. She had a print scarf over her head. She was under the sheets. There was an intravenous needle in her arm, which may have been carrying morphine. There was an attempt to keep her comfortable, but there was no sense that she was taking her own life, that this was some kind of assisted suicide. There did not seem to be any rush. A visitor had the sense that Jackie was art-directing these last moments of her life in her own very dignified way.

In repose, her face was completely smooth and translucent. Her mouth was slightly open, and there was the sound of a delicate exhalation. As the Gregorian chants continued to play, various members of the family filtered in and out of the room. Everybody was talking in hushed tones.

Carly felt privileged that the family had allowed her to be in the room with Jackie. She spoke to Jackie in a low and comforting voice, telling her how much she loved her. Maurice stood at the end of the bed, observing. Bunny, not far away on a settee, was praying.

"During the time I was sitting with Jackie and holding her hand," Carly later told a friend, "I felt as though I had a direct communication with her—an experience that was deep, personal, and untainted by self-consciousness. And as I opened the door and left the room, and walked through the halls, and said good-bye to the family members, I started crying."

Outside on Fifth Avenue, Carly and Joe Armstrong were assaulted by the lights of a hundred cameras. The crowds had grown even larger on the street, and it was impossible not to feel the sudden shift from the personal to the public. It was a sensation that Jackie's friends had experienced many times before—that whether she liked it or not, she was part of history. And as Carly and Joe disappeared into the throngs of Fifth Avenue, it seemed to them that once again Jackie was being taken over by the world.

NOTES

ONE: THE SUNDOWN OF CHIVALRY

The description of Theodore H. White's trip to Hyannis Port, his heavy drinking, his telephone calls to his mother's doctor, his thoughts upon seeing John F. Kennedy's widow, and his "Camelot" interview with Jacqueline Bouvier Kennedy for *Life* magazine are drawn from a variety of primary sources, including the author's own notes of a lengthy discussion that he had with White in 1985 about that famous interview.

In addition, Ralph Graves, assistant managing editor of *Life* in 1963, provided much corroborating material. In particular, Graves recounted for the author a discussion that he had with White many years after the "Camelot" interview about some of the unpublished details, including the fact that Jackie caressed the dead President's penis in Trauma Room No. 1 at Parkland Memorial Hospital in Dallas. David Maness, *Life*'s articles editor, is the source for the description of the telephone call that White placed to *Life* from Hyannis Port.

Further documentation for the missing portions of the "Camelot" interview came from Joan Braden, who learned during her interview for the John F. Kennedy Library's oral history project with Jackie's mother, Janet Auchincloss, that Jackie was menstruating on the day of the assassination. That section of Mrs. Auchincloss's interview has been suppressed by the Kennedy Library. The fact that Jack and Jackie slept together the night before the assassination is contained in William Manchester's tapes for *The Death of a President* (Harper & Row, 1967), according to Don Congdon, William Manchester's literary agent. Those tapes, which Manchester donated to the Kennedy Library, will not be available to the public until 2063.

Other details of the "Camelot" interview are taken from White's handwritten notes of his interview with Jackie. White donated these notes, known as the "Camelot Documents," to the Kennedy Library in 1969, but they were not available to researchers until May 1995, one year after Jackie's death.

Books that were used in this section include Theodore White's autobiography, *In Search of History* (Warner Books, 1978), and Joyce Hoffman's *Theodore H. White and Journalism as Illusion* (University of Missouri Press, 1995), which aided the author in his understanding of the Camelot myth and the ways in which Theodore White and Jackie collaborated in creating it.

The author conducted interviews with Theodore White's former wife, Nancy Hechtor, and his children, David and Hayden.

Descriptions of the weather in New York and Hyannis on November 29, 1963, were drawn from *The New York Times*, November 30, 1963.

TWO: BEYOND HER WILDEST DREAMS

The account of Jackie's Thanksgiving weekend in Hyannis Port, and how she coped with Caroline's reaction to her father's death, are drawn from several published sources: Rita Dallas's *The Kennedy Case* (G. P. Putnam's Sons, 1973), a memoir written with Jeanira Ratcliffe by the head nurse to Joseph P. Kennedy during the last eight years of his life; Robert Curran's *The Kennedy Women* (Lancer Books, 1964); Lester David's *Jacqueline Kennedy Onassis* (Birch Lane Press, 1994); C. David Heymann's *A Woman Named Jackie* (Lyle Stuart, 1989); and Marianne Means's *The Woman in the White House* (Random House, 1963).

Caroline's first words are quoted in *A Life in Pictures: Remembering Jackie* (*Life*, special commemorative edition, July 15, 1994).

The story about the white shark game that John F. Kennedy made up to amuse his daughter, Caroline, was recounted by Janet Auchincloss in her oral history housed at the John F. Kennedy Library.

The author first learned of Jackie's consultation with the psychoanalyst Erik Erikson during an interview with Peter Beard. The description of Jackie's consultation with Erikson is drawn chiefly from interviews conducted by the author and a research assistant with Erik Erikson's biographer, Dr. Lawrence Friedman; Erikson's children, Kai Erikson and Sue Erikson Bloland; Margaret Brenman-Gibson, a close colleague of Erikson's; and Richard Goodwin.

Other published sources for the chapter on Erik Erikson include "Configurations in Play," from Erik Erikson's *A Way of Looking at Things* (W. W. Norton, 1987); *Current Biography*; *History & Theory Magazine* (May 1, 1995); a *New Yorker* profile (1970); *Newsweek* (May 23, 1994); and *The New York Times* (May 13, 1994).

Two other excellent sources for details on Erikson's life and work were Margaret Brenman-Gibson's film *Erik Erikson: A Life's Work* and Dr. Richard Evans's film *Professor Erik Erikson*.

The scene of Jackie refusing to confess to a priest after JFK's death was recounted in Heymann's *A Woman Named Jackie*. Descriptions of the birthday parties Jackie gave Caroline and John Jr. in the White House were drawn from Heymann and from Wendy Leigh's *Prince Charming* (Dutton, 1993). Bunny Mellon's calling Jackie "a witch" is recounted in Wayne Koestenbaum's *Jackie under My Skin* (Farrar, Straus & Giroux, 1995).

Much of the material about Jackie's relationship with her father, John Vernou Bouvier III; her mother, Janet Auchincloss; and her *Vogue* Prix de Paris entry is derived from the author's previous book, *All Too Human* (Pocket Books, 1996). See the notes in that book, especially the notes to chapters two and three.

Additional interviews were conducted with Robin Duke and Charles Whitehouse.

THREE: NO PLACE TO GO

The account of Jackie and her children arriving back in Washington from Thanksgiving weekend in Hyannis Port is drawn from the *Boston Herald*, December 2, 1963.

Details of the changeover of the Oval Office after JFK's assassination are drawn from William Manchester's *The Death of a President* (Harper & Row, 1967) and Wendy Leigh's *Prince Charming* (Dutton, 1993). In interviews with the author, Horace Busby recalled the reactions of Harry Truman and the White House female press corps, and Jack Valenti explained how LBJ took pains not to look like a usurper. Accounts of this transition period are also drawn from the oral histories of Jacqueline Kennedy Onassis and Liz Carpenter, housed in the Lyndon Baines Johnson Library, and from Mary Barelli Gallagher's memoir, *My Life with Jacqueline Kennedy* (David McKay, 1969).

The original memo Jackie sent to Lady Bird Johnson from Hyannis Port, dated Sunday, December 12, 1963, is housed in the Lyndon Baines Johnson Library.

The description of Marie Harriman was drawn from an interview with Peter Duchin.

Jackie's family background and her life at Merrywood are described in the author's first Kennedy biography, *All Too Human* (Pocket Books, 1996). Nina Auchincloss Straight recalls how Jackie's bedroom in Hyannis Port copied her beloved Merrywood bedroom in J. C. Suares and J. Spencer Beck's *Uncommon Grace* (Thomasson-Grant, 1994).

"I suppose I was in a state of shock" is recounted in Jacqueline Kennedy Onassis's oral history in the Lyndon Baines Johnson Library.

JFK funeral preparations are described in Angier Biddle Duke's papers at the Duke University Library Private Collections in Durham, North Carolina.

The history of Lincoln and the burial of his children in Arlington and elsewhere is in *The New York Times*, December 5, 1963.

The account of Janet Auchincloss's involvement in the interment and reinterment of Jackie's two children beside their father in Arlington National Cemetery is drawn from the author's interviews with Janet's son, James Auchincloss, and with Charles Hayes, the son of John F. Hayes Jr., the funeral director of Hayes-O'Neill funeral home in Newport at that time.

Descriptions of Ed Zimny and the plane he piloted are drawn from Joe McGuinness's *The Last Brother* (Simon & Schuster, 1993). Cardinal Cushing talks about the part he played in the interment of Patrick Bouvier Kennedy in John Henry Cutler's *Cardinal Cushing of Boston* (Hawthorn Books, 1970).

Information on the relationship between venereal infections and infertility is drawn from the author's interview with Dr. Atilla Toth, a specialist in the field.

Janet Auchincloss's attitude toward Catholic prelates is derived from the author's interview with James Auchincloss.

"What could I have done? How could I have changed it?" comes from a conversation that Jackie had with Kitty Carlisle Hart, who recounted it to the author.

Other details of the Arlington reinterment are drawn from *The New York Times*, December 5, 1963.

FOUR: THE FREAK OF N STREET

The interior designer Billy Baldwin recounted his conversation with Jacqueline Kennedy in Georgetown in his memoir *Billy Baldwin Remembers* (Harcourt Brace Jovanovich, 1974).

"The smaller the better" is a quote from a previously unpublished letter from Jackie to Diana Vreeland, which is included in a private collection of letters that was offered for sale by Ursus Rare Books in New York City.

Benjamin Bradlee quoted the letter from Jackie to him and his then wife Tony in his memoir, *A Good Life* (Simon & Schuster, 1995).

In an interview with the author, Robert McNamara described the scene of his giving a portrait of JFK to Jackie after the assassination.

Details of the evening Jackie spent with Marlon Brando, her sister Lee, and George Englund were provided by a close friend of Brando's who wishes to remain anonymous.

The English words to the song "Danke Schoen" were written by Kurt Schwabach and Milt Gabler; the music was written by Bert Kaempfert. The song was recorded by Wayne Newton on the Capitol label.

Information on Clint Hill as a U.S. Secret Service agent was gleaned from a number of interviews by the author and his research assistants with Ham Brown, executive director of the Association of Former Secret Service Agents, and former U.S.S.S. agents Larry Newman, Paul Landis, Bill Livingood, and Frank Yeager.

Details on Clint Hill's years at Concordia College were kindly provided by Sharon Hoverton, Concordia College archivist, and college classmates Rudy Moe, Don Ylvisaker, and Hugh Kaste.

Mike Wallace's December 7, 1975, *Sixty Minutes* interview with Clint Hill, "Secret Agent No. 9," was kindly provided by Don Hewitt, executive producer of *Sixty Minutes*.

In 1978 the United States Secret Service commissioned a National Institute of Mental Health study of the effects of stress on S.S. agents. Although Dr. Frank Ochberg, associate director of the National Institute of Mental Health at the time, was not able to divulge any information about this confidential report, he was helpful in describing the type of post-traumatic stress disorder that an agent such as Clint Hill might have suffered after JFK's assassination.

Further background information on Clint Hill, stress, and the U.S. Secret Service was gleaned from a number of published sources, including George Rush's *Confessions of an Ex-Secret Service Agent* (Donald I. Fine, 1988), Dennis V. McCarthy's *Protecting the President* (William Morrow, 1985), and Rufus Youngblood's *20 Years in the Secret Service* (Simon & Schuster, 1973).

Periodical sources included the London *Mail on Sunday*, September 26, 1993; *U.S. News & World Report*, December 2 and December 23, 1963; *Newsweek*, December 9, 1963; and *Time*, October 6, 1975.

Information about Secret Service agents drinking the night before the assassination was gleaned from U.S.S.S. Chief Rowley's testimony before the Warren

Commission; Clint Hill's testimony was also available in *The Warren Report* (Associated Press, 1964).

The Associated Press also supplied photos of Clint Hill and other Secret Service agents.

Details on Jackie and Clint Hill's visit to the Jockey Club came from the author's interview with an eyewitness who wishes to remain anonymous. Further details on the Jockey Club itself came from interviews with Jack Scarella, former maître d', and Louise Gore, former owner of the Jockey Club. Background description of the Jockey Club was also gleaned from the *Washington Times*, January 8, 1991, and November 11, 1993, and from the January 1989 issue of *Cosmopolitan*.

FIVE: A GATHERING OF THE WRECKAGE

The narrative of Jackie's trip to Antigua is based on interviews with two eyewitnesses: Charles "Chuck" Spalding, an intimate of the Kennedys, and Paul Leonard, who has long served as Rachel Lambert "Bunny" Mellon's primary interior decorator.

Background on Bunny Mellon and her relationship with Jackie was gleaned from interviews by the author and his research assistants with Hélenè Arpels, Robin Duke, Peter Duchin, Mark Hampton, Kitty Carlisle Hart, John Loring, and I. M. Pei, and with others, who wish to remain anonymous.

Bunny Mellon is quoted as saying, "I remember kneeling . . ." in William Manchester's *The Death of a President* (Harper & Row, 1967).

In an interview with the author, Paul Leonard recalled that "Mrs. Smith" was the Secret Service code name used for Jackie in Antigua.

General background on Antigua and the Mellon property was gleaned from interviews with Barrie Pickering, an island resident; Victor Carmichael of the Antigua and Barbuda Tourist Board; and Jack Johnson of Johnson Construction in Antigua.

Principal published sources on Bunny Mellon and the Mellon family include a memoir by Bunny's father, Gerard Barnes Lambert, *All Out of Step* (Doubleday, 1956), Katharine Graham's *Personal Memoir* (Random House, 1997), David E. Koskoff's *The Mellons* (T. Y. Crowell, 1978), Billy Baldwin and Michael Gardine's *Billy Baldwin* (Little, Brown, 1985), and Paul Mellon's *Reflections in a Silver Spoon*, written with John Baskett (William Morrow, 1992).

Several articles on Paul and Bunny Mellon were particularly helpful: "Paul Mellon" in *Town & Country*, May 1978; "A Cool Mellon" in *Vanity Fair*, April 1992; and "A Most Generous Gentleman" in *Town & Country*, December 1994. Other articles appeared in the *Chicago Tribune*, December 14, 1990; *The Washington Post*, April 7, 1992; the *Washington Times*, January 2, 1997; *The Washington Post*, February 23, 1983; and Paula Dietz's "The Private World of a Great Gardener," *The New York Times*, June 3, 1982.

Principal published sources on the Mellons and Antigua include *Antigua and Barbuda: A Little Bit of Paradise* and articles in *Vogue*, May 1963; *Holiday*, March 1962; and *House Beautiful*, December 1959.

The Drew Pearson article about the possible marriage of Lee Radziwill and Aristotle Onassis was referred to in several published sources including Diana DuBois's *In Her Sister's Shadow* (Little, Brown, 1995), and Arianna Stassinopoulos's *Maria Callas* (Simon & Schuster, 1981).

The story recounted in "As Close as You Can Get," detailing events that occurred in Antigua and the relationship between Jackie and Robert F. Kennedy, came from interviews with Robert Kennedy's biographer James Hilty, and with Chuck Spalding, Charles Bartlett, William Manchester, Richard Goodwin, Joan Braden, Helen Thomas, and Lee Radziwill's biographer Diana DuBois.

"I'd read it quite a lot before" was from a June 2, 1976, tape-recorded interview with Jackie by Arthur M. Schlesinger Jr., which was quoted in his book *Robert Kennedy and His Times* (Houghton Mifflin, 1978). The Schlesinger book is also the source for the quote from Aeschylus' *Agamemnon*, which was a favorite of RFK's. Bobby's reliance on the wisdom of ancient Greek literature to deal with his grief is recounted in James Hilty's *Robert Kennedy* (Temple University Press, 1997). It was also recounted in Charles Spalding's oral history housed at the John F. Kennedy Library.

Pierre Salinger's recollection of Robert Kennedy's manic football game was drawn from Lester and Irene David's *Bobby Kennedy* (Dodd, Mead, 1986) and Peter Collier and David Horowitz's *The Kennedys* (Summit Books, 1984).

Robert Kennedy's statement "I thought it would be me" is recounted in Hilty's RFK biography.

Other published sources for this section include Lester David's *Jacqueline Kennedy Onassis* (Birch Lane Press, 1994), C. David Heymann's *A Woman Named Jackie* (Lyle Stuart, 1989), Frieda Kramer's *Jackie* (Award Books, 1975), and Edward DeBlasio's "The Friendship That Saved Two Lives," *Pageant*, July 1964.

Principal published sources for the relationship between RFK and LBJ include Heymann's *A Woman Named Jackie*, Michael R. Beschloss's *Taking Charge* (Simon & Schuster, 1997), Jerry Oppenheimer's *The Other Mrs. Kennedy* (St. Martin's Press, 1994), William vanden Heuvel and Milton Gwirtzman's *On His Own* (Doubleday, 1970), and Ronald Steel's *Walter Lippmann and the American Century* (Little, Brown, 1980).

Jackie talks about the RFK–LBJ relationship in her oral history housed in the Lyndon Baines Johnson Library in Texas.

Further details on the relationship between Jackie and Bobby were drawn from interviews with Charles Bartlett, Joan Braden, Paul "Red" Fay, James Hilty, and William Manchester.

The description of RFK as "in a trance" after the assassination is drawn from William Manchester's *Controversy and Other Essays in Journalism* (Little, Brown, 1976).

Murray Kempton's verdict on the relationship between RFK and JFK is drawn from Laurence Leamer's *The Kennedy Women* (Villard Books, 1994).

SIX: AN UNERRING SENSE OF STARDOM

The narrative in the "Mister Manchester" section is derived primarily from the author's interview with Don Congdon, William Manchester's literary agent, and from William Manchester's *Controversy and Other Essays in Journalism* (Little, Brown, 1976).

In "Disguises and Smiles," the description of Jackie's apartment at 1040 Fifth Avenue is drawn from the author's eyewitness notes based on his personal visits there on two separate occasions, and from articles that appeared in *The Washington Post*, May 26, 1994, and in *House Beautiful*, September 1994. Other published sources include Lester David's *Jacqueline Kennedy Onassis* (Birch Lane Press, 1994) and Frieda Kramer's *Jackie* (Award Books, 1975).

Nancy Tuckerman's stories about going apartment-hunting with Jackie disguised as a nanny, and of the day Jackie moved into 1040 Fifth Avenue, are contained in "A Personal Reminiscence" from Sotheby's 1996 auction catalog, *The Estate of Jacqueline Kennedy Onassis*.

Jackie's letter to Jim Bishop dated September 17, 1964, appears in Manchester's *Controversy and Other Essays in Journalism*.

Details about Jackie's contributions to Robert Kennedy's Senate campaign are recounted in Jerry Oppenheimer's biography of Ethel Kennedy, *The Other Mrs. Kennedy* (St. Martin's Press, 1994).

The background information on Jackie and Oliver Smith that forms the basis for "Lessons in Self-Improvement" was derived from numerous interviews by the author and a research assistant with Richard D'Arcy, Smith's friend and companion; Lloyd Burlingame, former chair of the New York University Tisch School Department of Design, who co-taught an advanced stage design class with Smith for twenty-two years; Aileen Mehle, the columnist "Suzy"; and Kitty Carlisle Hart.

Principal published sources include Lloyd Burlingame's "The Design Department of the Tisch School of Arts: A Chronology from the Perspective of the Chair 1971–1996"; "Remembering Oliver," a tribute to Oliver Smith compiled by American Ballet Theatre; Gerald Clarke's *Capote* (Simon & Schuster, 1988); Truman Capote's *Answered Prayers* (Random House, 1987); Charles Payne's *American Ballet Theatre* (Knopf, 1978); Bob Colacello's *Holy Terror* (HarperCollins, 1990); Charles Kaiser's *The Gay Metropolis* (Houghton Mifflin, 1997); George Plimpton's *Truman Capote* (Doubleday, 1997); Oliver Smith's obituary, *The New York Times*, January 25, 1994; and a series of five articles by Liz Smith titled "Jackie Comes Off Her Pedestal," which appeared first in the *New York World Journal Tribune* (December 1966–January 1967) and later in *Cosmopolitan*.

The details of Jackie and her sister Lee Radziwill's sibling rivalry that appear in "You Can't Know One without the Other" are derived from a series of interviews by the author with Kitty Carlisle Hart. The party is described in Charlotte Curtis's "The Radziwills Give a 'Teeny, Tiny Party'—for 100 Guests," *The New York Times*, April 21, 1965. Lee's apartment is also described in Mark Hampton's *Legendary Decorators of the Twentieth Century* (Doubleday, 1992), a book that was edited by Jackie.

Primary published sources for this section include George Carpozi's *The Hidden Side of Jacqueline Kennedy* (Pyramid Books, 1967); Diana DuBois's *In Her Sister's Shadow* (Little, Brown, 1995); C. David Heymann's *A Woman Named Jackie* (Lyle Stuart, 1989); Irving Shulman's *"Jackie"!* (Trident Press, 1970); the aforementioned Liz Smith articles; Laura Bergquist's "Jacqueline Kennedy Goes Public," *Look*, March 22, 1966; and Aileen Mehle's "The Jackie I Knew," *Good Housekeeping*, September 1994.

Jackie's explanation of why she did not vote in the 1964 election comes from the Jacqueline Onassis oral history located in the Lyndon Baines Johnson Library.

The material included in "Audition" was derived primarily from the author's interviews with Kitty Carlisle Hart. Primary published sources include Clarke's *Capote* and DuBois's *In Her Sister's Shadow*.

The story about Caroline's mouse was told by Teresa Gorman in the London *Mail on Sunday*, May 22, 1994.

SEVEN: THE OTHER JACK

The story of Jackie's romantic involvement with the architect John Carl Warnecke comes from a series of extended interviews that the author conducted with Mr. Warnecke himself. Other interviews were conducted with Marion Javits, Robin Duke, Paul Goldberger, and several sources who wish to remain anonymous.

Details of Jack Warnecke's involvement with JFK's memorial and with Lafayette Square come from a number of articles: Benjamin Forgey's "The Well-Rounded Square; Lafayette, Absorbing Change with Grace," *The Washington Post*, January 29, 1994; "John Carl Warnecke: An Athletic Architect," from the *New York Times* "Man in the News" column, October 7, 1964; Ada Louise Huxtable's "Design Dilemma: The Kennedy Grave," in *The New York Times*, November 29, 1964; and Sarah Booth Conroy's "Preserving Lafayette Square," in *The Washington Post*, May 26, 1994.

The material in "Dumping the Secret Service" and "A Cottage in the Woods" comes from the author's extensive interviews with John Carl Warnecke.

Details of Jackie's arrival in Hawaii were drawn from "4,000 Turn Out at Airport to Greet Jackie, Children," from the *Honolulu Advertiser*, June 6, 1966.

Information about Jackie's frame of mind at this time comes from Liz Smith's series of articles entitled "Jackie Comes Off Her Pedestal," which appeared in the *New York World Journal Tribune* in December 1966–January 1967.

Descriptions of the party Jackie threw for John Kenneth Galbraith come from an interview with William vanden Heuvel and an article in *Time*, October 1, 1965.

Details about Jackie's visit to Spain were derived from newspaper clippings and letters written by Jackie to Angier Biddle Duke when he was ambassador to Spain, which are housed in the Angier B. Duke special collections, William R. Perkins Library, Duke University.

Jackie calls Angier Biddle Duke her "knight in armor" in an undated letter (later marked "probably April 1966") from Jackie to Duke, which is contained in the A.B. Duke files at Duke University.

Primary published sources for the section on Jackie in Spain come from George Carpozi's *The Hidden Side of Jacqueline Kennedy* (Pyramid Books, 1967); *Time* magazine, April 29, 1966; and numerous newspaper articles, including *The Washington Post*, April 4, 1966; *The New York Times*, April 20, 1966; *Times-Post Services*, March 28, 1966; and *The Record American*, Boston, Massachusetts, April 13, 1966.

The narrative of Jackie's visit to Hawaii is drawn primarily from interviews with John Carl Warnecke; with Henry J. Kaiser's son Michael Kaiser and Michael's wife, Betsy Kaiser; and with Richard Goodwin.

Primary published sources for this section include James Spada's *Peter Lawford* (Bantam, 1991) and a number of articles that appeared in June and July of 1966 in *The New York Times*, the *Honolulu Advertiser*, and the *Star-Bulletin*.

Jackie's letter to the editors of the *Honolulu Advertiser* and the *Star-Bulletin*, thanking them for preserving her privacy during her Hawaiian vacation, appears in "Jackie Thanks Hawaii for Aloha," the *Honolulu Advertiser*, July 24, 1966.

Mrs. Henry J. Kaiser's story about John Kennedy Jr. appears in "John-John Kennedy Now Just Plain John," *The New York Times*, July 24, 1966.

The words to the song "Tiny Bubbles in the Wine" were written by Leon Pober; the music was composed by Leon Pober.

EIGHT: TARNISHED HALO

Details in the section "Out of Control" about Mike Cowles's trip to Hyannis Port to meet with Jackie about the *Look* serialization of Manchester's book come from an interview with William Attwood, *Look* editor in chief at the time. The interview is housed in the Columbia University Oral History Project. Published sources for this section include Stephen Birmingham's *Jacqueline Bouvier Kennedy Onassis* (Grosset & Dunlap, 1978) and George Carpozi's *The Hidden Side of Jacqueline Kennedy* (Pyramid Books, 1967).

William Manchester recounted the details in "Us Against Them" in his book *Controversy and Other Essays in Journalism* (Little, Brown, 1976).

The section "Taking Care of Business" is drawn from a series of interviews by the author with John Carl Warnecke.

Lloyd Shearer's article "Jackie Kennedy, World's Most Eligible Widow—Will She Marry Again?" appeared in *Parade*, December 4, 1966.

Published sources for "Acting on Her Own" include John Corry's *The Manchester Affair* (G. P. Putnam's Sons, 1967) and Cass Canfield's *Up and Down and Around* (Harper & Row, 1971). Periodical sources include James Reston's "The Death of Camelot" column, *The New York Times*, December 18, 1966, and Theodore White's letter to the editor, *The New York Times*, December 19, 1966.

The letters between Jackie and LBJ regarding the Manchester affair are housed in the Lyndon Baines Johnson Library.

The narrative of Jackie's first trip on the *Christina* was derived in part from the author's interview with Robert White, premier collector of Kennedy memorabilia. Mr. White shared details of unpublished memos and letters by both JFK and Jackie from this time period. Other material that appears in the section "An Unabashed Love Letter" appeared in the author's previous book, *All Too Human* (Pocket Books, 1996).

Primary published sources used in compiling the story of Aristotle Onassis's previous life and his entry into Jackie's include Frank Brady's *Onassis* (Prentice-Hall, 1977); Christian Cafarakis's *The Fabulous Onassis* (William Morrow, 1972); L. J. Davis's *Onassis* (St. Martin's Press, 1986); Nigel Dempster's *Heiress* (Grove Weidenfeld, 1989); Peter Evans's *Ari* (Summit Books, 1986); *Aristotle Onassis* (Lippincott, 1977), written by Nicholas Fraser et al.; Willi Frischauer's *Onassis* (Meredith Press, 1968); Doris Lilly's *Those Fabulous Greeks* (Cowles, 1970); and William Wright's *All the Pain That Money Can Buy* (Simon & Schuster, 1991).

The narrative in the section "Typical Jackie" was derived from a published interview with a friend of the Onassis family who wished to remain anonymous.

NINE: FALLEN IDOL

The portrait of Jackie and Ari's courtship is drawn chiefly from extensive interviews that were conducted by the author during several trips to Greece. Among those interviewed were Costa Anastassiadis, captain of the yacht *Christina*; Stefanos Daroussos, the yacht's chief engineer; Niki Goulandris, a close personal friend of Jackie's; and Stelio Papadimitriou, Onassis's second-in-command.

An interview with Robert McNamara was the source for the reactions of André Meyer and McNamara to the marriage of Jackie and Ari.

Primary published sources for this chapter include Frank Brady's *Onassis* (Prentice-Hall, 1977), Lester David's *Jacqueline Kennedy Onassis* (Birch Lane Press, 1994), John H. Davis's *The Bouviers* (Farrar, Straus & Giroux, 1969), Peter Evans's *Ari* (Summit Books, 1986), Frieda Kramer's *Jackie* (Award Books 1975), Jerry Oppenheimer's *The Other Mrs. Kennedy* (St. Martin's Press, 1994), Jean Stein and George Plimpton's *American Journey* (Harcourt Brace Jovanovich, 1970), and William Wright's *All the Pain That Money Can Buy* (Simon & Schuster, 1991).

Direct quotes from Vivian Crespi, Roswell Gilpatric, Karl Katz, and Lady Bird Johnson appear in Carl Sferrazza Anthony's *As We Remember Her* (HarperCollins, 1997).

The words to the song "Little Green Apples" were written by Bobby Russell; the music was written by Bobby Russell.

Details about Christina and Alexander Onassis in the section "The Perfect Match," about the Onassis wedding in the section "Esiah's Dance," and about the reception and honeymoon in the section "A Special Surprise" were drawn from anonymous sources and from newspaper articles published at the time.

The account of the prenuptial negotiations and final agreement between Jackie and Ari comes from extensive interviews with Stelio Papadimitriou.

TEN: THE PEONIES OF GREECE

In order to re-create Jackie's life on Skorpios the author relied on numerous interviews with eyewitnesses such as Costa Anastassiadis, captain of the yacht *Christina*; Stefanos Daroussos, chief engineer of the *Christina*; Niki Goulandris, Jackie's good friend; and Paul Leonard, Jackie's decorator on Skorpios.

Primary published sources for life on Skorpios include Carl Sferrazza Anthony's *As We Remember Her* (HarperCollins, 1997), Billy Baldwin's *Billy Baldwin Remembers* (Harcourt Brace Jovanovich, 1974), Peter Evans's *Ari* (Summit Books, 1986), *Aristotle Onassis* by Nicholas Fraser et al. (Lippincott, 1977), C. David Heymann's *A Woman Named Jackie* (Lyle Stuart, 1989), and Kitty Kelley's *Jackie Oh!* (Lyle Stuart, 1979).

Jackie's thoughts about her life on Skorpios in "The Journey to Ithaca" section are contained in an unpublished letter from Jackie to Niki Goulandris dated August 25, 1970, which was kindly provided to the author by Mrs. Goulandris.

The thoughts on Jackie and Ari's relationship attributed to Alexis Miotis, director of the Greek National Theater, appear in Heymann's *A Woman Named Jackie.*

Jackie's letter to Arthur M. Schlesinger Jr. describing the Greek character appears in Anthony's *As We Remember Her.*

C. P. Cavafy's poem "Ithaca" is published in *The Complete Poems of Cavafy* (Harvest Books/Harcourt Brace Jovanovich, 1989).

The narrative about the cabal against Jackie, and Onassis's renewed relationship with Maria Callas, is drawn from interviews with Stelio Papadimitriou as well as a number of published sources, including Frank Brady's *Onassis* (Prentice-Hall, 1977), Lester David's *Jacqueline Kennedy Onassis* (Birch Lane Press, 1994), L. J. Davis's *Onassis* (St. Martin's Press, 1986), Nigel Dempster's *Heiress* (Grove Weidenfeld, 1989), Evans's *Ari*, *Aristotle Onassis* by Fraser et al., Willi Frischauer's *Onassis* (Meredith Press, 1968), Heymann's *A Woman Named Jackie*, Kelley's *Jackie Oh!*, Doris Lilly's *Those Fabulous Greeks* (Cowles, 1970), and Arianna Stassinopoulos's *Maria Callas* (Simon & Schuster, 1981).

The narrative in the section "An Even Dozen" is derived from interviews with Hélenè Arpels.

ELEVEN: THE FALL OF THE HOUSE OF ATREUS

Kitty Carlisle Hart's story about Jackie visiting a veterans' hospital is drawn from Carl Sferrazza Anthony's As We Remember Her (HarperCollins, 1997), and from the author's own interview with Mrs. Hart.

The narrative of Jackie and Ari's dinner at the Coach House restaurant is drawn from an interview with an American friend of the Onassis couple who wishes to remain anonymous.

Details of Jackie's consultation with a heart specialist are drawn from the author's interview with Dr. Isadore Rosenfeld. Information about using Resusi-Annie to learn CPR techniques was provided by Dr. Laurence Inra and Eugene Lucchese, emergency medical service supervisor at the New York Hospital.

Primary published sources include Anthony's As We Remember Her, Stephen Birmingham's Jacqueline Bouvier Kennedy Onassis (Grosset & Dunlap, 1978), Frank Brady's Onassis (Prentice-Hall, 1977), Peter Duchin's Ghost of a Chance (Random House, 1996), Peter Evans's Ari (Summit Books, 1986), C. David Heymann's A Woman Named Jackie (Lyle Stuart, 1989), Kitty Kelley's Jackie Oh! (Lyle Stuart, 1979), Arianna Stassinopoulos's Maria Callas (Simon & Schuster, 1981), and William Wright's All the Pain That Money Can Buy (Simon & Schuster, 1991).

The narrative of Ari's remorse and guilt over Alexander's death in the section "Hubris" was drawn from the author's interviews with Stelio Papadimitriou and Peter Duchin.

TWELVE: LOVE, DEATH, AND MONEY

Material for this section, which describes the turmoil in Ari and Jackie's marriage after Alexander's death, Ari's illness and death, and Christina's settlement with Jackie of the disputed will, is drawn from interviews with Stelio Papadimitriou, Eleanor Lambert, Peter Beard, Jack Anderson, Les Whitten, Bill Fugazy, Tom Bolan, Dr. Isadore Rosenfeld, Niki Goulandris, and David Banfield.

The narrative of Jackie and Ari's visit to the Guinness home in Lantana, Florida, is drawn from an article by Aileen Mehle in Good Housekeeping, September 1994.

Primary published sources for the background on Loel and Gloria Guinness are Sally Bedell Smith's Reflected Glory (Simon & Schuster, 1996), Annette Tapert and Diana Edkins's The Power of Style (Crown, 1994), and Veronique Vienne's "In a Class by Themselves: Fourteen Women of Style," Town & Country, November 1994.

The description of the Guinness house was drawn from All Out of Step (Doubleday, 1956) by Bunny Mellon's father, Gerard Lambert, who designed and built the house.

Information about myasthenia gravis came from an article by James F. Howard Jr., M.D., professor of neurology, University of North Carolina at Chapel Hill, published on the Myasthenia Gravis Foundation Homepage.

Onassis's illness and treatment were reported in The New York Times, November 12, 1974; December 20, 1974; and February 5, 6, 7, 11, 13, and 20, 1975. His death was reported in *The New York Times*, March 16 and 17, 1975. Steven V. Roberts's article on Onassis's funeral appeared in *The New York Times*, March 19, 1975.

The material in "A Sweeping Indictment" is drawn primarily from interviews with Jack Anderson and Les Whitten. Mr. Anderson provided the author with copies of his "Merry-Go-Round" articles on Jackie's spending habits, a series of United Feature Syndicate columns dated April 14–April 17, 1975. Les Whitten's handwritten and typewritten notes were provided to the author by Marie Boltz, assistant, Lehigh University Special Collections.

John Corry's article about the planned Onassis divorce appeared in *The New York Times*, April 12, 1975; details of the will on June 8, 1975; and Nicholas Gage's article about the settlement between Christina and Jackie on September 20, 1977.

Nude photos of Jackie were published only in Europe until *Hustler* magazine broke the story in the United States, according to John Heidenry's *What Wild Ecstasy* (Simon & Schuster, 1997).

The narrative of Judith Campbell Exner's appearance before the Senate Select Committee on Intelligence Operations, chaired by Frank Church, was drawn from the following periodicals: "Church Denies Cover-Up of a Kennedy Friendship," *The New York Times*, December 16, 1975; "Kennedy Friend Denies Plot Role," *The New York Times*, December 18, 1975; "Addendum to the Kennedy Years," *The New York Times*, December 21, 1975; William Safire's "Murder Most Foul" column, *The New York Times*, December 22, 1975; "A Shadow over Camelot," *Newsweek*, December 29, 1975; "Closets of Camelot," *Newsweek*, January 19, 1976; Lewis Lapham's "The King's Pleasure," *Harper's*, March 1976; "Kennedys: More Pillow Talk," *Newsweek*, March 1, 1976; and Nicholas Gage's "Link of Kennedy Friend to Mafia Still a Puzzle," *The New York Times*, April 12, 1976.

Details of Jackie's dealings with Christina and Artemis were drawn from interviews with Stelio Papadimitriou and anonymous sources.

Principal published sources include Stephen Birmingham's *Jacqueline Bouvier Kennedy Onassis* (Grosset & Dunlap, 1978); Frank Brady's *Onassis* (Prentice-Hall, 1977); Bob Colacello's *Holy Terror* (HarperCollins, 1990); Lester David's *Jacqueline Kennedy Onassis* (Birch Lane Press, 1994); L. J. Davis's *Onassis* (St. Martin's Press, 1986); Nigel Dempster's *Heiress* (Grove Weidenfeld, 1989); Peter Evans's *Ari* (Summit Books, 1986); *Aristotle Onassis* by Nicholas Fraser et al. (Lippincott, 1977); C. David Heymann's *A Woman Named Jackie* (Lyle Stuart, 1989); Kitty Kelley's *Jackie Oh!* (Lyle Stuart, 1979); Frieda Kramer's *Jackie* (Grossett & Dunlap, 1979); Laurence Leamer's *The Kennedy Women* (Villard Books, 1994); Wendy Leigh's *Prince Charming* (Dutton, 1993); Arianna Stassinopoulos's *Maria Callas* (Simon & Schuster, 1981); and William Wright's *All the Pain That Money Can Buy* (Simon & Schuster, 1991).

THIRTEEN: THE MYSTERIOUS M. T.

The account of Maurice Tempelsman's background, business dealings, and developing relationship with Jackie was drawn from interviews with a number of friends and business associates of Tempelsman's who wish to remain anonymous. In addition the author interviewed Hélenè Arpels; Arnaud de Borchgrave; Frank Carlucci, former political officer at the U.S. Embassy in Kinshasa, Congo, former deputy director of the CIA, and former secretary of defense; Larry Devlin, former CIA station chief in Kinshasa; Roy Furmark; Jeffrey Gartner, dean of the Yale Business School; Brendan Gill; Brandon

Grove, U.S. ambassador to Zaire, 1984–1987; Robert Oakley, U.S. ambassador to Zaire, 1979–1982; Michael Schatzberg, author of a book on Mobutu; Sue Schmidt; Alex Shoumatoff; Adlai Stevenson Jr.; Jack Valenti; Dr. Herbert Weiss, director of Central Africa Project, Columbia University; and Melissa Wells, U.S. consulate general of Brazil, former U.S. ambassador to Zaire.

In an interview with the author, Rabbi Arthur Schneier discussed in general terms the legal requirements of a Jewish divorce or "get."

The author also drew on accounts in periodicals for his description of Tempelsman's relationship with Jackie. These include the author's own cover story in the August 1989 issue of *Vanity Fair* titled "Jackie, Yo!"; Paula Span's "The Man at Jackie's Side: In Maurice Tempelsman, the Sophisticated Lady Has Finally Met Her Match," *The Washington Post*, May 26, 1994; "The Man Who Loved Jackie; With Savvy, Cultivated Maurice Tempelsman, Jacqueline Kennedy Onassis at Long Last Found a Safe Haven—and Serenity," *People*, July 11, 1994; Jessie Mangaliman's "Jacqueline Kennedy Onassis—A City Mourns; Family Was Her Priority; Jackie's Companion—A Loyal, Caring Advisor," *Newsday*, May 21, 1994; Sandra Sanchez's "Longtime Friend: 'Journey Is Over,' " *USA Today*, May 24, 1994; Susan Baer's "Jacqueline Kennedy Onassis: 1929–1994; Onassis's Longtime Companion Was Considered Family," *Los Angeles Times*, May 24, 1994.

Periodical sources for the description of Maurice's business dealings in Africa and elsewhere include "Maurice Tempelsman's African Connections," *Fortune*, November 15, 1982; "Maurice Tempelsman: Diamonds and Diplomacy," *Jewelers Circular Keystone*, June 1989; "To De Beers on Prices: Don't Kill Golden Goose," *Jewelers Circular Keystone*, September 1989 and August 1991; Vladimir Kvint's "Sorry Mr. Oppenheimer," *Forbes*, February 15, 1993; Rita Koselka's "Brand Name Diamonds?" *Forbes*, April 28, 1986; Leon Dash's "Zaire Gambles by Resigning Diamond Cartel," *The Washington Post*, November 11, 1981; Howard W. French's "In Africa, Wealth Often Buys Only Trouble," *The New York Times*, January 25, 1998; James Ring Adams's "Citizen Kennedy's Energy," *The American Spectator*, December 1997; "U.S. Diamond Dealer Turns Peacemaker," *Africa News*, August 15, 1997; John Elvin's "Angolan Angle," *The Washington Times*, September 20, 1990; Jim McGee's "Polishing Off a Ban on S. African Diamonds," *The Washington Post*, January 25, 1990; *The Orange County Register*, June 29, 1989; and the London *Mail on Sunday*, May 22, 1994.

Primary published sources for this section include Carl Sferrazza Anthony's *As We Remember Her* (HarperCollins, 1997), Lester David's *Jacqueline Kennedy Onassis* (Birch Lane Press, 1994), C. David Heymann's *A Woman Named Jackie* (Lyle Stuart, 1989), and Michael G. Schatzberg's *Mobutu or Chaos* (University Press of America and Foreign Policy Research Institute, 1991).

Two excellent sources for information on Mama Mobutu's funeral were Thomas M. Callaghy, professor of political science, University of Pennsylvania, and Crawford Young, professor of political science at the University of Wisconsin and co-author with Thomas Turner of *The Rise and Decline of the Zairian State*.

Primary published sources for details of Gbadolite and Mobutu's fabulous palace there include Colette Braeckman's *Le Dinosaure: Le Zaire de Mobutu* (Fayard, 1992) and a book by Pierre Janssen, one of Mobutu's sons-in-law, titled *À La Cour de Mobutu* (Editions Michel Lafon, 1997).

The author also drew on accounts in periodicals for details on Mobutu's life in Zaire, including "Rebel With a Cause," *Vanity Fair*, August 1997, and articles in *The New York Times* and *The Washington Post*, September 8, 1997.

FOURTEEN: SINGLE WORKING WOMAN

The account of Jackie and Lee Radziwill's falling out over Lee's aborted marriage to Newton Cope was drawn from Diana DuBois's *In Her Sister's Shadow* (Little, Brown, 1995) and Taki Theodoracopulos's *Princes, Playboys & High-Class Tarts* (Karz-Cohl, 1984).

The story of Jackie's involvement with historic preservation and the Municipal Art Society was drawn from an extensive interview with Brendan Gill shortly before his death. Background for this period of her life was provided by Gregory Gilmartin's *Shaping the City* (Clarkson Potter, 1995).

The narrative of the party Jackie and Pete Hamill attended in Soho in March 1980 was drawn from interviews with the hosts of the party, John and Julienne Scanlon, and the co-host, Patsy Denk Powers.

Pete Hamill recounts details of his problems with drinking and fatherhood in his memoir *A Drinking Life* (Little, Brown, 1994). The author's interview with friends of Jackie's who requested anonymity also provided insight into Jackie's relationship with Hamill. The New York *Post*'s printing of Hamill's scathing column about Jackie marrying Onassis is recounted in Kitty Kelley's *Jackie Oh!* (Lyle Stuart, 1979).

Dustin Hoffman's comment on receiving his first Oscar was quoted in Jack Mathews's "Oscar at 60: He Stands for Popularity, Not Excellence," *The Washington Post*, April 12, 1988.

Jackie's comment about journalists was made to the author at a Christmas party he attended at Jackie's apartment in 1981.

Insight into Jackie's work as an editor at Doubleday was drawn from an extensive interview with John Loring, the former design director of Tiffany & Company, and from interviews with other publishing colleagues who wish to remain anonymous.

Insight into Jackie's frame of mind in the mid 1980s was drawn from an interview with one of her authors, the psychoanalyst Dr. Stephen Appelbaum.

Jackie defined her own idea of happiness in an article that appeared in Ms. magazine in March 1979. Gloria Steinem's thoughts about Jackie's life as a working woman appeared in that same issue of Ms., and were reprinted in her collection of essays *Outrageous Acts and Everyday Rebellions* (Holt, Rinehart & Winston, 1983).

Susan Douglas, professor of media and American Studies at Hampshire College, relates her ideas about Jackie as a transitional figure for early feminists in *Where the Girls Are* (Times Books, 1994).

The narrative of Jackie's growing reliance on Maurice Tempelsman in "The Power behind the Throne" was drawn from the author's interviews with Hélenè Arpels and with a number of friends of the couple who wish to remain anonymous.

Details about Tempelsman's heart attack and follow-up treatment were drawn from an interview with one of his friends. The author also drew upon a number of published sources, including the American Heart Association's *Guide to Heart Attack Treatment, Recovery, and Prevention* (Times Books, 1996), Robert E. Kowalski's *8 Steps to a Healthy Heart* (Warner Books, 1992), Siegfried Kra's *What Every Woman Must Know about Heart Disease* (Warner Books, 1996), and Harvey Wolinsky and Gary Ferguson's *The Heart Attack Recovery Handbook* (Warner Books, 1988).

FIFTEEN: THE TIME OF HER LIFE

The narrative on Jackie's transformation from haunted to happy in "The Best Disguise" is drawn from the author's extensive interview with John Loring. The account of Jackie's life on Martha's Vineyard is drawn from interviews with summer and winter residents of the island, including Gus Ben David, director of the Felix Neck Wildlife Sanctuary; Joan Braden; Art Buchwald; David Flanders, Flanders Real Estate; Ralph Graves; Louise Grunwald; Adriana Ignacio; Robert McNamara; I. M. Pei; Richard Reston, editor and publisher of the *Vineyard Gazette*; and Alfred Vanderhoop, whose family owned part of the disputed Gay Head property.

Details of Jackie's purchase of the Gay Head property and the subsequent suit and settlement with the Wampanoag Indians were also drawn from accounts published in the *Vineyard Gazette*, August 1978, January 1989, and March 1990.

Bunny Mellon described her landscaping for Jackie's Gay Head property in Paul Deitz's "The Private World of a Great Gardener," *The New York Times*, June 3, 1982.

Details of Jackie's relationship with her children are drawn from the author's interviews with Peter Beard and with a number of other friends who wish to remain anonymous.

Primary published sources for information on John F. Kennedy Jr.'s life include Wendy Leigh's *Prince Charming* (Dutton, 1993), Lester David's *Jacqueline Kennedy Onassis* (Birch Lane Press, 1994), and C. David Heymann's *A Woman Named Jackie* (Lyle Stuart, 1989).

The narrative about Jackie in "The Man Who Won Art Buchwald" was drawn from interviews with Art Buchwald and with a guest at the Katharine Graham luncheon who wishes to remain anonymous.

The section "A Real Trooper" is drawn from the author's extensive interview with Tillie Weitzner, Jackie's yoga teacher.

SIXTEEN: TOUCHED BY THE SUN

The narrative of Jackie's diagnosis and treatment for cancer was drawn from the author's interviews with medical personnel involved in Jackie's treatment who wish to remain anonymous.

Other details come from a number of published sources including Lois Romano's "Reliable Source" column, *The Washington Post*, November 24, 1993; Christopher Andersen's *Jackie after Jack* (William Morrow, 1998); Carl Sferrazza Anthony's *As We Remember Her* (HarperCollins, 1997); Lester David's *Jacqueline Kennedy Onassis* (Birch Lane Press, 1994); and C. David Heymann's *A Woman Named Jackie* (Lyle Stuart, 1989).

Frank Sinatra's first *Duets* album was released in 1993 by Capitol Records. The words to the song "Guess I'll Hang My Tears Out to Dry" were written by Sammy Cahn; the music was composed by Jule Styne; the words to "In the Wee Small Hours of the Morning" were by Bob Hilliard; the music was by David Mann.

Information on non-Hodgkin's lymphoma was drawn from Laurence K. Altman's "Lymphomas Are on the Rise in U.S. and No One Knows Why," *The New York Times*, May 24, 1994, and Geoffrey Cowley's "A Varied but Brutal Disease," *Newsweek*, May 30, 1994.

The narrative of Maurice providing breakfast for Jackie after her radiation treatments was drawn from Elizabeth Gleick's "The Man Who Loved Jackie," *People*, July 11, 1994.

C. P. Cavafy's poem "Ithaca" appears in *The Complete Poems of Cavafy* (Harvest Books/Harcourt Brace Jovanovich, 1989).

Brooke Astor's letter from Jackie was read on the *Charlie Rose Show* about Jackie, May 20, 1994.

The words and music to "Touched by the Sun" were written by Carly Simon.

The narrative in "Final Exit" is drawn from the author's interview with close friends of Jackie's who wish to remain anonymous.

BIBLIOGRAPHY

Abramson, Rudy. *Spanning the Century: The Life of W. Averell Harriman 1891–1986.* New York: William Morrow, 1992.

Adler, Bill. *The Kennedy Children: Triumphs and Tragedies.* New York: Franklin Watts, 1980.

Andersen, Christopher. *Jackie after Jack: Portrait of the Lady.* New York: William Morrow, 1998.

Anthony, Carl Sferrazza. *As We Remember Her: Jacqueline Kennedy Onassis in the Words of Her Family and Friends.* New York, HarperCollins, 1997.

———. *First Ladies: The Saga of the Presidents' Wives and Their Power.* Vol. 2. Morrow, 1991.

Baldridge, Letitia. *Of Diamonds and Diplomats.* Boston: Houghton Mifflin, 1968.

Baldwin, Billy. *Billy Baldwin Remembers.* New York: Harcourt Brace Jovanovich, 1974.

Baldwin, Billy, and Michael Gardine. *Billy Baldwin: An Autobiography.* Boston: Little, Brown, 1985.

Beard, Peter. *Longing for Darkness: Kamante's Tales from "Out of Africa."* San Francisco: Chronicle Books, 1975, 1990.

Beschloss, Michael R. *Taking Charge: The Johnson White House Tapes, 1963–1964.* New York: Simon & Schuster, 1997.

Biddle, Livingston. *Our Government and the Arts: A Perspective from the Inside.* New York: American Council for the Arts, 1988.

Birmingham, Stephen. *Jacqueline Bouvier Kennedy Onassis.* New York: Grosset & Dunlap, 1978.

———. *The Late John Marquand: A Biography.* Philadelphia: Lippincott, 1972.

Bishop, Jim. *The Day Kennedy Was Shot.* Reprint. New York: Bantam, 1969.

Boller, Paul F., Jr. *Presidential Wives: An Anecdotal History.* New York: Oxford University Press, 1988.

Bouvier, Jacqueline, and Lee Bouvier. *One Special Summer.* New York: Delacorte Press, 1974.

Braden, Joan. *Just Enough Rope.* New York: Villard, 1989.

Bradlee, Benjamin C. *Conversations with Kennedy.* New York: W. W. Norton, 1975.

———. *A Good Life: Newspapering and Other Adventures.* New York: Simon & Schuster, 1995.

Braeckman, Colette. *Le Dinosaure: Le Zaire de Mobutu.* Paris: Fayard, 1992.

Brady, Frank. *Onassis: An Extravagant Life.* Englewood Cliffs, N.J.: Prentice-Hall, 1977.

Buck, Pearl S. *The Kennedy Women: A Personal Appraisal.* New York: Cowles Book Company, 1970.

Cafarakis, Christian. *The Fabulous Onassis: His Life and Loves.* New York: William Morrow, 1972.

Canfield, Cass. *Up and Down and Around: A Publisher Recollects the Time of His Life.* New York: Harper's Magazine Press/Harper & Row, 1971.

Capote, Truman. *Answered Prayers: The Unfinished Novel.* New York: Random House, 1987.

———. *A Capote Reader.* New York: Random House, 1987.

Carpozi, George. *The Hidden Side of Jacqueline Kennedy.* New York: Pyramid Books, 1967.

———. *Jackie & Ari: For Love or Money?* New York: Lancer Books, 1968.

Cartledge, Paul. *The Greeks.* New York: Oxford University Press, 1993.

Cassini, Oleg. *In My Own Fashion: An Autobiography.* New York: Simon & Schuster, 1987.

Cavafy, C. P. *The Complete Poems of Cavafy.* Translated by Rae Dalven. Reprint. New York: Harvest Books/Harcourt Brace Jovanovich, 1989.

Clarke, Gerald. *Capote: A Biography.* New York: Simon & Schuster, 1988.

Clinch, Nancy Gager. *Kennedy Wives, Kennedy Women.* New York: Dell, 1976.

Cohn, Roy, and Sidney Zion. *The Autobiography of Roy Cohn.* New York: St. Martin's Press, 1988.

Colacello, Bob. *Holy Terror: Andy Warhol Close Up.* New York: HarperCollins, 1990.

Collier, Peter, and David Horowitz. *The Kennedys: An American Drama.* New York: Summit Books, 1984.

A Concise Compendium of the Warren Commission Report on the Assassination of John F. Kennedy. New York: Popular Library, 1964.

Corry, John. *The Manchester Affair.* New York: G. P. Putnam's Sons, 1967.

Curran, Robert. *The Kennedy Women: Their Triumphs and Tragedies.* New York: Lancer Books, 1964.

Curtis, Charlotte. *The Rich and Other Atrocities.* New York: Harper & Row, 1976.

Cutler, John Henry. *Cardinal Cushing of Boston.* New York: Hawthorn Books, 1970.

Dallas, Rita, with Jeanira Ratcliffe. *The Kennedy Case: The Intimate Memoirs of the Head Nurse to Joseph P. Kennedy during the Last Eight Years of His Life.* New York: G. P. Putnam's Sons, 1973.

David, Lester. *Jacqueline Kennedy Onassis.* New York: Birch Lane Press, 1994.

David, Lester, and Irene David. *Bobby Kennedy: The Making of a Folk Hero.* New York: Dodd, Mead, 1986.

David, Lester, and Jhan Robbins. *Jackie and Ari: The Inside Story.* New York: Pocket Books, 1975.

Davis, John H. *The Bouviers: Portrait of an American Family.* New York: Farrar, Straus & Giroux, 1969.

Davis, L. J. *Onassis: Aristotle and Christina.* New York: St. Martin's Press, 1986.

The Decade of Women: A Ms. History of the Seventies in Word and Picture. Edited and produced by Suzanne Levine and Harriet Lyons, with Joanne Edgar, Ellen Swett, and Mary Thom. New York: G. P. Putnam's Sons, 1980.

Dempster, Nigel. *Heiress: The Story of Christina Onassis*. New York: Grove Weidenfeld, 1989.

Douglas, Susan J. *Where the Girls Are: Growing Up Female with the Mass Media*. New York: Times Books, 1994.

DuBois, Diana. *In Her Sister's Shadow: An Intimate Biography of Lee Radziwill*. Boston: Little, Brown, 1995.

Duby, Georges. *William Marshal: The Flower of Chivalry*. Translated by Richard Howard. New York: Pantheon Books, 1985.

Duchin, Peter. *Ghost of a Chance: A Memoir*. New York: Random House, 1996.

Epstein, Edward Jay. *The Rise and Fall of Diamonds: The Shattering of a Brilliant Illusion*. New York: Simon & Schuster, 1982.

Erikson, Erik H. *A Way of Looking at Things: Selected Papers from 1930–1980*. Edited by Stephen Schlein. New York: W. W. Norton, 1987.

Evans, Peter. *Ari: The Life and Times of Aristotle Socrates Onassis*. New York: Summit Books, 1986.

Exner, Judith, as told to Ovid Demaris. *My Story*. New York: Grove Press, 1977.

Fay, Paul B., Jr. *The Pleasure of His Company*. New York: Harper & Row, 1966.

Fenton, John H. *Salt of the Earth: An Informal Profile of Richard Cardinal Cushing*. New York: Coward-McCann, 1965.

Foreman, Norma Ruth Holly. "The First Lady as Leader of Public Opinion: A Study of the Role and Press Relations of Lady Bird Johnson." Ph.D. diss., University of Texas at Austin, 1971.

Foster, Mark S. *Henry J. Kaiser: Builder in the Modern American West*. Austin: University of Texas Press, 1989.

Fraser, Nicholas, et al. *Aristotle Onassis*. Philadelphia: Lippincott, 1977.

Friedan, Betty. *The Second Stage*. New York: Summit Books, 1981.

Frischauer, Willi. *Onassis*. New York: Meredith Press, 1968.

Galbraith, John Kenneth. *Ambassador's Journal: A Personal Account of the Kennedy Years*. Boston: Houghton Mifflin, 1969.

Gallagher, Mary Barelli. *My Life with Jacqueline Kennedy*. New York: David McKay, 1969.

Galella, Ron. *Jacqueline*. New York: Sheed & Ward, 1974.

Garvey, Barbara Oney. "A Rhetorical-Humanistic Analysis of the Relationship between First Ladies and the Way Women Find a Place in Society." Ph.D. diss., Ohio State University, 1978.

Giglio, James N. *The Presidency of John F. Kennedy*. Lawrence: University Press of Kansas, 1991.

Gilmartin, Gregory F. *Shaping the City: New York and the Municipal Art Society*. New York: Clarkson Potter, 1995.

Graham, Katharine. *Personal History*. New York: Random House, 1997.

Grobel, Lawrence. *Conversations with Capote*. New York: New American Library, 1985.

Gutin, Myra Greenberg. "The President's Partner: The First Lady as Public Communicator, 1920–1976." diss., University of Michigan, 1983.

Hall, Gordon Langley, and Ann Pinchot. *Jacqueline Kennedy: A Biography*. New York: Frederick Fell, 1964.

Hamill, Pete. *A Drinking Life: A Memoir*. Boston: Little, Brown, 1994.

Hamilton, Nigel. *JFK: Reckless Youth.* New York: Random House, 1992.

Hampton, Mark. *Legendary Decorators of the Twentieth Century.* New York: Doubleday, 1992.

Harding, Robert T. *Jacqueline Kennedy: A Woman for the World.* New York: Encyclopedia Enterprises, 1966; distributed by Vanguard Press.

Heidenry, John. *What Wild Ecstasy: The Rise and Fall of the Sexual Revolution.* New York: Simon & Schuster, 1997.

Heilbrun, Carolyn G. *The Education of a Woman: The Life of Gloria Steinem.* Reprint. New York: Ballantine Books, 1996.

Hersh, Seymour, M. *The Dark Side of Camelot.* Boston: Little, Brown, 1997.

Heymann, C. David. *A Woman Named Jackie.* New York: Lyle Stuart, 1989.

Hilty, James W. *Robert Kennedy: Brother Protector.* Philadelphia: Temple University Press, 1997.

Hoffmann, Joyce. *Theodore H. White and Journalism as Illusion.* Columbia: University of Missouri Press, 1995.

Janssen, Pierre. *À La Cour de Mobutu.* Paris: Editions Michel Lafon, 1997.

Johnson, Lady Bird. *A White House Diary.* New York: Holt, Rinehart & Winston, 1970.

Kaiser, Charles. *The Gay Metropolis: 1940–1996.* Boston: Houghton Mifflin, 1997.

Kramer, Frieda. *Jackie: A Truly Intimate Biography.* New York: Grosset & Dunlap, 1979.

Kelley, Kitty. *Jackie Oh!* Secaucus, N.J.: Lyle Stuart, 1979.

Kennedy, Rose Fitzgerald. *Times to Remember.* Garden City, N.Y.: Doubleday, 1974.

Kitto, H. D. F. *The Greeks.* Harmondsworth, Middlesex: Penguin Books, 1951, 1963.

Klein, Edward. *All Too Human: The Love Story of Jack and Jackie Kennedy.* New York: Pocket Books, 1996.

Koestenbaum, Wayne. *Jackie under My Skin: Interpreting an Icon.* New York: Farrar, Straus & Giroux, 1995.

Koskoff, David E. *The Mellons: The Chronicle of America's Richest Family.* New York: T. Y. Crowell, 1978.

Kowalski, Robert E. *8 Steps to a Healthy Heart.* New York: Warner Books, 1992.

Krock, Arthur. *Memoirs: Sixty Years on the Firing Line.* New York: Funk & Wagnalls, 1968.

Lambert, Gerard Barnes. *All Out of Step: A Personal Chronicle.* New York: Doubleday, 1956.

Lawford, Patricia Seaton, with Ted Schwarz. *The Peter Lawford Story.* New York: Carroll & Graf, 1988.

Leamer, Laurence. *The Kennedy Women.* New York: Villard Books, 1994.

Leigh, Wendy. *Prince Charming: The John F. Kennedy, Jr. Story.* New York: Dutton, 1993.

Lewis, Lloyd. *Myths after Lincoln.* New York: Harcourt Brace, 1929, 1940.

Lilly, Doris. *Those Fabulous Greeks: Onassis, Niarchos, and Livanos.* New York: Cowles, 1970.

Lippmann, Walter. *Public Persons.* Edited by Gilbert A. Harrison. New York: Liveright, 1976.

Manchester, William. *Controversy and Other Essays in Journalism, 1950–1975.* Boston: Little, Brown, 1976.

———. *The Death of a President: November 20–November 25, 1963.* New York: Harper & Row, 1967.

Martin, Patricia Miles. *Jacqueline Kennedy Onassis.* New York: G. P. Putnam's Sons, 1969.

Martin, Ralph G. *A Hero for Our Time: An Intimate Story of the Kennedy Years.* New York: Fawcett, 1983.

————. *Seeds of Destruction: Joe Kennedy and His Sons.* New York: G. P. Putnam's Sons, 1955.

McCarthy, Dennis V. *Protecting the President: The Inside Story of a Secret Service Agent.* New York: William Morrow, 1985.

McGuinness, Joe. *The Last Brother: The Rise and Fall of Teddy Kennedy.* New York: Simon & Schuster, 1993.

Means, Marianne. *The Woman in the White House.* New York: Random House, 1963.

Mellon, Paul, with John Baskett. *Reflections in a Silver Spoon: A Memoir.* New York: William Morrow, 1992.

Morgan, Robin, ed. *Sisterhood Is Powerful: An Anthology of Writings from the Women's Liberation Movement.* New York: Vintage Books, 1970.

Mossman, B. C., and M. W. Stark. *The Last Salute: Civil and Military Funerals, 1921–1969.* Washington, D.C.: Department of the Army, 1971.

Nevins, Deborah, ed. *Grand Central Terminal: City within the City.* Fwd. by Jacqueline Kennedy Onassis. New York: Municipal Art Society of New York, 1982.

Nowakowski, Tadeusz. *The Radziwills.* New York: Delacorte, 1974.

Ogden, Christopher. *Life of the Party: The Biography of Pamela Digby Churchill Hayward Harriman.* Boston: Little, Brown, 1994.

Onassis, Jacqueline. "Being Present," *The New Yorker.* January 13, 1975, 26–28.

————. "A Visit to the High Priestess of Vanity Fair." New York: Metropolitan Museum of Art, 1977.

————, ed. and intro. *The Firebird and Other Russian Fairy Tales.* New York: Viking, 1978.

Oppenheimer, Jerry. *The Other Mrs. Kennedy: Edith Skakel Kennedy; An American Drama of Power, Privilege, and Politics.* New York: St. Martin's Press, 1994.

Payne, Charles. *American Ballet Theatre.* New York: Knopf, 1978.

Plimpton, George. *Truman Capote.* New York: Doubleday, 1997.

Porter, Katherine Anne. *The Collected Essays and Occasional Writings.* New York: Delacorte, 1970.

Potter, Jeffrey. *Men, Money & Magic: The Story of Dorothy Schiff.* New York: Coward, McCann & Geoghegan, 1976.

Rainie, Harrison, and John Quinn. *Growing Up Kennedy: The Third Wave Comes of Age.* New York: Putnam, 1983.

Reich, Cary. *Financier: The Biography of André Meyer; A Story of Money, Power, and the Reshaping of American Business.* New York: William Morrow, 1983.

Rhea, Mini. *I Was Jacqueline Kennedy's Dressmaker.* New York: Fleet, 1962.

Rogers, Warren. *When I Think of Bobby: A Personal Memoir of the Kennedy Years.* New York: HarperCollins, 1993.

Rush, George. *Confessions of an Ex-Secret Service Agent.* New York: Donald I. Fine, 1988.

Schatzberg, Michael G. *Mobutu or Chaos: The United States and Zaire, 1960–1990.* Lanham, Md.: University Press of America; Philadelphia: Foreign Policy Research Institute, 1991.

Schlesinger, Arthur M., Jr. *Robert Kennedy and His Times.* Boston: Houghton Mifflin, 1978.

————. *A Thousand Days.* Boston: Houghton Mifflin, 1965.

Salinger, Pierre. *P.S., A Memoir.* New York: St. Martin's Press, 1995.

————. *With Kennedy.* Garden City, N.Y.: Doubleday, 1966.

Schneir, Miriam, ed. *Feminism in Our Time: The Essential Writings, World War II to the Present.* New York: Vintage Books, 1994.

Shaw, Maud. *White House Nannie: My Years with Caroline and John Kennedy, Jr.* New York: New American Library, 1966.

Shulman, Irving. *"Jackie"!: The Exploitation of a First Lady.* New York: Trident Press, 1970; Pocket Books, 1971.

Smith, A. Merriman. *Merriman Smith's Book of Presidents.* Edited by Timothy G. Smith. New York: W. W. Norton, 1972.

Smith, Sally Bedell. *Reflected Glory: The Life of Pamela Churchill Harriman.* New York: Simon & Schuster, 1996.

Sorenson, Theodore C. *Kennedy.* New York: Bantam, 1965.

Spada, James. *Peter Lawford: The Man Who Kept the Secrets.* New York: Bantam, 1991.

Sparks, Fred. *The $20,000,000 Honeymoon: Jackie and Ari's First Year.* New York: Bernard Geis Associates, 1970.

Stafford, Jean. *A Mother in History.* New York: Pharos Books, 1992.

Stancioff, Nadia. *Maria: Callas Remembered.* New York: E. P. Dutton, 1987.

Stassinopoulos, Arianna. *Maria Callas, the Woman behind the Legend.* New York: Simon & Schuster, 1981.

Steel, Ronald. *Walter Lippmann and the American Century.* Boston: Little, Brown, 1980.

Stein, Jean, and George Plimpton. *American Journey: The Times of Robert Kennedy.* New York: Harcourt Brace Jovanovich, 1970.

Steinem, Gloria. *Outrageous Acts and Everyday Rebellions.* New York: Holt, Rinehart & Winston, 1983.

Stern, Sydney Ladensohn. *Gloria Steinem: Her Passions, Politics, and Mystique.* New York: Birch Lane Press, 1997.

Suares, J.C., and J. Spencer Beck. *Uncommon Grace.* Charlottesville, Va.: Thomasson-Grant, 1994.

Tapert, Annette, and Diana Edkins. *The Power of Style: The Women Who Defined the Art of Living Well.* New York: Crown, 1994.

Thayer, Mary Van Renssalaer. *Jacqueline Bouvier Kennedy.* Garden City, N.Y.: Doubleday, 1961.

———. *Jacqueline Kennedy: The White House Years.* Boston: Little, Brown, 1967.

Theodoracopulos, Taki. *Princes, Playboys & High-Class Tarts.* Princeton: Karz-Cohl, 1984.

Thom, Mary. *Inside Ms.: 25 Years of the Magazine and the Feminist Movement.* New York: Henry Holt, 1997.

Thomas, Helen. *Dateline: White House.* New York: Macmillan, 1975.

Time/Life editors. *Remembering Jackie.* New York: Warner Books, 1994.

Travell, Janet. *Office Hours: Day and Night.* New York: World Publishing, 1968.

Truman, Margaret. *First Ladies.* New York: Doubleday, 1997.

vanden Heuvel, William, and Milton Gwirtzman. *On His Own: RFK 1964–1968.* Garden City, N.Y.: Doubleday, 1970.

Vidal, Gore. *Two Sisters.* Boston: Little, Brown, 1970.

Von Hoffman, Nicholas. *Citizen Cohn.* New York: Doubleday, 1988

Vreeland, Diana. *D.V.* Edited by George Plimpton and Christopher Hemphill. New York: Knopf, 1984.

Vreeland, Diana, with Christopher Hemphill. *Allure.* Garden City, N.Y.: Doubleday, 1980.

Walker, John. *Self-Portrait with Donors: Confessions of an Art Collector.* Boston: Little, Brown, 1974.

Warhol, Andy. *The Andy Warhol Diaries*. Edited by Pat Hackett. New York: Warner Books, 1989.

Warren Commission. *The Warren Report; Report of the U.S. President's Commission on the Assassination of President John F. Kennedy*. Washington, D.C.: U.S. Government Printing Office, 1964.

Watney, Hedda Lyons. *Jackie O*. New York: Leisure Books, 1979.

West, J. B., with Mary Lynn Kotz. *Upstairs at the White House: My Life with the First Ladies*. New York: Coward, McCann & Geoghegan, 1973.

The White House Gardens: A History and Pictorial Record. New York: Great American Editions, 1973.

White, Theodore H. *In Search of History: A Personal Adventure*. New York: Warner Books, 1978.

Wills, Garry. *The Kennedy Imprisonment: A Meditation on Power*. Boston: Little, Brown, 1982.

Wilson, Edmund. *The Sixties: The Last Journal, 1960–1972*. New York: Farrar, Straus & Giroux, 1993.

Witcover, Jules. *The Year the Dream Died: Revisiting 1968 in America*. New York: Warner Books, 1997.

Wright, William. *All the Pain That Money Can Buy: The Life of Christina Onassis*. New York: Simon & Schuster, 1991.

Young, Crawford, and Thomas Turner. *The Rise and Decline of the Zairian State*. Madison: University of Wisconsin Press, 1985.

Youngblood, Rufus. *20 Years in the Secret Service: My Life with Five Presidents*. New York: Simon & Schuster, 1973.

INDEX